Dear Reade

The book yo
St. Martin's
Times calls "
a fascinating account of
has captured the national
of bestselling true crime
Crowley, who explores the ~~~~ ~~~~~ between a prominent Manhattan surgeon and the disappearance of his wife fifteen years earlier in THE SURGEON'S WIFE. Suzy Spencer's
BREAKING POINT guides readers through the tortuous twists and
turns in the case of Andrea Yates, the Houston mother who
drowned her five young children in the family's bathtub. In
Edgar Award-nominated DARK DREAMS, legendary FBI profiler
Roy Hazelwood and bestselling crime author Stephen G.
Michaud shine light on the inner workings of America's most
violent and depraved murderers. In the book you now hold,
NEVER SEEN AGAIN, acclaimed author Jeanne King exposes the
hidden secrets behind what appeared to be the perfect family—
until one of them disappeared.

St. Martin's True Crime Library gives you the stories behind
the headlines. Our authors take you right to the scene of the
crime and into the minds of the most notorious murders to show
you what really makes them tick. St. Martin's True Crime
Library paperbacks are better than the most terrifying thriller,
because it's all true! The next time you want a crackling
good read, make sure it's got the St. Martin's True Crime
Library logo on the spine—you'll be up all night!

Charles E. Spicer, Jr.
Executive Editor, St. Martin's True Crime Library

NEVER
SEEN
AGAIN

**A RUTHLESS LAWYER, HIS BEAUTIFUL
WIFE, AND THE MURDER THAT TORE
A FAMILY APART**

JEANNE KING

St. Martin's Paperbacks

NEVER SEEN AGAIN

Copyright © 2008 by Jeanne King.

ISBN: 0-312-94866-2
EAN: 978-0-312-94866-5

Printed in the United States of America

St. Martin's Paperbacks edition / May 2008

St. Martin's Paperbacks are published by St. Martin's Press, 175 Fifth Avenue, New York, NY 10010.

10 9 8 7 6 5 4 3 2 1

For my son, Christopher,
who is always there for me

Table of Contents

Table of Contents

Acknowledgments

I am deeply grateful to Police Chief Ronal Serpas of the Metropolitan Nashville Police Department and to Don Aaron, his public information manager. It was through their help that I gained unfettered access to members of the department investigating the Janet March case.

I especially want to thank Sergeant Pat Postiglione and Detective Bill Pridemore, the two members of the elite Cold Case unit of the homicide squad whose mission was to bring closure to the investigation. Thanks go to Captain Mickey Miller and Detective Brad Corcoran for being so gracious with their time in speaking with me. And I thank Amy Raines on Don Aaron's staff for her invaluable assistance in providing many of the photographs for this book.

I am forever grateful to lawyers John Herbison, Fletcher Long, Ed Fowlkes, and Bill Massey for accommodating me throughout the writing of this book and giving me down-to-earth remembrances of events. They were simply terrific. Both John and Fletcher spent much time with me reconstructing key points of the case, and I am deeply appreciative of their time.

Janice Boone, the assistant to John Herbison, was an

absolute gem. She helped track down bits of information about the case and gave me what seemed like hundreds of hours of advice. I especially want to thank her.

To my dear friend and colleague, Larry Brinton—the host of WSMV-Channel 4's "Word On The Street," whose stories capture the goings-on in Nashville and who shared with me his extensive ten year-plus history of the case—all I can say is thank you, Larry, for your constant help, for your humor, and for your words of advice and wisdom as the book was taking shape.

I would also like to thank reporter Dennis Ferrier for the interviews he conducted with Janet's brother, Mark Levine, which were aired on WSMV-TV, and for allowing me to share them with our readers.

I extend my thanks to Susan Niland, the spokeswoman for the Nashville District Attorney's office. And my hat goes off to Tom Thurman, the Nashville district attorney, and to Katy Miller, the assistant DA, who together presented a dynamite case to the jury in the trial of Perry March. They brought the case to a successful conclusion by leaving nothing to chance.

My thanks also go to Dorinda Carter, spokesperson for the Tennessee Department of Corrections, who set me straight on Perry's deed once he got to the big house and got himself tangled up in trouble.

Thanks are extended to Sheila Burke of the *Tennessean,* who covered the story every day for her newspaper, for answering my many queries. A special thank-you also to Willie Stern, who wrote a series of articles for the *Nashville Scene* that gave a wealth of background about the case.

I also want to thank Carolyn Purcell and her colleagues at *Court TV,* and Kathleen O'Connell at CBS News' *48 Hours* for their help.

In writing the book, I relied on interviews with former friends of Perry March and also with his college law professor, Donald Langevoort. Documents used in the book were provided by the Nashville police or were made available through court transcripts. I also utilized the pre-sentence reports of both Perry March and his father, Arthur, and was privy to the victim impact statements made by Janet's parents, Lawrence and Carolyn Levine, and by her brother, Mark Levine. Most of the quotes attributed to Perry come either from interviews he gave to reporters over the ten years he was at large or when he testified at the probate hearing deposition.

In Mexico, I could not have made it without the able assistance of reporter Dale Palfrey and her wonderful husband, Wayne, the director of the Oak Hill School, which Perry's two children, Sammy and Tzipi, attended. Dale in particular came to my rescue several times and got me through the maze of Perry's six years in Ajijic, Mexico. Thanks to Dale's journalistic nose, I met up with lawyer Henri Loridans, who set me straight on some of Perry's questionable business dealings down there. Joel Rasmusson was also very helpful, giving me an earful on Perry's life in Ajijic. He detailed Perry's exploits in the village and put me in touch with other expatriates who refused to be directly quoted in the book—they still fear Perry, even though he is in prison. Thanks to Joel, I was able to interview Thomas Delangre on the record, who at one time was married to Carmen Rojas, Perry's second wife.

In the chapters on Perry's life in Mexico, I relied extensively on material found in a CD prepared by the Committee to Bring Perry March to Justice, called *Perry Avram March: Master of Fraud and Corruption*. The authors of that CD provided thirteen chapter reports, numbering over 150 typed pages, which were made available to authorities in Mexico and Nashville. Due to Perry March's continuing reach into Mexico, they have respectfully declined to be identified.

Steve Somerstein, my legal adviser and dear friend, provided frequent explanations of the law and was always available to answer a question. He was truly generous with his time, and I am more than appreciative and thank him dearly.

To my many newspaper colleagues at the Manhattan Criminal Court building press room in New York City, thank

Acknowledgments

you all for putting up with me and for the superb and invaluable assistance you gave as the book project progressed. Thanks go to Dareh Gregorian, Laura Italiano of the *New York Post*, Barbara Ross of the *New York Daily News*, Samuel Maull of the Associated Press, Juliet Papa of Radio Station WINS, Irene Cornell of WCBS Radio, Anemona Hartocollis of the *New York Times,* and Karen Freifeld of *Bloomberg News*. Also a thank-you to my former Reuters colleague, Ellen Wulfhorst.

I extend appreciation and thanks to my friends Patricia O'Connell and Felice Cohen for reading portions of the manuscript and making suggestions. And a huge thank-you to my true-crime aficionado in Los Angeles, Yvonne Adler, for the extraordinary support she gave me as the book was being written.

I am particularly indebted to those who loved Janet March—especially her parents and her brother, who, painfully, shared their memories of her during the course of this case—and I thank them for being so open during their testimony.

I also want to thank film producer Sue Pollock, who introduced me to my agent Jane Dystel of Dystel & Goderich Literary Management. Jane graciously—and quickly—opened the door for me at St. Martin's Press. She is not only incredible but watched over the project like a mother hen. I truly appreciate her support and enthusiasm.

At St. Martin's Press, the book was in the expert hands of Charles Spicer, Executive Editor of St. Martin's True Crime Library, and my editor, Yaniv Soha, who, through shrewd editing, did an exceptional job poring over the manuscript to fine-tune the copy and make it sparkle, catching many typos. Thank you for your hard work.

Finally, thanks to my son, Christopher, for being there when I need you the most.

—Jeanne King

NEVER
SEEN
AGAIN

1

"I'm Not the Monster I've Been Made Out to Be"

Perry March walked awkwardly toward the Northwest Airlines departure gate at Los Angeles International Airport, a white terry-cloth towel thrown over his hands to disguise the handcuffs binding his wrists. He was slovenly dressed. He had not shaved in almost a week.

If Perry was embarrassed by his unusual circumstances, he tried hard not to show it to the other passengers in the terminal, who hardly gave the unkempt man a glance. As he neared the Jetway, he felt the chain belt around his waist tighten. That's when two six-foot detectives on either side of him abruptly grabbed him under the arms and hustled Perry down into the cabin. It was nearly 10 a.m. They were the last passengers to board the plane that morning of August 12, 2005, for what was to be for Perry the first leg of the flight to Memphis, then on to Nashville before reaching his final destination—a jail cell.

Perry's deep dark eyes darted around the cabin of the crowded Airbus A319 as the detectives nodded for him to take the window seat in the last row of the jet.

Looking like a death row inmate about to keep a date with "the needle," Perry seemed bewildered, as though in a daze.

Until now, he was used to controlling not only his own life, but other people and events. Yet here he was on a jet, cuffed and chained and trapped with nowhere to run. Next to him, calling the shots, were two no-nonsense detectives.

As he sat strapped in his seat in disbelief, Perry March had to wonder whether what was happening to him was a bad dream, and whether he would soon wake up. After all, he had had a beautiful wife. Two adoring children, Samson, called Sammy, and Tzipora, known as Tzipi—Hebrew for "bird." He was a graduate of the prestigious Vanderbilt University Law School. He was a brilliant lawyer who'd worked for one of Nashville's most influential law firms. He was well-respected by his affluent friends and for the most part enjoyed the lifestyle of the idle rich.

But as the jet roared down the runway, the deafening sound of the powerful engines jolted Perry back to reality— that he was under arrest for murdering his wife, Janet Levine March, almost ten years earlier.

During the flight, Perry at first quietly read a magazine, dozed briefly, and ate a snack supplied by the airline. About forty-five minutes into the trip, he nervously started up an unusual conversation with 54-year-old Sergeant Pat Postiglione, the twenty-seven-year veteran of the Nashville Police Department next to him in the center seat. Postiglione's 52-year-old partner, Bill Pridemore, a thirty-year veteran with the department, was close by in the aisle seat, within earshot of the conversation.

"I'm ready to close this chapter in my life if we can work out a deal." Perry seemed to be reciting. "My attorneys will be contacting the police again soon." He went on nervously, eager to see if he had pushed the detective's buttons.

The deal he outlined was simple: "What if I plead guilty that I killed my wife, Janet, on August fifteenth, 1996, and in exchange do no less than five years and no more than seven years in prison?"

Postiglione was surprised by what Perry, a brilliant corporate lawyer, was saying, and he elected to listen.

The two detectives had been on many of these trips, picking

up prisoners from different cities and bringing them back to Nashville, and it was not unusual for prisoners to remain completely silent from the airport to the plane until they were put in jail. "Until now, I've never had a prisoner talk about making a plea deal," Postiglione later said. But that was not the case here.

Perry talked non-stop. It was obvious to Postiglione that Perry was very interested in knowing what type of evidence prosecutors had against him—whether it was circumstantial or if there was any physical proof of his guilt.

Postiglione reminded him that only Tom Thurman, with the district attorney's office, could make such a plea agreement. It was obvious to the seasoned detective that Perry had an agenda, and that this was his method of controlling the situation.

Both homicide detectives, members of the elite Cold Case Unit, had spent countless hours over the past several years attempting to bring closure to the mysterious 1996 disappearance of Janet Levine March that started out as a missing persons case and ultimately turned into a murder investigation.

Postiglione, a transplanted New York City resident, had been born and raised in an Italian neighborhood in the borough of Queens. He'd spent a good part of his youth in the middle- to upper-class neighborhood of Forest Hills, and as a young boy, had wanted to be a police officer solving homicide cases, particularly after his cousin was murdered. But when he applied to the NYPD, the waiting list was long, so he went into construction.

A vacation trip to Nashville prompted him to apply to the Metro police force, where in 1980 he was accepted as a patrol officer. Eventually he made detective and in 1987 was assigned to Homicide.

And here he was, seated next to Perry March, a man accused of murdering his wife in 1996.

After munching his snack, Perry wasted no time settling into his new situation: attempting to work a compelling con on the cops. He had it all mapped out, and began speaking at length to Postiglione about the charges against him. He had already dropped the first rather absurd bombshell. The next phase started by his asking Postiglione about a picture that had appeared in a Mexican newspaper in 2004, which he had sent to prosecutors a year earlier. It showed a female spectator with three friends watching the Olympics in Athens, Greece. Perry and his new wife, Carmen Rojas, were adamant that the woman in the photo was Janet, and that it was proof she had been alive when she'd left Nashville. For months they had been showing the photo to anyone who would pay attention.

"Did the police check it out?" Perry persisted. "She looks like Janet, and she could be alive, maybe in Quebec."

"It was checked out enough to determine it was not your wife," Postiglione replied routinely.

Perry wouldn't give up, certain that Janet had been in Athens. But like all those who practice to deceive, he got tripped up and forgot the obvious. When reporting Janet missing, he'd told police she had taken her passport with her. Since it had been found in her purse when the Volvo was located, Perry had no explanation as to how Janet could have gotten to Athens, much less Canada or even Mexico, without it.

But it didn't stop him from questioning the strength of the case against him. "Have you been able to establish that Janet is dead? How strong is the case against me? Do you have any physical or direct evidence? Can you be sure she's dead? Have you found her?"

"If we didn't think Janet was dead, you wouldn't be sitting here charged with her homicide," said Postiglione wryly.

"Well, are you charging me because the civil suit declared her dead? Is that why the police department is charging me with her death?"

Postiglione patiently explained that the civil suit had nothing to do with his investigation. "Am I the only one indicted?" Perry asked in disbelief.

Perry had initially denied any involvement in Janet's

disappearance. But as the five-hour flight wore on and the plane neared Nashville, he began getting worried, realizing he was running out of time and that the detective didn't appear to be interested in listening to any of his arguments for a plea bargain.

But he persisted in attempting to discuss the evidence with the detective, and Postiglione was just as persistent in not answering any of his questions.

"I understand, but I wanted to tell you anyway so you could tell Tom Thurman," Perry emphasized in an effort to sound sincere.

So Perry raised the ante one more time. "Look, I will plead guilty even though I'm not guilty, so I can avoid the possibility of being convicted and sentenced to thirty years," he said.

Then the questions came fast and furious. Perry asked about the prison facilities in Tennessee. Was it possible to go to a minimum security prison?

Then he switched gears. "Speaking in hypothetical terms, what if it was an accident? If I were to admit culpability to something along those lines, would it still be second-degree murder?"

Perry became antsy when informed again that it was Thurman's decision. "I need you to get with him as soon as possible tonight, and discuss the possibility of a plea. But Tom has to be reasonable and honest with me. He has to lay his cards on the table and convince me that his case against me is strong.

"After all, I might be able to get an acquittal, and I'm not sure I want to roll the dice, get convicted and do thirty years."

Perry explained that if he did more than 7 years in prison, he would lose his wife, Carmen. She would not wait for him, and then he would not get to see the 4-year-old daughter he had with his new wife.

More than once, Perry emphasized how he wished he "had taken care of this nine years ago," because prison would then be behind him. "But now I'm going to take the high road, do the right thing, be a man, and do the time. I know it won't be a 'Martha Stewart'–type prison; but a minimum- to medium-security prison with the possibility of conjugal visits is do-able, provided I'm treated with respect, and not being duped."

Then, just as Postiglione was beginning to believe he had heard it all, Perry started in about August 1996 and "the Janet incident," as he referred to her disappearance. Perry admitted to the detective that he had "never been involved in any other criminal-type activities." As a lawyer, he should have realized he was implicating himself, and doing a good enough job on his own of convicting himself.

When Postiglione suggested that sometimes people hurt those they love in a moment of anger, Perry became agitated. "You don't have a witness saying they saw me killing Janet?" he asked.

"You know, I intensely loved Janet, but she wasn't the angel she was made out to be by the media, and I'm not the monster I've been made out to be. There are two sides to every story.

"You know specifics about the case that I don't know, and I know specifics about the case that you don't know."

He went on to mention a newspaper article he had read in which someone claimed to have seen him with a dead dog, and Perry said, "That's ridiculous, and was done to smear me." He also denied stories that he'd wrapped Janet in a rug and thrown her in a Dumpster or an incinerator.

After embarking on the last leg of the flight, from Memphis to Nashville, the conversation took another turn. Perry was now sitting between the two officers.

Pridemore, who taught Sunday school, was immersed in *Rabbi Paul*, a book about the Apostle, when Perry interrupted him to say, "You know, Paul was Jewish."

"I'm aware of that," Pridemore politely replied.

"You know, I'm Jewish too," Perry said.

"I know that."

"When this is all over, I'd be happy to come to your Sunday school class and talk about Paul."

Pridemore and Postiglione looked at each other, disbelieving.

At times during the short flight to Nashville, Perry appeared to be getting edgy and stressed. He was tenacious, though, about discussing his proposed plea agreement. "I'm not being arrogant, but rather just honest. I know what's best for me and I'm going to be the best attorney in that courtroom. You tell Tom Thurman that if we can work out a deal, I will answer their questions completely and honestly, and be one hundred percent truthful," he said with resignation in his voice. "All I want is to be treated with respect by all involved. Anything less and we go to trial."

After the flight touched down and they arrived at the Criminal Justice Center booking room in downtown Nashville at a little after 8 p.m, Perry confided that he would "seriously consider a plea if certain conditions are met. To be honest, I'm scared shitless about this."

Two hours later Perry was taken to night court, where the commissioner told him he would not be allowed to post bond until his arraignment.

That night, Davidson County sheriffs took Perry to one of the twenty-two cells in the Special Management Unit of the jail, set aside to protect him from other inmates, and placed him on suicide watch.

When court time rolled around five days later, Perry shuffled into a crowded criminal courtroom, handcuffed, his feet shackled, wearing a bright yellow prison-issue jumpsuit. He pleaded not guilty to all charges.

As he gave Judge Steve Dozier his vital statistics—his date of birth and Social Security number—Perry looked around the room. Seeing Postiglione and Pridemore seated in the front row, he gave them a sinister smile as if sending them a signal that his plea deal conversation on the plane had been merely a game—though he'd enjoyed pulling their strings. Through his lawyers, Perry denied the airborne confession of a plea.

As word spread that Perry had been returned to Nashville and was in police custody, Janet's parents, Larry and Carolyn

Levine, breathed a sigh of relief. For the first time in almost a decade, they believed there would be justice for Janet.

"We've waited a long time for this. We're not sad. Let's put it this way: I'm sad for our grandchildren," Carolyn Levine told WTVF, Channel 5 upon learning that Janet's husband was locked up.

2

A Marriage from Hell

Perry spent the ninth anniversary of Janet's disappearance in a barren 6-by-9-foot cell in the Davidson County jail in downtown Nashville, not far from the honkytonks on Lower Broadway and the popular Tootsies, where such legendary country music greats as Patsy Cline, Minnie Pearl, Garth Brooks, and Reba McEntire got their start.

Confined in this rather bleak, isolated area of the jail since his arrest, Perry was in protective custody, watched over by his jailers 24/7 with lights on overhead to make sure he didn't take his own life. Aside from reading a book and getting an hour a day for recreation or making limited phone calls to those on his approved list, the once up-and-coming lawyer sat on his cot with its almost paper-thin mattress staring at cold steel bars, surrounded by nothing more than a commode and a stark metal writing desk attached to a sink. The accommodations were in sharp contrast to the lush five-acre, million-dollar, French-style country home he'd once shared with wife, Janet, at 3 Blackberry Road in the stylish Forest Hills neighborhood of West Nashville.

Janet had called the house she designed her "dream home." In a rare interview with Nashville reporter Dennis

Ferrier of television station WSMV, her brother Mark recalled that "she had designed it so that the rays of sunlight would hit on a different area, so that there would always be bright light in the house."

A gifted artist, her paintings decorated the walls of almost every room, so you could almost feel her presence wherever you went in the house.

The isolation in his cell gave Perry a jolt of reality, and time to reflect on his former life and his humble beginnings.

Perry's grandfather, Paul Marcovich, a Romanian immigrant, had settled in East Chicago, Indiana, about 20 miles northwest of Chicago, Illinois, at the turn of the century. It was a town which, during the peak of the great Industrial Revolution, was truly designed to meet the needs of its workers, where four out of five of its citizens were foreign born.

Like many immigrants seeking the American dream, Marcovich worked at three jobs. He became moderately wealthy, reportedly owning real estate, a bank, a pharmacy, and many other lucrative small businesses. Marcovich and his wife, Pearl Cohen, had two sons, Arthur, born in 1928, and Martin, born two years later in 1930.

Arthur earned a pharmacy degree at Ohio Northern University in Ada, Ohio, in 1948, then in 1950 joined the U.S. Army and remained in the military until 1978, retiring with the rank of lieutenant colonel.

While in the military, Arthur met and married his wife, Tzipora Elyson, an Israeli immigrant from Minsk, Ukraine. The couple had three children.

Their first child, Perry, was born on January 14, 1961, in East Chicago, followed by Ron in 1964, and Kathy in 1965.

Sometime in 1956, Arthur legally shortened his name to March, his attorney Fletcher Long says, because the army didn't know how to correctly spell his legal name and "kept screwing up his monthly check."

In 1970, when Perry was 9 years old, tragedy struck when his mother died suddenly of a "barbiturate overdose" which some believe was actually a suicide. Arthur's explanation at the time was that a physician had prescribed the painkiller Darvon to help ease her pain after she got a cut on her head, and he claimed that his wife subsequently had an allergic reaction to the medication and died of anaphylactic shock.

Tzipora's East Chicago death certificate lists her cause of death as "accidental," while the state death certificate indicates that a "partially empty bottle of Darvon" was found in her bedroom.

Arthur never remarried, and he raised the three kids as a single parent with help along the way from various nannies.

Although the March family was Jewish, Perry's father sent him to La Lumiere, one of the finest college preparatory schools in the Midwest. The coeducational Catholic high school is situated 8 miles north of La Porte, Indiana, on 155 rolling acres along a picturesque country lake fed by natural springs. As one of 145 students, Perry excelled in all of his academic studies.

In high school, he became a versatile athlete. To build his self-confidence and relieve stress, he picked up a first-degree black belt in karate. He also found time to play tennis, learn to strum the guitar, ski, mountain bike, and earn four varsity letters in wrestling and three in soccer.

By his senior year, he scored high on his pre-college exams and was attracted to the University of Michigan for its exceptional Chinese studies program. It was there that he received an undergraduate degree in Asian Studies.

Perry's professors described him as bright and personable. While at the University of Michigan, he took two specialized Chinese language courses from the National University of Singapore and another through Shanghai East China, and to this day he speaks fluent Chinese and Mandarin in addition to Spanish and Hebrew.

It was at the U of M's Ann Arbor campus that Perry and Janet met as undergraduates in 1982. They were introduced by Janet's roommate, Stacey. A year earlier, Janet had graduated from the University School of Nashville, where she was vice president of her class. Friends remember her as soft spoken, with a distinctive, pleasing Southern accent.

She was smart, popular, and creative, a talented commercial artist who wanted to become a magazine illustrator.

Janet exhibited her artwork at several local restaurants. From the mural on the walls of the Tin Angel restaurant on Nashville's chic West End to the art gallery in the Jewish Community Center, Janet's paintings and illustrations of children's books have kept her memory alive for friends.

Perry, on the other hand, was not exactly an altar boy at college. While an undergraduate at Michigan he was accused by a woman of smacking her in the face with his fist. When confronted a year after Janet's disappearance with the allegations during an interview with Willy Stern of the *Nashville Scene* alternative weekly, Perry shrugged off the incident, saying, "She was a slut. I fucked her for a few months. Then she came back from vacation, told me she had the crabs, and I dumped her."

The woman denied having had sex with Perry, and never reported the supposed encounter to police or campus security.

Perry had some rough edges, but most classmates considered him high-energy and painstakingly thorough. He was also at times belligerent, stubborn, and greedy. Perry was jokingly referred to as "the classmate most likely to be indicted for securities fraud."

After Perry graduated from Michigan in 1984, he moved to Chicago. Janet followed him to the Windy City, where she attended the Art Institute. It was here the two college sweethearts became inseparable and began living together. He became a futures broker after taking a course through the National Association of Securities Dealers and took a job at the Oppenheimer & Co. brokerage firm as a management trainee.

Janet was homesick and wanted to move back to Nashville, urging her parents to pay Perry's tuition so he could attend law school at Vanderbilt University. They agreed, and Perry went on to win honors at Vanderbilt and make the Law Review. "He was quite committed and hard-working and wanted to be a good lawyer," recalls Donald

Langevoort, his former Vanderbilt law professor, now at Georgetown University in Washington, DC.

"I got to know Perry quite well. He did legal research with my wife. He was an excellent student, a terrific law student, and I'm just saddened by his current situation."

The first time Perry met his future family should have instantly raised a red flag. Mark can still remember the day he met his future brother-in-law for the first time. "We were playing a board game," Mark told Nashville reporter Dennis Ferrier of television station WSMV. "Perry covered the rules. The first time he beat me, the second time he beat me. After all, he knew the game well and had been playing for years. The third time around, I started to figure it out and I started winning. I'm winning the game and I'm about to make a . . . bad move. My mom, who was watching us play, had also figured the game out, and shook her head no, like 'Don't go there.'

"I picked up on her signal and said to myself, 'Oh yeah, I see the threat.'

"My mom probably shouldn't have told me that, but it was a game. But with that, Perry stood up and became very upset and agitated, and said to my mom, 'You can't help him.' He was serious.

"I said, 'I'm sorry, Perry. I won't do it again. I promise. It's just a game.'

"And Perry said, 'No, no, no, you can't help him.'

"And with that, he stood up and walked away from the game. That happened the first day I met him, and this was the day he was trying to impress the family with his character—over a game?"

While it was apparent that Perry had a short fuse, the Levines chose to close their eyes to their future son-in-law's failings. Instead they created an elegant engagement party and a distinctive, lavish, and romantic wedding for the couple in 1987. The picture-perfect pair settled down in Nashville. A year later, Perry graduated from Vanderbilt, and received two lucrative offers from top New York–based law firms: Cravath, Swaine & Moore and Shearman & Sterling.

Instead he chose the very staid, blue-ribbon Bass, Berry & Sims, a prominent firm many considered Waspy, where Perry reportedly became the first Jewish attorney. In joining the firm, one of the largest in Tennessee, Perry became one of over 200 attorneys. His starting salary was $42,500.

Sammy was born three years after they married. Daughter Tzipora—named after Perry's mother—arrived four years later.

The Marches made a nice-looking couple, settling into a largely Jewish neighborhood in the Belle Meade area of West Nashville, a few miles from Janet's parents.

Janet's career as an artist began to take off. She was very sure of herself and full of life. As an independent young woman, she was caring and witty, meticulous about her work, and not at all shy in expressing her opinion. She started selling some of her paintings and had been hired to do some commercial illustrations, Perry told CBS News' *48 Hours Investigates* in 2002.

"I think she would have done more of that, if she lived," Janet's mother, Carolyn Levine said. "As people saw her work, there was a demand for it. Janet had a wonderful sense of humor, and I have a number of sketches where you can see the humor in her art. There was something whimsical about it. And she did like to use bright, vivid colors. Her work is full of very happy figures."

While both Janet and Perry were intelligent, their loving friends often referred to her as a dreamer, while Perry was thought of as level-headed and practical.

By 1990 trouble appeared to be brewing at the March home. For openers, finances had become a problem. Important bills were not being paid. Perry also began to resent Janet's constant nagging and her insistence that if he really loved her, he would change his everyday lifestyle habits to please her.

More than once, Janet made it known to Perry during their frequent quarrels that she wanted him to turn off the television or the CD player so they could have time to speak with each other without interruption. There were times when

Janet complained that she felt Perry didn't need her. And there were other irritants—the telephone's ringing off the hook when all she wanted was to talk with her husband, or when Perry would forget her birthday or neglect to come home with a box of candy or red roses on Valentine's Day.

About that same time, court records show that Perry was becoming increasingly abusive toward Janet—physically, verbally, and emotionally.

To get away from what he perceived as Janet's maddening demands, Perry sought solace by stepping out almost every night and spending more and more time away from home. He claimed to police that his excursions, often over the night at hotels, were merely a chance to get some sleep.

Be that as it may, in the months before Janet vanished, police learned that Perry had become something of a womanizer, and more than once had been spotted around town with a number of attractive women, having cozy candlelight dinners or leaving a late night movie theater.

With their marriage growing difficult, both Janet and Perry felt comfortable talking to Carolyn Levine. In many ways, Perry, who had lost his own mother at an early age, viewed Carolyn as a surrogate. He looked to her for a solution to his troubled marriage. But the couple was arguing so much that she suggested he move out of the house.

When family mediation didn't pan out, Perry underwent several years of psychiatric treatment at Janet's insistence. He began seeing Nashville psychiatrist Dr. Thomas Campbell for about thirty sessions from November 1992 to March 1994.

Dr. Campbell met again with Perry in 1996 and after four sessions that included Janet, characterized her as having an aggressive, domineering side. Nevertheless, he suggested that the warring couple consider a trial separation. Campbell described the last session as "volatile," especially when Janet brought up why Perry had left his former law firm, Bass, Berry & Sims.

Perry had not leveled with the psychiatrist, and merely told him that he'd left the firm because someone had become overly melodramatic and reacted excessively in the office. In short, he had played down the incident.

Mark remembers one of the last conversations he had with his sister, two months before her death, at a family reunion. Janet told him that she had given Perry an ultimatum: if he didn't get better rather quickly and stop the abuse, she was going to get a divorce.

Perry had become wild with anger upon hearing those words, and glaring at her, said in a low, sinister whisper, "I'll kill you."

Janet told her brother she was stunned by Perry's threat. She said she challenged the remark. "What did you tell me? Did you just say you're going to kill me?"

When Perry didn't reply, Janet raised her voice and said, "Perry, don't lie to me. Did you tell me you're going to kill me?"

"Yeah, I said it. So what!" he had responded.

Mark choked up as he related the story to Nashville reporter Dennis Ferrier, and confided that to this day he feels guilty about dismissing Janet's remarks and not taking what she had told him more seriously. "I thought it would be a nasty divorce. I thought he would try fighting her tooth and nail for the children. I knew he could be mean, but never in my wildest dreams did I imagine that he could kill her."

Whenever she learned that the couple had been arguing, Janet's mother would shrug her shoulders, saying, "So what else is new?" The situation had become so explosive that Carolyn Levine offered to pay for an apartment for Perry to live in, so that he and Janet would not be physically together.

In early August, Janet kicked Perry out of the house. At first he tried renting a spare condo from Paul Eichel, a former law client. When that wasn't available, he began checking into local hotels. According to police investigators, Perry spent his nights at either the Hampton Inn near Vanderbilt University or at the Budgetel Inn the week before Janet disappeared.

Perry admits staying at each of these hotels, but claims he

never rented a room until after the children were asleep in their own beds, and that he was always back at his home by seven in the morning so that the kids would not be aware that he had been gone all night.

Janet did not disclose any of her marital problems with her close girlfriends, preferring to keep a stiff upper lip, carrying on as normal a life as she could under the circumstances. Her only confidante was her mother.

A year before becoming the city's most talked-about murder mystery, Janet had designed, planned, and decorated her dream home, a 5,300–square foot stone house. It had been privately financed with a $300,000 note from her parents and money Janet contributed from her personal funds, which was why the home was listed only in her name.

"She spent a good deal of time making sure it was correctly built, and oversaw every detail," says Carolyn Levine.

The value of the house was close to a million dollars when it was completed, but less than a year after Janet's disappearance it sold for only $726,000 to a local lawyer, perhaps because of the notoriety attached to it.

During a fight to keep the house from being sold, Perry testified at a probate court hearing three months after she disappeared that it was Janet's "crowning achievement as a designer and brilliant student of architecture."

Mitchell Barnett, the architect who helped Janet design and construct the home, says that "she was in control of the project, and Perry showed little interest in it."

Janet's life was not only centered on her thriving talent as an artist and designer of her new home. "She was also a great mother," says Barnett, who witnessed her daily interactions with her children as the home was being built.

Janet's friends also remember her as a devoted mother. She may have been a working mom, but it didn't stop her from attending school programs or setting up play dates for them with her friends' children, they said.

Despite her seemingly successful life, her gorgeous dream home, and two good-looking children, Janet was depressed over the state of her marriage. She told her mother she was contemplating divorcing Perry and had in fact made an 11 a.m. appointment with divorce attorney Lucinda Smith for August 16.

Janet might have hastened her proceedings toward divorce if she had been aware of the problems Perry had faced at Bass, Berry & Sims. He has never disclosed to his lawyers what prompted him to write anonymous sexually explicit letters to an attractive coworker. But that's precisely what he did, and it was the beginning of the end for Perry, who until this aberration had seemed to be on track to becoming a partner in the firm.

Paralegal Leigh Reames, a willowy blonde with long, straight shoulder-length hair, arrived at her desk on the twenty-fifth floor of the firm on July 19, 1991, and found several single-spaced pages of explicit writing on her chair that disturbed her.

The anonymous letter started off addressing Reames as "Dearest Leigh." It wasted no time getting to the point, which was to express a desire to have oral sex with her. The writer told her he wanted "to have hours and hours of licking and sucking" and "to inhale the essence of you," to devour her and caress her "soft belly."

Reames was highly offended. Not only was she uninterested in pursuing any type of relationship with this individual, she was a happily married woman. She brought the matter to the attention of her supervisor, who turned it over to the law firm's security investigation unit. A trap was set up utilizing two closed-circuit cameras.

The culprit turned out to be Perry March. But before he was caught red-handed, he fired off two more anonymous letters to Reames.

In his second, three-page, single-spaced missive, Perry bared his soul, saying he felt

> *like the lucky leprechaun who has seen the rainbow and knows what lays* [sic] *beyond. And like the leprechaun, I wonder if I'll ever find it. I want to taste your arms. The pure sexiness of your body grips me.*

Even though I know that I am playing the fool here, I am wildly singing to heaven inside.

I know that your reasons to communicate elude me, but I will suffer the crash and burn of pure disappointment gladly to be granted a few short days of dreaming of you again. I feel like a prisoner on death row with his sentence commuted. Not that my dreams of you ever left me Leigh, they were only tarnished with my sadness. How my heart broke.

Oh Leigh, I am so torn by this. I stop myself from bursting with excitement by reminding myself that you may want only to chastise me for my thoughts or to discover me. Your name rolls through my mind like a mantra, being chanted over and over again.

Nothing you can say can vaguely approach the self-inflicted torment I am in. I am depressed enough with this obsession with you. You can never comprehend my ache, my eternal disappointment when I knew that a kiss from you would never come my way.

The smell of your body, the touch of your skin, the taste and feel of you are always at my call. You are my horizon. How utterly sad it is to know your dream. Your ultimate fantasy, your obsession will never be yours.

Perry's writing read as eloquently as a romance novelist's. He goes on in his letter to describe his mad passion for Leigh:

I thought that, like a parched man in the desert, a mirage had appeared before me. There it was, so simple, so trivial. I feel like a puppy whose master has finally come home to play.

Perhaps sensing that Reames was more than upset about his unorthodox approach, Perry says:

Then I caution myself. I check my enthusiasm. I reign [sic] it in. Leigh, I wallowed in guilt and shame. Lower

*than low, as the song goes. I just can't believe I did
something so selfish to you, to the one I want to hold so
dearly. I now realize just how mean I have been to you.
I know how sweet you are. I know how my letter must
have upset you. I am sure that it caused you pain and
discomfort, and my intrusion was so galling. Please
understand that what has depressed me so has been a
combination of, first, the knowledge that I will never
caress you, and, second, the knowledge of how I may
have upset you. I can struggle alone with my internal
pain, knowing my fantasies are lost . . .*

*When I say I want you so intensely it hurts, I know
that it is in large part to who you are. I want to make
love to you because I am attracted to you, all of you.
Don't misunderstand. I am not changing the focus of
my desire for you. I am just acknowledging that there
is more to my longing than I gave credit to. The
thought of my tongue buried within you excites me
more than anything else in the world. I say this so that
you can understand why it is that I feel so badly; to
taste you is my day dream, to cause you upset chills
me.*

The letter goes on and on, Perry sounding desperate, acting like a car with no brakes heading for a dead end crash.

*Never has a woman so occupied my mind, just for the
merest glimmer of a chance to be with you. Please
don't lose sight of my feelings for you, my desire for
you—I am not some little boy who made a mistake and
deserves a scolding. I am a grown man who is obsessed with the desire to hold you and love you. I know
my mistakes, and I freely admit them. But again, nothing you can say will ever make me regret telling you
the things I have told you. All in all, I have done nothing but write you a love letter—how wrong is that??
What crime have I committed, what sin must I con-
fess? I have never wished you ill . . . I want nothing but*

*your happiness. If I could, I would give you stars. I
tremble at the thought of pleasing you. I would give
my soul to hear you say my name as you climax.
Please don't try to destroy my world.*

Concerned he might be revealed as the anonymous letter-
writer, Perry suggested that if Reames wanted to contact
him, she should go to the law firm's library on the twenty-
sixth floor and look for a set of books titled *Institute on Federal Taxation*, published by Matthew Bender.

*Please find volume no. 28 on the bottom shelf which is
for 1970. Please put your message to me in the back of
that book, and then reshelve it. No one ever uses them,
these books are old and in the archives, so chances are
almost certain that what you place there will not be
discovered by anyone other than me. I will check the
book periodically. I chose this location and book because you work in the tax group, and if you should
have trouble locating it, someone can help you without
raising suspicion.*

Perry ends the letter by reminding Reames that

*these next days will be sweet for me, regardless of your
message. My fantasies would dim the brightest comet.
I will think of you constantly. I will pray fervently. I
will seduce you and love you and drink you every moment of the day and night. You have given me a present, and that present is the thought of you undiminished
by rejection . . . remember Leigh—I would worship
you like no one ever has. Say what you will, my dearest, you will forever be my truest longing.*

In his final letter to Reames, in which he asks her to "re-
consider" her decision to communicate with him, he suggests
that she check out from the library *Tax Management: Estates,
Gifts and Trusts Portfolio* #134-4th, titled "Annuities." Perry

instructs her to insert a library check-out card signed by her in its place saying,

> *I will periodically notice if it is gone. If so, I will contact you to let you know how to reach me anonymously.*

After the internal investigation's closed-circuit camera showed Perry leaving a note for Reames in a book, he was given a choice of either voluntarily resigning or being fired. Perry quit.

Shortly after he left Bass Berry, a staff memo was sent around the office praising Perry for his fine work and wishing him well in his new endeavor of practicing corporate law. No one at the firm has ever acknowledged publicly that the sexual harassment case ever took place.

Angered at the way the firm handled the incident, allowing Perry to leave on such flattering terms, Reames also quit.

Reames sued Perry in civil court over the letters, but in the end agreed to an out-of-court settlement because Perry wanted the matter kept private, and didn't want Janet to learn of his indiscretion.

A confidentiality agreement between Perry and Reames was reached. As part of the settlement, BB&S agreed not to reveal the reason for his departure. That meant that when he sought employment at Levine, Mattson & Geracioti, the law firm of his father-in-law, Lawrence Levine, Perry came with glowing references. He told his friends he'd moved to his father-in-law's smaller firm because he wanted to pursue his own legal interests.

Perry was to pay Reames $24,000 over the course of four years, but got behind in his monthly installments, still owing her $12,500. The correspondence surrounding the case, including the sexually explicit letters themselves that had led to his forced resignation, was returned to Perry and stored on his personal computer at home.

On August 13, 1996, two days before Janet disappeared, Perry wrote Reames and her husband a letter on his home computer saying that he was establishing his own law firm. He pleaded for still more time to make good on the remaining portion of the settlement, saying that he planned to pay it in full on or before October 1.

"Cash flow is tight right now as my expenses are building for this, but I will also pay as much as possible before the final payment."

In the letter, Perry asked the couple to calculate "what you believe I owe in principal, interest and penalty and indicate your willingness to accept it in full satisfaction of my obligation to you." He asked that the couple send the information to his office marked "Personal and Confidential."

3

"That Effing Janet Has Ruined My Life"

After living in hotels for a couple of weeks, Perry returned home on Tuesday, August 13, 1996. He stopped by his in-laws' home with Janet and the children. What should have been a time of reconciliation turned into another war of words. It didn't matter to Perry that he and his wife were bickering at the home of his in-laws. The fight started up about Perry's lack of responsibility around the house. There were lots of issues on Janet's plate, and point by point she itemized what Perry needed to take care of. And as the hours wore on at the Levines', the fight escalated.

Janet was irritated over Perry's lack of dependability and the fact that he was not conscientious about sharing the routine tasks of running the house with her. "She criticized me for not changing the light bulbs, that I failed to balance my checkbook or clean the basement. She was ticked off about a variety of things that she seemed to feel I had dropped the ball on during our marriage," Perry recalled.

The squabbling about money matters continued back at the Marches'. For months, Janet had been after him about returning an overdue videotape to Blockbuster. Then there was the Bell South telephone bill that he consistently failed to pay. And the $3,000 tuition bill for Sammy's new private school was coming due. By the next day, Janet was determined to find out why Perry couldn't pay the bills to run the house.

But what had really gnawed at her over the last few years was the mystery surrounding Perry's departure from Bass Berry five years earlier. Was it caused by a fling he was carrying on with a woman at the firm? Was it still going on? Janet suspected the worst, but had no proof.

When Ella Goldshmidt, a Russian immigrant who was the nanny to the March children, Sammy and Tzipi, arrived at the house on Wednesday, August 14, she found Janet in an emotional state—"not herself," Goldshmidt said.

Perry had already left for the office. Janet was working on Perry's computer in his darkened study.

"When I came in that morning, Janet had a gray, stone-like face. She had circles under her eyes. As long as I knew her she emitted light, but she was particularly upset on the last day I saw her."

Janet told the nanny that she was going to be working on the computer all day and was not to be interrupted, not even by the children—an unusual request for her.

In fact, it was the first time that the nanny had seen Janet at the computer in the six years she'd worked for the family. She described Janet as "an ideal mother who never failed to sacrifice her time" for her children. "She was smart, caring, and devoted. I never heard her demand anything from her children without explaining why."

The police theorized that while working at the computer, Janet must have found Perry's August 13 letter to the paralegal in which he indicated he was having trouble coming up with the balance he owed from the settlement agreement. By delving further into Perry's computer that day, she'd probably found his secret files and discovered the lurid letters he had written to Reames.

Shocked after reading the letters, Janet made copies of them and placed them in an envelope with her name on it, and squirreled them away among her art supplies in her studio for safekeeping. Her plan no doubt was to use the contents of the letters as ammunition in her divorce action against Perry.

On the morning of August 15, Perry left for his office early. Janet started the day off by making phone calls and getting ready to deal with the two cabinet-makers, John Richie and John McAllister, who were coming later in the day to work on countertops and make some repairs. In the morning she spoke with one of her best friends, Laura Rummel, a Realtor who says Janet sounded "hurried and distracted."

In the afternoon, unbeknownst to Perry, Janet contacted Marissa Moody, whose 6-year-old son Grant was friends with Sammy in pre-school. Janet planned a play date for the boys for the next day and suggested that the kids get together around nine in the morning.

The rest of the day was spent with Richie and McAllister installing a countertop at the March home. Janet supervised the men and at one point asked if they would tighten a loose pipe. When Perry came home, Richie borrowed a pair of pliers from him to make the necessary repair. If Janet was seething about the explicit letters she had found, she never let on to anyone about them, not even her mother.

Perry's recollection of what took place at his home shortly before Janet vanished is vague at best. When questioned on November 20, 1996, at a probate court hearing, in a sworn deposition, the answer he often gave to the examiner was, "It's been a long time now. It's been over three months. I don't remember."

In the ten years that followed, he refused to be interviewed or speak to police about his wife's disappearance. The hearing is the only official account of what transpired between Perry and his wife on the day she disappeared, and of any interactions that took place before and after.

He recalled coming home from the office at about four or four-thirty that afternoon. "Sometime during the day, my wife routinely called me at the office and requested that I come home early. When I got home, the kids were playing in the back. Janet was inside the house dealing with two cabinet workers.

"I played with the kids outside, puttered around and watched them while Janet worked with the cabinet people. I helped the workmen fix the faucet. And at some point I went out to the Steven's grocery store near the split of Highway One Hundred and Seventy to pick up some dinner. I don't remember if the cabinet men were still there."

Perry recalls cooking the dinner, but as to what he cooked, "I don't remember. I have no idea. I fixed the children dinner."

When they caught a glimpse of her before eating dinner with their father, it would be the last time that Sammy or Tzipi would ever see their mother again.

"Janet did not eat with me or the children that evening because she was working in her studio on a painting," Perry said.

After supper, he gave the kids baths and put them to sleep.

It wasn't until about seven o'clock that evening after tucking the children in for the night that he and Janet had any conversation about their marriage, says Perry, who didn't recall the details of how the argument started.

"It's a matter of semantics," he told Jon Jones, the examiner who had been retained by the Levines to question Perry after Perry filed a probate petition to gain access to his wife's bank accounts and his children's trust funds. His precipitous filing made the Levines suspicious of their son-in-law, prompting them in turn to file a wrongful death suit against him.

"The answer to your question is, Janet was upset. I did not argue, but I believe she was upset with me, and she did argue," Perry told Jones.

"How did it begin? Janet wanted to discuss her continuing issues with our marriage. It was routine that Janet had lists of issues, things she wanted to discuss, recurrent themes, and she wanted to bring them up and talk about them. I sat at the kitchen table. She talked for a while, asked me what I was going to do, and left."

But Perry was evasive as the hearing went on, never once

offering any specific details of what had upset Janet that evening.

"The truth is that I did not have an argument. The truth is that Janet did, but it's hard to dance with only one person. So someone observing it may say it was an argument between a husband and wife, but I can tell you that my demeanor was the exact same as it is here today with you, sir. If Janet was upset, which— She grew upset and she grew emotional and passionate. That was her nature. It is her nature to do that."

"You never lost your temper on August fifteenth, is that correct?" Jones asked Perry.

"Correct."

"You never went into a rage or became emotionally upset and lost control of yourself on August fifteenth?"

"Correct."

"You did not do anything in the heat of passion?"

"Correct."

And was Perry in full control of his emotions? he was asked.

"We obviously were upset with each other during our conversation before she left. And I'm not sure if I was upset with her or she was upset with me about other issues when I came home. But—correct me if I'm wrong—the tenor of your question is, Was I upset or angry, or was there anything of that nature going on that evening? And the answer is . . . We had a general disquiet, a general sense of upsetness between the two of us. Things weren't right in our marriage. I probably was upset to some degree with her from the moment I even came home. But it was a general issue in our marriage at that time that we both had unresolved tensions with each other."

Perry kept pussy-footing around the term "argument."

"Did you yell at her?"

"No, I did not yell back."

"Did you throw anything at her?"

"Not at all."

"Did she throw anything at you?"

"No, not that night."

"Did she talk about divorce?"

"No. That night I don't believe she did."

Perry was asked a series of questions on whether he had ever hit his wife. "No, I never struck Janet," he replied.

"You never struck Janet with a fist or open hand at any time in your life?"

"To the best of my recollection, Mr. Jones, I have never struck my wife. It has always been something that I am proud of. I have never struck my wife."

"That's not something you could possibly forget, is it?"

"Mr. Jones, as I sit here today, I don't believe I ever struck my wife. As I sit here today, I tell you that I do not believe I ever struck my wife."

"I didn't ask you if you believed it. I asked you if you did. Do you know that you never struck her?"

"Yes, I think I believe I do know I never struck her."

"Did you ever choke her?"

"No."

Perry's responses were mind-numbing, and as the hours of interrogation wore on, he continued to give ambiguous answers. "The general tenor was, how was I going to make up to her for the period of time that she claimed I had deserted my duties to the household?"

He did admit though that he may have physically hurt Janet when he grabbed her arm and moved her out of the way, or took something from her which she was holding back from him. "I, you know, held her arm in a firm manner, which might be construed to be twisting. But certainly never with the intent of inflicting bodily harm on my wife."

Perry didn't "believe" that he and Janet talked about money that last night, and he claimed he wasn't under any financial pressure and did not have any outstanding unpaid bills or debts "other than routine monthly bills."

He then was forced to admit that he had what he said was "a ten-thousand-dollar payment due at some point in the near future . . . that was in settlement for a disputed claim of harassment when I was at Bass, Berry and Sims."

Perry acknowledged under oath that the debt was to

Leigh Reames, but "I don't believe it was a pressing matter on August fifteenth that I owed the debt." He insisted that the overdue payment "was disputed. I had a legitimate claim, I believe, and I still believe, to this day that I may not pay that debt based on breaches of confidentiality."

"Did you tell your wife about that debt?" Perry was asked.

"Yes."

"When?"

"I don't recollect. On a number of occasions though. On at least two or three occasions," Perry replied.

But when pressed about when he had discussed the debt with Janet, his best response was that "sometime early in the process I told her about the situation. Couple of years ago. And then I know specifically she and I discussed it at length when we were on our last trip to Quebec together, and that was sometime I believe in February or March of this year. And then I believe it was again sometime in July, I mentioned it briefly. It may have been June or July."

Perry claimed that he'd talked about the final payment "on this thing" to Janet, but was hard-pressed to offer any details about the conversation other than to reveal that he had set up a separate bank account under his name in which he made payments to Reames.

He denied setting up the account so Janet would not learn of the indebtedness, and swore that he'd talked to her about it and that "she certainly knew about it."

The argument between Perry and his wife ended "with her being upset. My staying calm, sitting at the kitchen table, with her asking me to leave for the evening.

"My answer to her was, 'Are you sure you want me to leave?'

"Her response was, 'Yes, I want you to go to a hotel.'

"I got up, I went to the phone. I called the Hampton Inn. I made a reservation. I hung up the phone.

"She got up, and she said, 'You're not going again on my time and my money.' And she took my credit card from me. She took my wallet from me. She grabbed the stuff. She ripped up the card. She handed me back my driver's license and my cash. And she walked into my study where— She was there for a short period of time. I heard her. I sat at the kitchen table.

"I heard the printer. She walked out of my study. She walked upstairs. I don't know how long she was upstairs, but it was a relatively short period of time. I stayed at the kitchen table.

"She came downstairs. She had the bags. She handed me the note that she had typed and asked me to read it and sign it. I did so. She turned around. She said something to the effect of 'It's your turn. See ya.' And she left.

"That was the last time I saw my wife."

According to Perry, the word processing program that he and Janet used had a file stamp of the last time it had been saved on the computer. "I know that the note that Janet typed and printed and gave to me on the night she ran away, the file stamp was eight-seventeen at night."

At 9:11 that evening, Perry called his brother Ron March in Wilmette, Illinois. "Ronnie, she's done it. She's pissed off. She packed her bags. She's driven off. She's left. And I'm worried. What should I do?"

" 'Perry, just don't worry about it. Don't worry about it at all. Whenever she comes back, she'll come back. If she's not back, call me in the morning,' " Perry quoted his brother as saying.

"He was a little brusk with me, kind of hung up the phone on me, and that was it. That was the tenor of the conversation."

The call, according to telephone records, lasted three minutes.

Perry was worried, he explained to the probate examiner, "because my wife had never packed her bags and driven off before. She's stormed out of the house and driven off before. Squealing tires and all kind of stuff, but she's never packed her bag. And she also handed me a note that said 'twelve-day vacation' on the top. So I was a little bit more worried this time than normal."

"And you didn't tell your brother anything to the effect that 'Janet and I had an argument and I've killed her and what should I do?'" Perry was asked.

"Mr. Jones, your question is offensive."

But what really set Perry off was when he was asked if he was involved in an ongoing sexual relationship with anyone. Perry's initial response was to say "it's none of your business." When ordered to reply, he said, "I think you're vulgar and insensitive, and I will not answer that question."

After hanging up the phone with his brother that night, telephone records indicate that Perry next reached out to his sister Kathy at 9:18 p.m. His sister, Perry says, "had a different feel for Janet. She's not as charitable towards Janet. Her response was, 'Good. Maybe she'll, you know, go off and have a nice weekend and get her head together, come back. But don't worry about it. Talk to you tomorrow.'"

During the deposition Perry at times squirmed, hesitated in answering, rested his head in his hands, or blinked his eyes before answering a question posed to him. He often referred to Janet in the past tense and would modify his answers.

After Perry's calls to his siblings, and a fast call to mutual friend Laura Rummel to say that Janet had left home, it was three hours before anyone heard from him again. Police who questioned Perry weeks later asked him about the critical three hours.

His answers were not very convincing: he claimed he'd watched television, but couldn't remember what he saw that night.

It was midnight on August 16 inside the lavish home of the Levines in the exclusive area near Edwin Warner Park when the phone rang. "It was Perry," says Carolyn. "He seemed excited. I was kinda shocked to receive a call at that hour. We have phones on either side of the bed, and we looked at the clock and that's how we know what time it was."

Perry was never able to offer a logical explanation as to

why he'd waited almost three hours to call Janet's parents with news that she had left home. At one point he indicated that it was because he and his wife had agreed not to involve her parents in their problems. But the Levines were already aware of their day-to-day marital difficulties. In the end, he claimed he'd called at that late hour thinking maybe Janet was spending the night at her parents' home.

"Perry told me that he and Janet had an argument and that she drove off. They had been arguing so much that when he told me they had another argument, I said, 'Perry, don't worry about it. I'm sure she just wants to cool off. She's probably driving around the block. Call me when she gets back.'

"He told us that maybe she was riding around the block. I didn't doubt what he told me that night. I was sure that she would be back. They had argued many times before, so this was not unlike any other day, except that she had never gone away in her car and taken off."

But Janet didn't come back in the morning.

Carolyn Levine said that Perry's story that night "was believable. At the time, I don't think I could think of anything else. My mind was not going to accept what I inevitably came to believe."

Whether Perry told his mother-in-law then that Janet had left home with suitcases, Carolyn Levine wasn't too sure, but eventually she learned that her daughter had taken some bags with her.

Perry got up about five-thirty or six that morning. "I woke up whenever my kids woke up," says Perry. "They had a fitful night. I took care of them. I got dressed. I sat around steaming at Janet. I took care of the kids. Then I calmed down.

"I said, 'Fine. To heck with it.' I waited for Ella to come. Actually I called her and had her come to my house a half hour early."

He then phoned Carolyn Levine to say that Janet had not returned during the night.

Perry was working in his study, located on the same floor as the kitchen, when unexpected guests arrived. He was at a loss for words and called his mother-in-law in a panic.

"What's wrong?" she asked,

"Marissa Moody is at the door with her son, Grant. I don't know what to tell her. She says her son has a play date with Sammy."

"Why not let the child play with him?" she suggested.

"But this was supposed to be the day when I bring Sammy to the office," Perry replied.

"Well, Perry, I imagine he would prefer to play with his friend than sit at your office all day long," she offered.

The fact that Janet had arranged the play date convinced her family and friends that he'd had no plans to go anywhere that day.

Moody says she saw a rolled-up oriental rug about knee-height in the study and that when she saw Perry, he was agitated, and hurried them out of the house. Sammy was bouncing up and down on the carpet. Janet was nowhere to be found in the house. Tzipi was playing in the side yard with the nanny, Ella. And it was Sammy who let Moody and her son into the house.

What Moody remembers most was Sammy bouncing up and down on the dark-colored rug.

The nanny also noticed the rug blocking the entrance to the kitchen when she got to the house that day. She thought it unusual because she did not know where it had come from.

Perry, on the other hand, claims Moody was never in the house that day and couldn't have seen any carpet. "What roll of carpeting? I have no idea what you're talking about." He at one point questioned the nanny, asking her if she had ever noticed the rug. But even his young son recalls seeing it.

For the last two years, Deneane Beard had worked for Janet part-time as a $75 once-a-week house cleaner earning extra money while she attended nursing school. Her husband, David Beard, is a detective in nearby Williamson County.

Janet was "meticulous, she liked organizational skills," Deneane says. When she arrived at the house that day, around 8:30 that morning, she says she didn't see the rolled-up carpet. Perry specifically told her not to clean the children's playroom, which opened onto the area where Moody said she'd seen the rug. "Don't go in there, the playroom is too messy," Perry instructed her.

What really stood out to her that day, and what she found unusual was that Janet usually left quite a bit of her long, shoulder-length hair behind in the bathroom when she showered. "Janet's hair was missing in the bathtub. There wasn't any hair to clean up on that morning." In fact, the house, particularly the kitchen area, was exceptionally spotless, even though it had been a week since her last visit to clean the March home. It was as though somebody had already scoured the place with a disinfectant.

Word about the missing rug leaked out to the news media and became "topic A" in Nashville. Was it possible that Sammy had actually been jumping on his mother's 104-pound corpse, concealed inside the rug? Did the rug simply disappear?

For years, witnesses came forward to police reporting sightings of such a rug. Some pin-pointed the location, saying it was last seen in a trash bin near a Belle Meade market. One informant claimed he'd seen Perry at a park near his home rolling a dog inside the rug.

As tense as the situation was for Perry, once Ella Goldshmidt arrived at the house, he took off to the office, leaving the nanny to care for the March children and Grant. Goldshmidt later claimed quite adamantly that Janet's routine whenever she left town was to have her parents take care of the children, and Goldshmidt would help in looking after them. And Janet never left town without informing Goldshmidt that she would be gone.

Perry remembers that Friday at the office this way: "I sat around. I did my work. I checked at home to see if Janet had come home. I checked with Carolyn to see if she had heard from Janet. I checked with Larry to see if he had heard from Janet. I called Vanderbilt Plaza. I called the Hampton Inn. I called the Union Station Hotel just to see if she had checked in somewhere to chill out. I did work for [a] client. And I came home early."

Carolyn was concerned about what he told the children about Janet's absence. After all, she told him, they had never gotten up before to not find their mother at home.

"I told them that she had a large art project and she had to leave early before they woke up, and that she wouldn't be back until they go to sleep," Perry claimed.

Perry told his mother-in-law that that was what he'd also told Goldshmidt and Beard when they arrived for work, though both women later said that Perry told them that Janet had gone to California for a few days.

What really disturbed Larry and Carolyn Levine was when they learned that Perry had told the children that their mother ran away and abandoned them. "That was an outright lie. Janet loved those children, and to my knowledge she had never left the house at night and not come back, ever," Carolyn says.

Carolyn Levine was sure her daughter was coming back. It was so unlike Janet to go anywhere and not let her know. Carolyn stayed by the phone all day. Every time she talked with Perry that day, he dished out more details of what had happened the night before.

Carolyn Levine later admitted she had been suspicious of Perry from day one—that something had happened and that he was the cause of it. "I believed that she would be back, but in the back of my mind, I had suspicions, because I knew the treatment that Janet had undergone for a number of years by her husband, and so I had suspicions. Her leaving home like Perry said was not like her.

"In my wildest dreams, I didn't think Perry would be capable of killing his wife."

Carolyn said that her daughter had tried for five years to make the marriage work. It was more than Perry's abusive treatment. "There was emotional and psychological abuse. Perry would belittle her in front of me, in front of her friends, in front of others. Let me put it this way: he was not good to her."

Perry told his mother-in-law that on the night Janet left, she had packed a gray suitcase and two light overnight cases, and that she had handed him a note typed on the computer.

The next day, Perry faxed a copy of that note to Carolyn Levine. It was the twelve-day to-do list. "Later in the afternoon, he told me that Janet had taken her passport and fifteen hundred dollars in cash.

"The minute I heard that she had taken her passport, I told my husband, and he immediately said he was going out to the airport."

"If she took her passport, maybe she went somewhere," Larry Levine later said. But Janet's father returned home empty-handed, disappointed at not having found his daughter or the Volvo.

Perry told Carolyn that "he knew exactly" what Janet had worn when she left—khaki shorts and a navy short-sleeve top with buttons in the front and no collar. Later, he said he was mistaken and didn't remember what she'd been wearing when she left.

By Sunday night, August 18, Carolyn was really getting anxious. "It was so unusual for Janet. She just wouldn't leave the kids without somebody knowing where she was." If Perry was worried, he didn't show it. He reminded his in-laws, as his sister Kathy pointed out, that since Janet had written a twelve-day note, "we shouldn't do anything, and let's wait twelve days." The Levines meanwhile wanted to report their daughter missing to police.

That day, Perry called his father in Ajijic (pronounced, ah-hee-heek), Mexico. In fact, according to phone records, he placed two calls. The first call at 5:11 p.m. lasted four minutes, and the second call was at 10:18 p.m. and lasted three minutes. After speaking with his son and learning from him that Janet had taken off to points unknown on vacation, he decided to visit Perry in Nashville to help him take care of the kids.

"I was distraught that my wife had run away and he was very concerned and volunteered to come up to help," Perry says.

He arrived in Nashville around August 21 from Ajijic in his Ford Escort station wagon after making the tedious four-day, 2,270-mile trip.

No one recalls seeing Grandpa March on August 25, the day of Sammy's sixth birthday party in Dragon Park, but he could have been in attendance. What father and son might have been doing in the days before Perry reported Janet missing on August 29 would be a source of suspicion for detectives once the investigation got underway.

Around the 21st of August, the Levines were still of a mind to seek out the police, but Perry insisted, "No, let's give her more time." He called his brother, Ron, and had him speak with Carolyn. Ron told her that the police couldn't be trusted. To try to convince her, Carolyn said, Ron related a story to her about Chicago police.

"I said to Ron,' 'We live in Nashville, Tennessee. We're a small community, not Chicago, and I don't believe those kinds of things would happen here.' But he said, 'Don't go to the police.'"

What concerned Larry Levine was something he noticed the day he'd accompanied Perry to the Nashville airport in another attempt to look for Janet's Volvo. As the two men drove around the parking lot, Perry looked straight ahead, making no effort to locate the car. Perry's blasé behavior was the first sign for Larry that his son-in-law could have been responsible for Janet's disappearance.

The moment the police were brought into the picture on August 29, Perry changed his sentiments and blamed the delay in notifying authorities on the Levines. "The Levines forbade me from bringing in the police," Perry said.

And for good measure, he added, "That effing Janet has ruined my life."

4

"I'll Be Vindicated"

The disappearance of Janet March didn't become known to police until August 29, when Perry March and his father-in-law, Lawrence Levine, a prominent lawyer, walked into the Criminal Justice Center police headquarters in downtown Nashville, accompanied by Levine's son, Mark, also a lawyer, to file a missing persons report. By then, Janet had been missing for two weeks.

For nine years, Perry's story was that on that hot sweltering August 15 evening in 1996, he and his wife, Janet Levine March, had had what he called a "routine" argument. She'd told him she was going on vacation and typed a twelve-day to-do list for him to deal with while she was away. Among the items on the list were such mundane household chores as cleaning his closet and the garbage area, paying bills, and making sure to feed the children nutritious food three times a day. The twenty-three-item list, titled "Perry's Turn For Janet's 12 Day Vacation" ends saying, "I agree to do all of the above before Janet's Vacation (in response to Perry's cowardly, rash and confused vacation) is over," and she made him sign it, Perry told the police.

He said that Janet had then packed three suitcases, her

passport, and a plastic bag of marijuana, and taken $5,000 cash—or perhaps it was $1,500. Perry changed the amount of money Janet had with her, depending on whether he spoke with the media, the police or his in-laws.

But Perry was very consistent that she'd stormed out of the house, gotten into her new gray four-door Volvo 850 sedan saying, "Bye, see ya," and vanished. Janet has not been heard from or seen since that night.

He told his two young children that "Mommy ran away and we don't know where she is." Friends were told that Janet "took off." That pretty much was Perry's story.

"Perry had not wanted to go to the police. He was very nervous, very worried about police tactics and the media, and he said he wanted to go to a private investigator," Carolyn Levine recalled. He also insisted that "if we reported something to the authorities it would end up embarrassing Janet," and that by publicly reporting her missing, it would make the situation worse."

The Levines agreed to Perry's request and at first sought out a private investigator. Perry kept insisting he still did not want to report Janet missing, saying he feared embarrassing her. But as the days passed, the Levines gave him an ultimatum.

"My husband and my son said to Perry, 'We are not waiting any longer,'" Carolyn Levine related. "'We are going to the police. You can go with us if you want, or if you don't want, we're going anyway.'"

Almost from the start, Perry was a prime suspect. Police theorized that Perry's two-week delay in reporting Janet missing had given him ample time to dispose of the body and clean up any tell-tale signs of the murder.

He told police he had wanted to wait the two weeks to report her missing, figuring she was off "somewhere" having a good time on a twelve-day vacation and would return on her own when she was ready.

The police and Janet's family doubted that she had written the to-do list.

Since the note indicated she would be gone twelve days,

that meant she should be home by Tuesday, August 27. However, it also meant she would miss her son Sammy's sixth birthday party on Sunday, August 25, which she had already arranged to take place at Fannie Mae Dees Park, the "Dragon Park" on Blakemore Avenue near Hillsboro Village that kids like because they could play around the sculptured dragon.

A week before her disappearance, Janet had sent invitations to about twenty kids and their parents to attend what she thought would be a fun day to have with family. Janet had also arranged for pizza and drinks, and for cake and ice cream to be served. But Janet wasn't there. The party went on without her.

When Janet was a no-show, Perry and his in-laws made up a story that she was in California with an earache and couldn't fly home. But Janet's friends doubted the story, saying it was unbelievable that she wouldn't be at the birthday party for Sammy. And she certainly wouldn't have taken off without telling anyone, particularly her mother. But what really made Janet's family and friends suspicious about her disappearance was that the day after Sammy's birthday party, on Monday, August 26, he was starting a new school, The University School of Nashville, which Janet had attended as a young child.

"For Janet to miss Sammy's first day of school was not conceivable," her mother says.

Shortly after Janet disappeared, Elliot Greenberg, a client and one of Perry's best friends, gave an interview to the *Tennessean* about him. "When he first told me Janet was missing, he had tears in his eyes. Perry's very reserved; typically, he won't exhibit that kind of behavior in public," he said.

Meanwhile, Perry kept calling Larry Brinton, Nashville's well-known news reporter and distinguished television host on WSMV-TVs "Word on the Street," who has spoken to him more than 500 times in the last ten years, offering to profess his innocence to television viewers. "Perry could look you in the eye and say he didn't kill his wife, but the truth of the matter is that nobody believed anything he said," Brinton stated.

On one occasion, when Brinton told him that police might not be able to charge and indict him for murder until Janet's body was located, Perry's spontaneous response was to blurt out, "What are the police thinking? That they are going to find my business card on the body?"

"No," Brinton replied. "But if they find her wrapped up in a carpet, you might have problems."

Perry had no answer and promptly hung up the phone. It was such off-the-cuff remarks that made those who knew Perry consider him manipulative, aggressive, and tenacious.

In retrospect, Larry Levine later called his delay in calling the police "the biggest mistake we ever made. But," he says, "Perry kept telling us, 'Maybe she went here, maybe she went there.' . . . We believed him."

Once the police were called in, Perry began complaining to Larry Levine that the helicopters flying over his property were keeping him awake at night. He badgered his father-in-law to use his influence to call off the police.

"Perry, I don't want to call off the police. I want them to find Janet. They are doing their job. Secondly, I couldn't call off the police if I wanted to," Mark recalled his father telling Perry.

David Miller, assigned to the Missing Persons Unit, was the first detective to work the case, and was the lead detective on it for five months. Though retired now, and living in Florida, the gray-haired, bespectacled investigator says it still haunts him.

"As the case developed, it became a high-profile case with the media and reporters and photographers camped outside the March home . . . seeking any scraps of information," says Miller.

In the beginning, Miller and his team concentrated on parking lots in Nashville and at the airport. They checked hospitals, the county morgue, and the surrounding areas of Nashville, including Memphis, Hendersonville, as far north as Clarksville, south to Chattanooga, east to Knoxville and even into neighboring Kentucky to determine if Janet could be a DOA (dead on arrival) victim or a patient at a nearby hospital. Interviews were conducted with employees of self-storage facilities to see if Janet's body had been dumped there. The FBI was called in on the case and made flyovers using infrared sensors to detect body heat in dense-foliage areas and swamps. Even U.S. Army military helicopters went out looking for Janet, searching Otter and Richland Creeks and other rural areas in and around the March home.

Miller's team did not neglect searching area parks such as the Percy Warner and Edwin Warner Parks, Long Hunter State Park, and St. Cecilia Academy, and they even went so far as to check out a quarry in Alabama. They were all gone over with a fine tooth comb. A tip from a psychic that Janet's body might be in Radnor Lake, not far from the March home, also yielded nothing. "Every portion of Perry March's property and even the exterior of his neighbor's property was searched, not once but twice," says Miller.

Everyone in Nashville had a theory or claimed to have made a sighting of Janet. A state prisoner got into the act, suggesting police look for Janet's body along an area of the Cumberland River that snakes around downtown Nashville. "We brought divers in and searched the area for three days and came up empty," said Miller.

Cadaver dogs were brought in to assist in the search, as was the Bloodhound Search Organization, a private volunteer group that assists police with missing persons cases. The investigation was exhaustive, canvassing the local trash-hauling firms of BFI and Sanfill of Tennessee, where detectives learned that their Dumpsters are emptied regularly; in fact some Dumpsters are unloaded and cleaned out daily, meaning that there would be no chance of recovering a body.

Janet's credit cards were checked and there was no activity on any of them, including her ATM card and bank account, which showed no withdrawals.

Two weeks after reporting Janet missing, Perry gave his

first interview to *The Tennessean,* one of the leading daily newspapers.

"I am innocent," he declared. "If she was captured by Moonies, if she didn't do this on her own, I'm going to hug her and I'm going to bring her home, and I'm going to do whatever I have to do to make her whole again."

"The statement may have sounded like he was sincere and really meant what he was saying," says Larry Brinton. "But those who know Perry best say people should never lose sight of the fact that Perry has a big ego, loves being in the limelight, and tries to impress people."

On September 7, police got their first break in the case. Tim Mason, a homicide detective in the Criminal Investigative Unit, received a phone call from two tenants of the Brixworth Apartments on Harding Road in Belle Meade, 3 miles from the March home.

They reported a Volvo parked at building 131, near the rear of the apartment complex. It was Janet's car and it was locked.

Finding it backed into the parking spot immediately raised police suspicions, because it meant that whoever had parked it did not want the license tag visible to passers-by.

Some Brixworth tenants said they had not seen the Volvo, while others said they had seen it in the parking lot for two weeks. The police determined that neither Perry nor Janet had any friends living at the complex, although Perry insinuated that his wife might have been cheating on him with someone there. Perry also tried to imply that his wife had been seen there, "probably buying drugs."

Peter Rodman, a resident of the complex, came forward after Janet's car was found saying he'd seen a suspicious white man with curly hair, resembling Perry, on a bicycle standing still in the parking lot at about 1:30 the morning of August 16.

Perry owned a mountain bike and was an avid bicyclist, but denied any suggestion that he'd been near the Brixworth Apartments.

Detective Brad Corcoran, a twenty-year veteran with the

Metro Police Department was assigned to the Crime Scene Investigation Unit at the time the Volvo was discovered. It was towed to the forensic lab at 501 Second Avenue North so it could be examined in a controlled temperature environment, where Corcoran could photograph it, dust it for latent fingerprints, and run luminol tests to detect any presence of blood.

"In processing the car, I noticed that the outside of the vehicle had the appearance that it had been sitting for a while. It was covered with dirt, dust, and pollens. There were also cobwebs in the wheels and around the trunk area. There was rust buildup on the rotors on the disk brakes. It had been rusted over and had the appearance that the car had not been moved or driven in quite a while. If the brakes had been applied, the rust would not have built up," he explained.

After his chemical analysis, Corcoran inventoried the contents of the car. Janet's identification was found inside her purse in the left-hand front pocket of the door of the car, he said. The baby seat of Janet's 2-year-old daughter Tzipora was on the back seat, right behind the driver's seat. A baby stroller and a bag of diapers were found, along with a black suitcase containing various types of clothing belonging to Janet, including white socks, a bikini swimsuit, and three sundresses. A canvas bag was found behind the driver's-seat in the floorboard area containing toiletry items.

A pair of Janet's white sandals was neatly situated side-by-side below the driver's seat, which the detectives thought was an odd placement, perhaps intended to give the impression that Janet had been pulled out of the car forcibly.

Corcoran found her passport, along with $61, fifty of which were found in the glove compartment and the rest in Janet's purse. Nowhere in the car was the $5,000 or $1,500 that Perry claimed Janet had taken with her when she'd left the house.

A few days after the Volvo was found, Perry allowed police to examine his Jeep. Corcoran said he photographed it and collected physical evidence from inside it, observing that it had been driven recently.

The detective found two fibers and a strand of hair in the trunk area, which he sent to the FBI for further analysis. Significantly, the interior of the Jeep smelled like a cleaner or disinfectant had recently been applied.

The day the Volvo was located was an extremely difficult time for Carolyn and Larry Levine. Speaking about that Saturday, even ten years later, brings tears to Carolyn's eyes. Choked with emotion, her thoughts stir painful wounds in her memory. For the Levines, and for Janet's many friends, the discovery of the car meant that she was dead.

They collectively posted a $25,000 reward for information leading to the location of Janet or her body, the police announced.

"Perry's demeanor changed after the car was found," Carolyn recalls. As she learned after he left Nashville, in late September, he had retained well-known criminal attorney Lionel Barrett to represent him (two days *before* the missing persons report was filed).

Carolyn was taken down to the forensic lab where the Volvo had been towed. What caught her eye in checking the contents of Janet's gray overnight bag was that she had not brought a hairbrush, bras, or toothbrush. Those missing items suggested to detectives that a man, not a woman, had packed the suitcase.

Police wanted to have a sit-down interview with Perry at headquarters to take a statement, but he refused and distanced himself from the investigation. He kept saying he didn't have time. Finally, Detective Miller did the next best thing. He met with Perry at the Levines' home on September 10, where he found him "very nervous."

Mark recalled in his interview with Nashville TV Channel 4 that the day Miller had driven up to the Levines' home to question him, Perry turned white. "He started shivering, stuttering, unable to speak. He appeared almost light-headed, as if all the blood had rushed out of his head . . . faint, sweaty. He started to stand up, but fell back in his chair."

Perry must have thought that the detective was at the

Levine house to arrest him, because he blurted out, "Call my brother, Ronnie. Call Ronnie."

Miller didn't arrest him, but instead advised Perry of his Miranda and Fourth Amendment rights. Perry said that as an attorney, he understood them.

But Perry stonewalled the detective and instead hand-wrote his statement and mailed it. "It was not a normal procedure in a homicide investigation," Miller said, "and it is the only statement police have ever had from Perry."

"That was a big flag for me," said Miller's supervisor, Captain Mickey Miller (no relation) who oversaw the investigation. "First the finding of the car took away Perry's theory that his wife had left him. It just appeared to us that the car was staged. Then his statement didn't have anything of interest in it. It was a very prepared statement. It didn't sound like a grieving husband whose wife had disappeared."

By September 12, five days later, Perry's defense lawyer provided police with the twelve-day to-do vacation note that Perry claimed his wife had written on his computer before she took off. As the investigation wore on and detectives picked up other clues, more and more they were inclined to mistrust anything Perry March was telling them.

The detectives had suspicions that Janet did not type the to-do list. "Janet was the kind of person who would normally handwrite notes and lists. If she were going on a trip, she would leave a list for me about what needs to be done with the children," says Carolyn Levine. Usually she would leave a detailed list about what to feed them, when to feed them, when to bathe them, and when they went to sleep. Those notes weren't typed on a computer, but were handwritten.

"The last time she used the computer was when she was building the house, and then she used our computer in our home to make out lists of things that needed to be done at the house such as accountant expenses."

Carolyn was familiar with Janet's writing style, and instinctively knew that her daughter had not written the to-do list, because she never used capital letters at the start of a sentence. "And on the note, that Perry faxed to me, it's all capitalized. It's all numbers. It has the date at the bottom. Janet didn't date things at the bottom. She dated everything at the top. I have many examples of her writings and I know how she wrote," Carolyn emphasized.

The detectives probed further. There was no mention in the note of Janet arranging a play date with Marissa Moody's son Grant for August 16, or of Sammy's birthday party, which Janet had organized before disappearing. There were more and more inconsistencies that disturbed detectives.

The biggest was catching Perry in a transparent lie. Several days after Janet disappeared, police discovered that he'd had the tires on his Jeep Cherokee replaced with new ones.

Perry's propensity to mouth off tripped him up. "It was on my list, it was on my list," he tried to convince detectives. But changing the tires wasn't on the to-do list, and the more he lied about it, the deeper a hole he was in.

The explanation he gave investigators was that Janet worried that the tires were bald, and in the event of rain, the Jeep could slip and skid and cause an accident.

But the tires didn't need to be fixed. In fact, Robert Armstrong, the manager of the tire shop, informed Perry that his current set were still in good condition and questioned why they were being changed. Perry said he just didn't like the type of tires on the car and wanted "a set of Michelins." And he told Armstrong to get rid of his old tires, that he didn't want them returned to him even though they were still in good condition.

On September 17, search warrants were obtained for both the March house and a condominium near Vanderbilt University that Perry rented from a friend. "They came to my house with their corps of paramilitary boot camp folks," Perry said sarcastically as he recalled the day the police arrived at his house in a show of force to execute the warrant.

"There were about seventy to one hundred paramilitary types swarming all over my house."

Seized as a result of the warrant was a stained bath mat, shirts, twenty computer discs, a magazine, a legal pad, a book on divorce, a knife, a shirt with a stain, plant material, and assorted notes. From the condo apartment, bottles of cleaning supplies, "a dark substance," were seized, a detective informed Captain Miller. "Also, a security guard had seen Arthur March, Perry's father, come out of the condominium carrying women's clothing and a pair of women's shoes. When we tried interviewing the father, he disappeared," he said.

Perry told his mother-in-law that he'd sent his father "up to Chicago because he has a big mouth and talks too much." As for why he rented the condominium, Perry gave a rather transparent reason: "So that when Janet comes back I'd have a place to go."

A bulldozer and a backhoe were brought onto the property to turn up the four to five acres of earth. Fifty police cadets assisted in the ground search, poking through the wooded landscape with sharpened probes as cadaver dogs and bloodhounds searched for signs of Janet.

Perry says the scene was like something out of some B detective movie. The police investigation had captured the public's attention and the media was on hand to record every detail. Red Cross food wagons were set up on the property to feed the huge corps of reporters and photographers and those assisting in the search.

Perry's lawyer had informed him a day earlier that unless he allowed police to come out and effect a third voluntary search of the house, they were going to issue a search warrant.

With police crawling all over the March home, Perry took in the surreal scene calmly sitting on the back porch smoking a cigar, giggling and laughing with his lawyer and his brother, Ron, ignoring the crucial hunt for clues going on before his eyes. "He seemed to enjoy watching the police on their hands and knees looking at the ground," said Detective Miller.

David Miller's boss, Captain Mickey Miller said that once Perry stopped cooperating, he couldn't be eliminated as a suspect. "It was his whole demeanor. He wasn't willing

to make a statement, supposedly he didn't seem that aggrieved that his wife was missing." Further incriminating
factors, such as "his unnecessarily having all the tires
changed on his Jeep, and the missing carpet" also did not
bode well for Perry.

"He had two weeks, which is a lot of time to get rid of a
body and get rid of a lot of crucial evidence," Mickey Miller
said. And what really jumped out at Miller and the other detectives was that Perry always referred to Janet in the past
tense.

While searching the house, Captain Miller decided to
play some mind tricks with Perry. He had one of his detectives, Kim Gooch, who bore a striking resemblance to Janet
March, put on outer garments similar to what Janet wore.
She had the same dark hair, the same features. "We then
posted her in a window behind a sheer curtain looking out to
where Perry was sitting, so that when he saw her face, it
gave the appearance of something out of a dream. We had
her do that several times. At first it didn't seem to be bother-
ing him, and it looked as if he didn't seem to have a care in
the world. But suddenly he stared at the window and shot a
glance at what he must have thought was Janet returning
from the dead.

"I thought he was going to wrench his neck out of place
when he first looked up, but then he regained his compo-
sure."

Miller still chuckles in recalling the scene. "Perry mo-
mentarily appeared shocked. It spooked him. He jumped up
from his seat and started shaking. He had to wonder whether
it really was Janet or was it her ghost?"

Perry recovered enough from the game police were playing with his head to admit, almost bragging, that his lawyer
had tipped him off the day before that the police were coming to the house again.

Police searched the computer and found that the hard
drive had been ripped out. Detective David Miller came
storming out of the house, screaming, "Where's the hard
drive, Perry?"

Perry said he then "knew I was the prime suspect in my wife's disappearance."

Perry denied ripping out the hard drive and suggested his father-in-law or father as the culprit. Both later denied any involvement, although Perry's father did have access to his son's home when he stayed there on the 14th and 15th of September while Perry went to Chicago with the kids to celebrate Rosh Hashanah, the Jewish New Year.

"My father is a character. He's a big old cuddly bear, and I had him put up 'no trespassing' signs to keep people away from the house. It had already become a media circus with reporters and press people all over my property. And if he was there to watch the house while I was gone, I promise you, no one would get in my house."

Perry did admit that during the time his father stayed at his home, the burglar alarm system had been turned off, and it was possible that his father had removed the hard drive without telling Perry. However, Arthur March denied any involvement in its disappearance.

At the height of the investigation, nearly two dozen detectives worked on the case. By 2006 the police department had conservatively spent over $500,000—more likely close to a million—on it.

Over the years, police got more calls about where the body was. They dug up a horse barn stall. They went out to Woodlawn Cemetery and found a grave marker of a woman who'd died the same day that Janet disappeared, and dug a hole right next to it, thinking that maybe the body would be underneath the casket. Detectives went to the Music City Mix Factory, which was owned by one of Perry's clients, Paul Eichel, because there was a tunnel there that led from the basement to the river.

On another occasion, police got a call from someone saying he had just seen a man put a woman's body in the trunk of his car outside Music City. Police rushed to the scene. Yes, it was true. A man had placed his drunken wife in the trunk of his car and was taking her home.

Police received a tip from Crime Stoppers about a man

named Clyde Maxwell Sumner who at one time worked on the March home and who, it was alleged, had provided Perry with a gun. Perry's lawyer felt that Sumner might have had a motive to kill Janet, particularly after he revealed in an interview with Miller that he'd had a sexual attraction to her, even spying on her from outside the home. Those allegations never panned out.

Sumner agreed to take a polygraph test.

"Did you kill Janet March?" he was asked.

"No."

"Do you know for sure who killed Janet March?"

Again, Sumner said "No."

Although he denied having anything to do with Janet's death or disappearance, the test reports showed that he was deceptive.

"No action was taken against Mr. Sumner, and after interviewing him a second time, we found him to be cooperative. And he was honest enough and was not an individual we wanted to go further with," says Miller.

Perry proposed several scenarios of his own for how Janet might have been killed. "People involved with the construction of our house that carry extreme animosity and feelings towards Janet," might be responsible, he said, coming up with names of those who'd worked at the house eighteen months earlier.

"I warned Janet on a number of occasions to attempt to modify her behavior and to attempt to modify her statements and interactions with the various subcontractors and contractors working on our job because she was creating a great degree of animosity, and it was counterproductive to the job and it was also dangerous to her."

Asked if he'd ever heard these people threaten to kill her or do her bodily harm, he responded, "I have heard of intimations of such. The contractor himself, Cooper Cate—and I am not disparaging or meaning to slander or libel anybody, but I feel that there are people out there who have extreme levels of hate and animosity towards Janet."

When asked to supply other names, Perry came up with

"Ron, the painter, who was head of the painting crew. And various subs who I don't know their names."

Perry explained Ron's alleged animosity: "My wife is very finicky. She's very precise, and demanding of workmen. And the painter did not meet her standards, and she demanded that he meet her standards, and they had a constant battle about what he should do and what he shouldn't do."

Perry said that he'd singled out the contractor based on "a disastrous working relationship. I never heard him threaten her directly, but to me, he did. He swore at Janet numerous times to me."

According to Perry, the threats were "implicit. Things like 'If I don't get paid, you'll see what happens.' Things of that nature." In the end, he had to admit that the contractor had been paid "legally everything he was supposed to" and never made any explicit threats to him about his wife.

While Perry was adamant that he'd told Janet about the threats from Ron, they were apparently not significant enough for him to bother to learn the painter's last name.

Perry came up with a couple of other possible suspects, such as the workman Janet had caught stealing chairs from the house, the carpenter found stealing materials for his own personal use, and another workman she caught making a birdhouse "on our time," though none of those claims was substantiated.

"There must have been over a hundred people flowing in and out of your project that Janet had day-to-day contact with. Do you think any of these people killed her?" Perry was asked.

"I don't know."

On the advice of his lawyer, Perry refused to take a lie detector test, claiming it wouldn't be accurate, since he was taking anti-stress medication. He said he stopped cooperating with police after they fingered him as a suspect.

Asked about whether he was responsible for his wife's death, he responded indignantly, "Absolutely not. I'm just sick of that question. It's offensive. Of course not. I want you to know that I have nothing to do with the disappearance of my wife."

In an interview late in 2006, lashing out at investigators and his in-laws in particular, Perry added: "Without a shred of evidence, my in-laws, the Levines, have taken away my house, my livelihood, my community. I've been wrongly accused. But you'll see, I'll be vindicated."

5

"I'll Be in Mexico for the Rest of My Life"

By September 19, 1996, after being named the prime suspect by police in his wife's disappearance, Perry packed up his belongings and, with Sammy and Tzipi, fled to Wilmette, Illinois, leaving behind pictures of Janet taken on his wedding day.

The Levines tried to get a restraining order to prevent him from taking the children out of state, but by the time they got to court, Perry and the children were long gone. "They were no longer in Nashville. We were told we were too late," said Carolyn.

And thus began the acrimonious dispute over custody and visitation of the two grandchildren, fought in two states and in federal courts for the nine years that followed.

Three months after the Janet March case became the most talked-about police investigation in the area, the Levines held a memorial service for their daughter at the West End Synagogue, a Conservative Jewish congregation serving Nashville.

The service overflowed with loving friends, relatives, and extended family members that included cousins, nieces, nephews, aunts, and uncles. Everyone who knew Janet was there—with the exception of Perry. He made himself present in other ways, though: he filed a frivolous lawsuit against Rabbi Ronald Roth for holding the service at the synagogue.

Janet's brother Mark, a Washington, DC, lawyer and host of *Radio Inside*, a popular political talk-radio show, gave the eulogy that expressed the depth of his feeling toward his sister, and his sorrow at losing her.

> Janet, what's going on? One day you're building a house, having morning coffee with Mom, calling to tell me a funny story, raising two sweet, beautiful children. The next day you're missing, dead, murdered. Your children held in isolation, suffering, crying out behind an iron curtain, not allowed to talk to anyone they love, unless a sufficient ransom is paid . . .
>
> Janet, I'm torn . . . between the lessons of your life and the horror of your death. In your life, you always trusted and gave people the benefit of the doubt. You made everyone, friends and strangers, comfortable, because you listened perceptively with an open mind and a compassionate heart. You didn't judge.

Mark's voice cracked as he continued:

> Your death makes me bitter and angry. Were you naïve to believe you could heal a bruised soul, a sick mind? That kindness could conquer manipulation and lies? I thank you for sharing your private moments with me. I only wish that I had somehow acted to prevent your worst fears from coming true.

It was obvious from these last remarks that Janet had had conversations with her brother about Perry, and had confided in him about the emotional and physical abuse she had endured. It was a moving service, as Mark spoke of Janet's humor, her advice, and her perspective on life, recalling how she was a beautiful romantic, a perfectionist, a storyteller, a comedienne, an imitator par excellence.

You were such a sweet and giving person, with your friends (you had a special relationship with your friends), with Mom and Dad, with me, and to your children, mostly to your children. I have never seen such a devoted mother in my life. You were so proud of Sammy, not because he was smart, but because he would share his toys with everyone in the class, because he would look after his little sister. You were so proud of Tzipi too, the way she was curious about the world around her, her special fondness for all kinds of animals. And sometimes Tzipi would be a little stubborn, wanting to do things her way. Yet you were always patient.

Before ending his tribute to his sister with reciting a verse from Psalm 37 about trusting in the Lord and being patient that evildoers will "soon wither," tears flowed from the congregation as Mark spoke about the bitterness he felt over losing Janet.

I can't believe that I'm an only child. I cannot hide my bitterness. I want to honor you and mourn for you. But I'm compelled to draft legal papers instead. I want to give you a decent burial, but I don't know where you are. And I pray to God that someday, I will be able to place dirt in your grave.

I cannot hide my contempt for the person who murdered you. Your death has rocked the core of everything I believe in.

Grief-stricken over the loss of their daughter and unable to have any contact with Sammy and Tzipi, the Levines, through a local lawyer and with the help of their son, brought an action for grandparent visitation rights in Chicago, because the grandparent visitation statute had been declared unconstitutional by the Tennessee Supreme Court in 1993.

By December, the Levines were granted the right to visit every other weekend, but only in Chicago. Later another order allowed the children to stay with their grandparents every other weekend from Friday to Sunday. That arrangement went on for two-and-a-half years. These visits took place at a condominium the Levines purchased in Deerfield, a nearby suburb of the Windy City.

In June 1998, an appellate court vacated the order, and as a result visits between the children and the grandparents were abruptly terminated. Over the next year, Sammy and Tzipi only saw Larry and Carolyn on four occasions, each visit lasting about one day, other than a weekend visit in February 1999.

Meanwhile, the litigation continued. The Levines were in the process of seeking permanent visitation rights when Perry's brother, Ron, who was also acting as his attorney, announced in court that Perry and the kids had left Chicago and were now living in Mexico.

Founded by the Natuatl Indians in the early 1400s, Ajijic, Mexico (population 5,000) is 30 miles south of Guadalajara, along the northern shore of Lake Chapala in western Mexico's Sierra Madre Mountains. And for Perry, it was paradise, with its laid-back charm, its nightlife, restaurants, cool lake breezes, and comfortable lifestyle. Perry felt he had found his niche, where he and his children could live away from the constant harassment and bitter custody battles of the Levines, who he felt were spearheading the drive to get police and prosecutors to have him arrested for their daughter's disappearance.

"It surprised the judge, and it was a shock to us," says Carolyn of Perry's move. Not only could they no longer see the children, but the Levines were not allowed to speak to them, even though they called every week.

Perry and the children had arrived on May 19, 1999. "I wanted to be near my father in his retirement, and my children needed a breath of fresh air," Perry told Larry Brinton who at the time was with NewsChannel 5 in Nashville. "I think I'll be in Mexico for the rest of my life, unless the Levines can make up some way to have me shipped out."

But he was aware of the Levines' attachment to their

grandchildren and took advantage of the legal squabbling over Janet's property to frustrate their visitation efforts with Sammy and Tzipi. Perry repeatedly disregarded two Illinois courts' visitation orders and as a result, was eventually held in both direct and indirect criminal contempt of court in Illinois. His reaction to the Levines' lawsuits was to refer to them as "frivolous" and "malicious harassment" . . . "to disrupt his home life with his children."

The Illinois judge in the case appointed a guardian *ad litem*—a person named by the court to protect the interests of minors in a lawsuit. The guardian observed and informed the judge that Perry "intended to use the children as pawns in a vendetta" with the Levines and that Perry was using visitation as a "price tag for legalistic maneuvering, posturing and unsuccessful interchange of settlement issues."

Another guardian *ad litem* reported to the Illinois court that Perry had said he saw no harm or danger in the children visiting their grandparents. However, he would not permit it without receiving something in return. According to that guardian, the Levines could have contact with the kids if they would "drop all ancillary civil litigation" against him and help him re-obtain his law license. Perry had warned the court before taking off for Ajijic that if they granted the Levines visitation without his requests being met, he would take the children out of the United States to either Singapore or Mexico.

After Perry took off to Mexico, there was a different order from the Chicago court. "It allowed us visitation once a month with the children in the United States," says Carolyn.

Perry complied with the order in June and July 1999, sending the children to the United States. The first time, Perry flew the children up with his father, although the Levines had purchased the ticket in Perry's name. When it was time to return the children to Mexico, Arthur March did not go back with them. "The children were sent back alone to Mexico, and they were pretty young at the time to be flying alone," says Carolyn.

But in August 1999, Perry said he was not sending the

children anymore, Perry's argument to the court was that the July trip "was horrendous on the children." The reasoning Perry gave reporter Larry Brinton was that on that last visit, the Levines had allowed Sammy and Tzipi to read all the newspaper clippings about their mother's disappearance, and he thought it was entirely inappropriate. Perry also told the court that the children had "suffered a seriously traumatic flight home to Guadalajara." Of course, Perry made no mention in his legal brief that his father was meant to accompany them back to Mexico with a ticket purchased by the Levines.

But what really may have precipitated Perry's impulsive move was an order by Anthony Young, a Chicago judge who had a noted child and adolescent psychiatrist and associate professor of clinical psychiatry at the University of Chicago, Alan Ravitz, conduct a re-evaluation of the matter.

In preparing his report to the judge, which became a part of the court record, Ravitz met with Carolyn and Larry Levine and performed a number of home visits at the Deerfield condominium that they had purchased.

Before his meetings, Ravitz also reviewed a psychological evaluation of Perry March that had been prepared by the court, and read through various newspaper articles, court documents, and correspondence between Perry and the Levines.

"I attempted to involve Perry March in the evaluation by calling his attorney, Vincent Stark, on two occasions and attempted to contact Perry directly by phone in Mexico on one occasion but he did not make himself available," Ravitz wrote the judge in his four-page report of September 10, 1999.

The psychiatrist pointed out in his report to the judge that Perry and Janet had "relied extensively on Carolyn and Larry to provide childcare. Sammy and Tzipi spent an unusual amount of time with their grandparents . . . on an almost daily basis.

"There is no question but that the children had an exceptionally close relationship with Larry and Carolyn and the extended family, most of whom lived in the Nashville area."

Although it was clear to the psychiatrist that the Levines "were quite hostile to Perry," it was also clear that they understood that the grandchildren had to be insulated from this hostility for their own welfare.

However, Ravitz also noted that "Perry and probably his father as well, are exposing the children to hostile and alienating comments about the Levines . . . making visitation more difficult. Finally, I must state that it is apparent to me that Perry is not supporting the children's relationship with their grandparents and his behavior is likely harmful to the children."

The conclusion that Ravitz reached and recommended to the judge was that the Levines continue to play a vitally important role in the lives of the grandchildren. "Larry and Carolyn remain the only connection that the children have to their mother's family and to deprive Sammy and Tzipi of this relationship would be cruel and harmful."

Ravitz also advised the judge that he had "grave concerns" regarding the effect that Arthur March may have on the children, and questioned whether Perry's father should have any regular contact with his grandchildren.

A month later Judge Young of the Circuit Court for Cook County (Chicago) granted the Levines permanent visitation rights, allowing visits in the United States, in Mexico, or any other foreign country. "It allowed us to have not only normal visitation, but to make up visitation that had been missed in the past," recalls Carolyn. The order specifically said that they could have thirty-nine days of uninterrupted visits with the grandchildren.

By then the custody battle was going full blast, and as the weeks turned into months, Perry's relationship with his in-laws further deteriorated and became contentious, if not hopeless.

It had all started back on October 30, 1996, two months after Janet disappeared, when Perry filed a probate petition in Nashville seeking to seize his wife's bank accounts and his children's trust funds. That attack provoked the Levines to fan the flames by filling a counter claim against their son in-law, alleging that Perry should get nothing because he was responsible for their daughter's death.

After months of legal bickering, the probate court turned the matter over to an independent conservator who awarded Perry $60,000 cash and the couple's two automobiles, and indicated in the decision that when and if Janet was formally declared dead, he could have a share of her estate.

Two years later, the Tennessee Court of Appeals reversed the conservator's decision, but by then Perry and the money were a thing of the past, and he and the assets headed South—to Ajijic, Mexico, 1,200 miles away.

By now the fight between Perry and his in-laws was beginning to heat up. In the midst of the custody battle, on July 21, 1999, nearly three years after Janet's disappearance, the Levines filed a wrongful death suit against Perry, alleging that he had killed Janet March. Perry never showed up for the trial and offered no defense, leaving the Levines' lawyer to argue against an empty chair in court. Perry's attorney, Lionel Barrett Jr., apparently on instructions from his client, sat in the spectator section of the courtroom, observing and listening to the proceedings.

The result was that in 2000, the jury awarded Janet's parents and her two children a gigantic $113.5 million, the largest personal injury decision in Tennessee history. By then, paranoia had set in and Perry claimed that the decision was the result of the Levines' connections with "powerful figures." He even accused Judge Frank Clement Jr., a highly respected jurist and the son of a former Tennessee governor, of using the verdict to bolster his political visibility with the public.

Perry ridiculed the jury for placing such a high value on Janet's life, calling her "an absentee housewife who never earned, other than gift or inheritance from her parents, more than $2,000 in any reported year of her life."

Of course, Perry, being shrewd and calculating, also knew ahead of time that the huge jury verdict would be thrown out on a technicality. At first, he filed an appeal, but because he failed to post the required bond, the verdict stood.

To even the score, Perry's father, Arthur, jumped into his son's ongoing war with his in-laws and filed a wrongful death suit against Larry and Carolyn Levine. According to psychiatrist Ravitz, the "document is absolutely bizarre in its language and allegations." Arthur accused Larry Levine specifically of murdering his daughter.

The litigation involving Perry and the Levines continued unabated for years, with numerous revisals and court-ordered awards. All the while, Perry was making a comfortable home for himself in Mexico.

6

Frauds, Scams, and Lies

Perry heralded his arrival to Ajijic by taking out a full-page display ad in the *Guadalajara Colony Reporter*, a weekly newspaper covering national and local news for English-language readers. The ad announced the "PriMedical™ Medical Clinic Project" and invited readers to a May 22 gathering to "Meet the administrators & developers: S. Samuel Chavez, Esq. & Perry A. March, Esq., doctorates of law."

The ad outlined an elaborate health-care program for seniors living in the Ajijic area, suggesting that once the project was funded, they would no longer have to rely on physician care in Guadalajara, which was an hour away. According to the prospectus, the project would be organized under the laws of Belize with a minimum investment of $1,250,000.

"Over 40 physicians will practice at the PriMedical Clinic, in every major medical discipline," the ad announced. It listed some thirty-six medical specialties including audiology, plastics and cosmetic surgery, neurosurgery, pathology, sports medicine, thoracic surgery, and obstetrics and gynecology.

It is doubtful that there would be much value to retirees,

who make up the core of the Ajijic population, for a sports medicine physician or an obstetrician or gynecologist. And despite Perry's ability to verbally snow people, after holding two meetings in an effort to solicit money from investors, he was unable to satisfactorily persuade them. At these meetings, when it began looking bleak, Perry's father, Arthur, would rush to the podium, bragging about his experience as "a doctor" (he was not), persuading people to throw money at his son's feet. The response was generally indifference.

But this didn't seem to faze Perry. Nor did it seem to bother him that within six months of his arrival in Ajijic, complaints against him were filed with the local immigration authorities by Americans and others, alleging that he was ripping off the tight-knit international community.

By 2005, Perry's file was some twenty inches thick with the names of over two dozen victims who were scammed out of an estimated $2 million. It allegedly includes accusations and evidence of his criminal activities in Mexico. Perry is believed to have hidden huge sums of his money in offshore bank accounts or in the accounts of his second wife, Carmen Rojas, money which his victims will likely never see again.

Shortly before leaving Chicago, Perry's license to practice law had been suspended. A year later, on August 28, 2000, Perry was disbarred after he was found guilty of embezzling funds from, and filing a frivolous lawsuit against, his father-in-law's-firm, for which he'd worked. March also took money from a client that was supposed to go to the firm, and failed to notify the client that his license was suspended on May 28, 1999.

Perry's first order of business in arriving in the land of paradise was to hitch up with another disbarred attorney, Samuel Chavez, a Mexican American lawyer who was a graduate of Purdue and the Indiana University School of Law.

The two lawyers were partners until about July 2000, after Chavez realized that Perry had stolen $85,000 from him. Chavez also believes that Perry was behind a shooting incident that, he says, "almost killed me."

During the fifteen months they worked together, Chavez & March, Ltd., established or tried to create a number of businesses. Among them were Guardian Security, C&M Insurance, PriMedical Health Care Systems, and Misty Mountain Extended Care Community.

C&M Insurance was set up to act as an agent for Reliance National, a well-known Mexican insurance company. The business would have been a success had the offices of the two partners in Plaza Bugambilias not caught fire in December 1999. Chavez & March submitted a $46,000 bill to Reliance, even though the fire was not in their office. The two lawyers alleged that several expensive paintings, office equipment, and important business records had been destroyed. Reliance evidently had some misgivings about the Chavez & March team and hired an investigator based in Guadalajara, about 35 miles away, who found a number of disturbing clues that led Reliance to conclude that it was a case of arson.

Perhaps the strongest evidence the investigator found was that an accelerant had been used to speed up the fire and increase the temperature so as to increase the size of the claim.

Needless to say, Reliance ceased to be their agents in January 2000.

Guardian Security, on the other hand, offered full service home and business security, a 24/7 monitoring service with bilingual operators. The business also sold and installed various types of alarm systems that cost anywhere from $2,500 to $3,000, with monthly fees running $25 to $35, to be paid a year in advance.

All went well until word trickled out through local newspapers to various expatriates living in Ajijic about Perry's past. It became apparent that he was a real detriment to the business. By late spring, Guardian's business declined, and sometime between August and December 2000, Guardian closed its doors.

Since all customers were on a prepaid annual contract from the date they signed up, everyone had some portion of their contract unfulfilled when the business collapsed.

David Johnston, a Canadian and a Chartered Accountant (similar to a U.S. Certified Public Accountant) lost the $37,000 he had invested in Guardian. He believes the business failed because it was starved for cash and that investor funds were misappropriated by the two lawyers.

Johnston made some effort to recover his Guardian investment, but was told after consulting a local lawyer in Mexico that there was very little, if anything, that could be done. As for March, he merely laughed off Johnston's losses, calling it a normal business risk.

After returning to Canada and re-assessing his loss, Johnston recognized that he had initially failed to exercise due diligence before investing in Guardian, and says, had he done so, he would have learned that both Chavez and Perry had been suspended and disbarred from practicing law in the United States. Also, he did not know that neither attorney was licensed to practice law in Mexico.

Perry's biggest victim was Bob Duncan, who lost some $575,000: $50,000 that he invested in Guardian, $75,000 that went into the PriMedical/Ajijic Clinic scheme, and the theft of $450,000 from Duncan's Belize bank account for which Perry held the necessary code number. After Perry stole the entire balance, he told Duncan that Duncan's wife, Diane, had taken the money. But the wife had not touched the account—she didn't have the code. And when Duncan demanded his money back, Perry told him to go to hell, and made the first in a series of threats to have him killed.

Presumably distraught over his losses and his wife ultimately divorcing him, it is believed that Duncan's death by hanging on October 19, 2002, was a suicide, although at least two of Duncan's acquaintances claimed he simply did not have the strength to hang himself.

It is estimated that the loss inflicted on retiree Gayle Cancienne, a resident of the Ajijic area since 1998, of about $450,000 was the second largest of any individual whom Perry defrauded. Gayle is the only victim to bring a civil action against Perry, filed in the spring of 2004.

Gayle's plan when she arrived in Ajijic was to live on her

investments, but because of Perry's fleecing her, she was forced to work in an Ajijic veterinary clinic.

"He robbed me actually, and took my property that was in the United States. I had homes that I owned in the United States [that] he talked me into putting into a corporation for tax purposes. He showed me papers which said that I was president or sole owner of the corporation, when in fact it was his corporation," Gayle later said in an interview with NewsChannel 5.

Her initial contact with Perry had come about when she went to see Chavez about the certification for the water well on her property in La Canacinta in the fall of 1999.

During that meeting, she told Chavez that her mother Lorena Boozer had recently died in Mexico and that her will had to be probated. All of her mother's assets were in the United States, including two houses, a condo, and a duplex in New Orleans. All these assets were to be given to Gayle, according to her mother's will.

Chavez introduced her to his partner, Perry, who he said could handle her problem. Perry in turn hired a local lawyer in New Orleans because most of the work had to be done there.

Gayle initially retained Perry and paid him a $15,000 fee. Later she handed over another $5,000 at his demand. He indicated that the best way to handle her financial affairs was to create a corporation using the name TRIN Ltd.

He listed the duplex with a Realtor, with Gayle specified as the owner. When it was sold, however, the owner was listed as Peppers Holdings, in documents that, it turned out later, Perry had forged, making himself appear to be the sole owner.

Gayle's plan, of course, was to sell off the properties, put the money in a tax-free Mexican bank, and live off the interest, which is what most retirees do in Ajijic.

The New Orleans duplex, although listed for $240,000, sold for $181,000, but Perry lied and told Gayle that the duplex had not been sold at all. When she called the attorney in New Orleans, she learned the deal had closed a few days earlier and that the money had been wired to Perry.

Gayle never got a cent of that money, she says, and it is this scam by Perry that would be the object of a civil suit against him, pursued with the help of lawyer Henri Loridans in a Chapala court.

In the spring and summer of 2002, Perry threatened to kill Gayle several times. This was after she had hired lawyer Rene Guzman to try to recover the $181,000 for the fraudulent sale. Guzman was the same attorney who'd helped the Levines gain temporary custody of their two grandchildren in 2000.

Gayle also hired a lawyer in Kansas City to block Perry's planned fraudulent sale of the house she owned in Missouri.

In many ways, Gayle was a "soft" target for Perry. She was not experienced in legal matters. Unfortunately, she was easily convinced by smooth-talking Perry, and she did not demand copies of any documents that he prepared for her.

Gayle had to move from Ajijic, where she had lived for nearly eight years, having lost so much money at Perry March's hands. At 62, she was forced to give up her retirement lifestyle and move back to the United States.

Perry's other ventures while in Mexico included the Misty Mountain Extended Care Community, which combined housing and medicine so that seniors could have independent, custom-tailored personal care in a warm and friendly community setting.

Like so many of the other business ventures that Chavez and Perry put together, the Misty Mountain project proved to be a financial dud. Investors were promised a gated community with lake views and twenty-four-hour skilled nursing on campus that would only cost between $50,000 to $85,000. The homes were never built, and investors lost a bundle.

The majority of Perry's victims were senior citizens who were not only fearful of his threatened reprisal, but also embarrassed by what had happened to them. It was a sad turn of events for the elderly victims of the Ajijic-Chapala area for several reasons. None of the victims had family or close friends in the area. Some lived alone, following the death of a spouse. Many worried that their children or relatives who lived Stateside might have the victim placed under financial or personal supervision.

Perry not only pocketed funds that rightfully belonged to the seniors, but took advantage of a landlord who rented him a house in La Floresta by stiffing him when he first arrived in Mexico in May 1999. He paid the first and last months' rent—$850 a month—and for the next nine months, stopped it altogether. Then he moved out, leaving behind a telephone bill of 30,000 pesos—roughly $3,000. Ironically, the property was owned by David Bautista, a public defender in Johnson City, Tennessee, although he did not know at the outset that Perry was his tenant. It was unclear why neither the owner nor Re/Max, the agent for the property, ever took any action to collect the back rent.

But apparently, Perry chalked up a long history of not paying bills in Mexico. When he and Sam Chavez broke up their partnership in July 2000, the owner of the multiple offices in Plaza Bugambilias told him to leave because he was eight months behind on the rent. Perry was also some eighteen months in arrears in the $1,100-a-month rent on another home where he, his children, and Carmen's children had lived.

It didn't take real estate agents in the Ajijic-Chapala area long to learn of Perry's terrible track record as a tenant. And by 2000, a small number of Ajijic residents who had been cheated, ripped off or seriously misled banded together in an attempt to have Perry deported. Peggy Turner was part of that group. A no-nonsense woman, she was so irate at Perry that she began calling him "O.J." to his face whenever she saw him in public.

At the urging of Ajijic locals, Nashville's Channel 4 news team ran three four-minute reports on Perry's nefarious activities in the spring of 2000. Perry refused to be interviewed by the Channel 5 reporter and he used a guard outside his Plaza Bugambilias office to keep the reporter and camera crew at bay. Inside his office, Perry hid behind a pair of dark sunglasses. Once when he walked out, he placed his hand over the camera lens and, as he rode off on his motor scooter, shouted to the reporter, "Eat shit and die!"

Don Hauser, identified in the piece as the pastor of the Lake Chapala Baptist Church, emphasized in the report that neither Chavez nor Perry was licensed to practice law in Mexico and that both had had their law licenses suspended in the United States. Hauser also pointed out that both lawyers were claiming to have a "doctorate of law." The signs in the front window of their office read: "Dr. Perry A. March" and "Dr. Sergio Samuel Chavez."

"Such advertising is misleading," Hauser said, as was their prospectus boasting that 500,000 people who lived in the area would be served by the PriMedical project when the area population is only around 15,000.

In his interview, Hauser, who was very active in efforts to have Perry deported in 2000, brought up the fact that Perry had brought his two children into Mexico illegally on a tourist visa without the written permission of their mother, who at the time had not been declared legally dead.

Esther Solano, the city councilor for Chapala and the former elected representative in the State of Jalisco legislature, also got involved in the deportation effort after getting a call from a wealthy American asking her to translate a draft contract he was about to sign with Chavez & March, Ltd. "It was a horrible, fraudulent contract," Solano says, and she warned her client not to sign it.

Solano became aware of Perry's activities when he tried selling houses in the nonexistent Misty Mountain care community. "It was plain fraud," she says. "He was preying upon the most vulnerable, the elderly." She was further moved to seek his deportation upon learning that Perry had used a power of attorney to defraud an American she knew.

After Chavez and Perry became aware of Solano's efforts to have them deported, a dead cat was thrown on her porch. She then received a threatening telephone call: "Mr. Art [presumably referring to Perry's father, Arthur March] has got you on his list, and he is going to eliminate you."

Joel Rasmusson, a United States citizen, cactus grower, and long-time resident of the Ajijic and Lake Chapala area, also spoke openly about Perry's activities. Rasmusson worked very hard with Solano and others to deport Perry in 2000. After four years, he pressed José Luís Gutiérrez, the head of immigration in Guadalajara, to send Perry north. Gutiérrez had previously refused to change Perry's status from FM-3 to FM-2, which would have allowed him to begin the process of becoming a permanent citizen, and cancelled his FM-3 visa in mid-2001. That forced Perry the following year to leave Mexico, but like a bad peso, he returned a few days later on a tourist visa.

Rasmusson admits that many of the cases of fraud he has looked into have been difficult to document because Perry was "careful not to leave incriminating paper trails. Perry would hold on to the original paperwork, saying he needed to make copies. Clients who tried to collect their documents and files often got nothing more than a brush-off," he says. "It's inconceivable to believe that so many people with no other common connection would cook up a conspiracy of this magnitude."

Perry lived a carefree life south of the border and there was never the slightest hint that he was worried about getting kicked out of Mexico. That is because bribery had become a way of life for him, and it is believed that he had many Mexican officials on his private payroll.

The Levines had also tried, back in 1999, to have the immigration authorities deport their former son-in-law, but were unsuccessful. Then in early May 2000, an FBI agent assigned to the U.S. Consulate in Guadalajara alerted the Levines that they expected Perry to be deported to the U.S., where he would be arrested and taken into custody. In fact, a story in the Guadalajara *Reporter* indicated that the FBI "wanted Perry in the worst way" and had been trying for several months to persuade the Mexican authorities to deport not only Perry, but Chavez.

An effort to forcibly deport Perry began on June 21, 2000—the same day that the Levines went to the Oak Hill School in the village of San Antonio Tlayacapan, adjacent to Ajijic, to pick up their two grandchildren.

Like a precision heist, six burly Mexican immigration officers rushed into Perry's office at 10:45 a.m. and took him into custody, claiming that his "migratory papers" were not in order. Before he could even look at the documents the officers held in their hand, two men grabbed his forearm, shoved him out the door of his office toward the plaza's courtyard, and hustled him into an unmarked silver Suburban waiting outside on the street.

Perry was terrified. "Where are we going? Where are we going?" he frantically asked. "The officers actually lifted me by my ears and off my feet," he said, recalling how they'd gotten him into the vehicle. Realizing they were headed toward the airport, which meant he would be tossed out of the country, Perry pulled a fast one and asked one of the officers if he could speak with his boss. A cell phone call was made. "Don't you see? They're using this arrest as a decoy," Perry screamed into the phone in Spanish. "They're taking my children out of this country. The whole purpose is to take me away from the kids."

After handing the phone back to the immigration agent, Perry was informed that there had been a terrible mistake. "Your paperwork is in order," he was told. It was obvious that once again, Perry had promised an official a bribe to "clear up the matter," and "changed their minds."

Meanwhile, after an hour of argument, school administrators handed Sammy and Tzipi over to a Mexican judge, who in turn gave them to the Levines. They headed to a small airport three hours away in Manzanillo, Jalisco, Mexico, where they took a domestic flight to Mexico City.

Hours later, they boarded a Delta Air Lines international flight to Atlanta and then connected to another flight to Nashville, traveling with the young grandchildren all night.

Perry, meanwhile, had arrived at the Oak Hill School about ten minutes after the Levines left. His father, Arthur, had followed them, but lost them en route to the airport.

The Levines later told police that, while speeding to the Manzanillo Airport with Arthur chasing them in his car, he'd pulled a gun on them at one point, warning them that they would never get out of Mexico alive.

As a result of the bad blood between their former son-in-law and his father, the Levines wasted no time once they were back home in having their attorney file with the local court an emergency petition for custody, and termination of parental rights, which, in layman's terms, meant that if granted, it would strip Perry of custody of his two children.

7

A New Life, a New Wife

A week after arriving in Ajijic, Perry met Carmen, a beautiful Salma Hayek look-alike and a divorcee with three children from previous marriages. She was married to Thomas Delangre at the time. It was crucial for Perry to quickly acquire a Mexican wife, because that would increase the chances that he could continue to reside and work in Mexico. Perry wasted no time pursuing her.

"I fell in love with Carmen five days after getting to Ajijic," he says.

There are two stories that have floated around the Ajijic–Chapala area about how the lovebirds met. One story has Arthur March hiring Carmen to clean Perry's house and look after his young children once he got to Ajijic. Another has Perry introducing himself to Carmen when she was hanging around the Plaza Bugambilias with other young women.

But one thing is for sure: they began living together in June 1999, a month after Perry moved to Ajijic.

Perry swept Carmen off her feet. Carmen was looking for a more affluent lifestyle, so Perry bought her a BMW, with Texas plates, and registered it in her name. (Carmen, who didn't have a driver's license, later crashed the car.)

Her tangled marital history plagued the two of them. She did not divorce Delangre until March 2, 2000, and married Perry twenty-nine days later on March 31, two days before Janet was declared dead by a Tennessee court.

Tom Delangre, an American citizen, met Carmen on a visit to Mexico in 1993. At that time, Carmen had a 6-month-old son, Daro, but was unmarried. She told Tom that Daro's father could have been any one of several men, but Tom treated the child as his own. They married on July 4, 1995. Their first child, a son called Thomas, was born June 18, 1994, a year before they married. They later had another child, a girl, Cynthia.

Tom and Carmen started a small business, making muffins in their home. Soon, his customers began calling him "Muffin Tom." In the fall of 2001, when Carmen opened the Café Media Luna with Perry, she featured muffins on the menu—the popular muffins Tom had taught her how to make.

In 1999 after Carmen and Perry became lovers, they pressured Tom to agree to a quick divorce by controlling his access to his two children. According to Tom, she refused to let him speak with his children and did not even allow him to give them gifts. "She told me Perry was very jealous. When I managed to talk to Daro at school one day, he told me that it was Perry that would not let me see my kids. According to Perry, it was Carmen's decision. And according to Carmen, it was her lawyer's decision . . ."

Carmen asked Tom for a divorce and said that as soon as he signed the papers, she would let him see the children again. "I told her that I had no problem with the divorce, but I had a right to see my children. Then Perry called me up and threatened me with 'WAR' since I had upset Carmen by insisting on seeing the children. He said that I'd be 'sorry,' if I kept trying to see the children. And he said that 'I haven't seen yet what he could do to me' and that if I wanted to challenge him, I would never see the end of it."

Perry kept telling Tom that once Tom signed the divorce papers, Perry would insist that Carmen let her ex-husband see the children. "By this point, I was used to both of them lying, I didn't believe him and told him so," says Tom in his September 12, 2000, affidavit.

What made the divorce and subsequent marriage of Perry and Carmen irregular? Both Carmen and Tom lived in Ajijic, yet the 2.5-page petition for divorce on grounds of incompatibility dated January 19, 2000, was filed in Zacoalco de Torres, some 78 km (48 miles) from where both parties resided. The divorce called for Carmen to be given custody of the two children, Thomas and Cynthia, and Delangre was to pay her 1,000 pesos a month for child support. The reason it was filed so far from where they lived was that Perry wanted to make it easy for her to get a quick divorce so he and Carmen could marry without any delay.

A week later, on January 26, the petition for divorce was ratified, but never signed, and was received by the required State of Jalisco official. By February 14, the Declaration of the Final Decision was issued, and was signed March 1, 2000.

The February 14 document stated that both spouses were free to remarry once the final decree was registered on March 2. However, according to attorneys familiar with Mexican divorce law, article 420 of the Civil Code of Jalisco requires a one-year waiting period before either spouse can re-marry.

In the divorce papers, Carmen lists her matrimonial home at Juarez #30 in Villa Corona in the town of Zacoalco. In reality she was shacked up with Perry at Calle Paseo del Mirador #38 in La Floresta, Ajijic, in the home that he rented, where his two children and her three children lived.

There were other misleading irregularities surrounding the document. For instance, the originals for the divorce paper were missing from Zacoalco's public records; Delangre states he never signed the final decree, only the January papers, and that he was not in Mexico when the final decree was filed—as required—with the appropriate government office in Chapala where he and Carmen were married in 1995.

According to Delangre's affidavit, Perry is alleged to have told him that he "paid off a judge in the other village," referring to Zacoalco "to expedite the divorce since a local Chapala divorce would take six months and we had a window of opportunity to do an illegal paper maneuver thanks to the judge, a friend of my partner, Sam Chavez."

Despite the divorce order clearly specifying that Delangre had a right to see his children, Carmen and Perry continued to refuse to let him see or talk to them. "I was also not allowed to send them birthday or Christmas gifts. I spoke to the school teacher and the director and they told me they have strict orders from Carmen not to let me speak or get near to the kids," he said.

Carmen and Perry also made false statements on their marriage license. For openers, a Tennessee court had declared Janet to be legally dead on January 14, 2000, but that ruling was later overturned by an appeals court on March 17, 2003, and she was not officially declared dead until May 20, 2004.

Also, both falsely stated they were living at Calle Santa Monica #20 in Ajijic, the address of Perry's father, Arthur. Perry then claimed that his parents were Mexican nationals living in Los Angeles, because he wanted to avoid the delay of several months required when a foreigner marries a Mexican citizen. (Perry's mother, an American citizen, had died in 1970.)

The marriage license also claimed that Carmen was single, not divorced, and that Perry was also single, even though he was technically a widower.

After they married, he sent a copy of the marriage certificate to immigration authorities. Under Mexican law, two years must elapse after a foreigner marries a Mexican citizen before the foreigner may apply for Mexican citizenship.

When Joel Rasmusson, who with other Ajijic residents was spearheading a group seeking to deport Perry, took this evidence of false statements to immigration authorities, Perry responded that it was all a clerical error. No action was ever taken against him. And when Rasmusson brought the strange but illegal divorce decree of Carmen and Delangre to the attention of the Mexican judicial authorities, they merely shrugged it off and reassigned the judge who'd presided over the divorce, Rodrigo López Solís, to a different district.

Alongside his marriage complications were Perry's peculiar activities concerning his efforts to open the Café Media Luna—a "bistro and café" that was essentially run by Carmen. On April 5, 2001, an application was made to the Municipality of Chapala seeking a license for the café. It opened in late October 2001, over the objections of the 700-member La Floresta homeowners' association and the Municipality of Chapala, who were most concerned about a business that might display large signs, create noise, or increase vehicular traffic and cause parking problems.

While Perry was remodeling the café, he was informed by the association's board of directors that they intended to press the municipality to deny him the necessary business license. Perry was arrogant when Luis Ramirez, the office manager of the homeowners' association, delivered the letter. Without even reading it, he tore it up, threw it on the ground, and lashed out with venomous remarks about the organization.

Despite warnings by the association and local government officials, Carmen and Perry went ahead and opened the café, only to have it shut down two weeks later.

The closure brought about a complicated, drawn-out legal conflict involving numerous applications to the municipality for a license that included Perry applying under different names, and dozens of appeals to the courts. Even with Perry's skill in manipulating the legal system, he was unable to get the café to re-open until late April 2004.

Given the intense competition for cafés and restaurants in Ajijic and throughout the entire Lakeside area, those who were seeking Perry's deportation questioned why he fought so long and hard for the café to re-open. "It would appear that Perry wanted to use the café as a place to make contact with gringos to see if they 'qualified' to become victims for one of his scams. After all, what could be a more innocent and casual encounter than in a coffee shop?" Joel Rasmusson said.

During one of Perry's protracted arguments, he claimed that the building where the café was located was actually his "home" and that he was entitled to run a café out of it. Over the next thirty months, Perry obtained injunctions issued by the federal courts blocking any action that might adversely affect his constitutional rights.

By December 2002, Carmen had again applied to the Municipality of Chapala for a license to run a restaurant that would also sell liquor and to have on its premises a beauty salon and real estate office. It was never made clear if all three businesses were to be operated at the same time, or whether Carmen would operate them one at a time. But again, she was not able to re-open.

It wasn't until the end of April 2004, after two-and-a-half years of legal battling, that the café was back in business. When it re-opened, it operated twelve hours a day, and Perry could often be seen waiting on tables, "chatting" with gringos, and plying his charm.

A month later, to prevent the homeowners' association and the municipality from closing down the café again, Carmen and Perry got an *amparo*—a type of ex parte injunction against government authorities where the plaintiffs believe that they are going to have their constitutional rights violated. The device is unique to Mexico and provides for mostly wealthy, well-connected people to delay or even evade the due process of law.

The homeowners' association argued to no avail that it had not been properly informed that a license for the café was issued. They appealed, but Perry thumbed his nose at his neighbors, drawing attention to his café by painting a huge sign on the wall surrounding the property.

Perry had used every trick in the book to keep the café up and running. It didn't concern him that as of late July 2004, he owed his landlord some $20,000 in rent.

The homeowners' association fought long and hard in the

courts and finally, after two-and-a-half years, the Mexican federal authorities closed down the restaurant the week of October 16, 2006, when a judge ruled in the association's favor.

Carmen initially tried hiding the seal placed on the front door by federal authorities by putting up a "Closed for Remodeling" sign, but it didn't take her customers long to realize that she had been permanently shut down by the government and was out of business.

8

The Custody Battle Rages On

To Perry March's way of thinking, the Levines were "out to get him." For nearly a decade, Perry was convinced that the Levines and their money were the driving force behind the police naming him the prime suspect in his wife's disappearance.

Every chance he got, Perry would describe himself to reporters as the Richard Jewell of Nashville, victimized by police allegations that he'd murdered his wife and disposed of her body. But unlike the security guard who was accused and later cleared of the Atlanta, Georgia, Olympic bombing, Perry's hatred of the Levines was so intense that all he had on his mind was retribution.

That meant publicly accusing his in-laws of kidnapping, and in legal documents calling them "tricksters" who use "sewer service tactics," referring to them as "mere 'grabbers' of money and things, money-lenders and money grubbers." For good measure, Arthur had suggested in court documents that it was actually Larry Levine who had murdered his own daughter.

That said, and with the name-calling out of his system, Perry's next order of business was to find a way to get his children back. Shortly after Perry had moved to Mexico, Larry Levine had contacted him about visitation rights and Perry offered to "sell" him full custody of his children in return for half of the Levines' total assets.

The thirty-nine-day Illinois court-ordered visitation period that allowed the Levines to pick up the children on June 21 in Ajijic, expired on July 30, 2000. The Levines refused to return the children to Perry.

He was in a dilemma and didn't know where to turn for help. That's when Lady Luck intervened. Robert Catz, a retired law professor living in Cadiz, Kentucky, had read about the case in the newspapers and contacted Vincent Stark, the lawyer representing Perry in Chicago on the visitation issue. Catz had been looking into other issues of how a particular federal judge was interpreting the Hague Convention Treaty and told Stark that as a result of his research, he was interested in trying to get Perry's children back to him.

Because the children were now living with the Levines in Nashville, a licensed Tennessee lawyer was needed. Catz said he would become involved in the case if Nashville lawyer John Herbison, a prominent criminal attorney well-versed in constitutional issues, was brought in as co-counsel. Because the newspapers and television blanketed the Nashville area with non-stop stories about Perry and the Levines, Herbison was very familiar with the removal of Perry's children.

Catz knew about earlier decisions by the Sixth Circuit and the U.S. Court of Appeals involving the Hague Convention as it pertains to retrieving children from a foreign country. Herbison did some preliminary research, then made a fast trip to Mexico to meet with Perry. "The idea was to use this vehicle to get the children back," Herbison said he told a delighted Perry.

The Levines hadn't returned the children to their father after the period of visitation ended, because on July 3, 2000, Judge Betty Adams Green of the Nashville Davidson County Juvenile Court had given them temporary custody of the children beyond the specified thirty-nine days.

The Levines also had made it known through detailed legal

documents that they were seeking to terminate Perry's parental rights and gain custody of their grandchildren by instituting proceedings in Tennessee based on a number of issues, including their fervent belief that their daughter had been murdered by her husband and that he had shown "brutality and emotional and psychological abuse toward the children."

In their petition, the Levines alleged that Perry exposed his children to criminal conduct and other improper activities, including violence, threats, fraud, and other crimes; that he consistently placed his interests above the interests of the children; and that he blamed his children for obeying the authorities in complying with the court-ordered visitation rather than running away as he had instructed them.

The Levines also contended that Perry "punished his children for expressing their love for the Levines"; had threatened to kill himself if they did not return to Mexico; attempted to make them forget their mother by withholding pictures of her from them; and continually told them that Janet had runaway and abandoned them.

The petition claimed that Perry lied to the children, telling them that the Levines had stolen their home, were evil, and "paid off the judge" to gain custody. It alleged that he had "grilled [the children] in his telephone calls, and questioned his son as to whether he had spoken to the Nashville police."

Finally, the Levines made allegations about specific threats from Perry, Arthur, and Carmen.

According to the Levines' petition, Arthur March had threatened them and their adult son, Mark, saying, "You'll never get out of Mexico alive." He'd further threatened Lawrence Levine to the effect that "We'll cut your balls off and slice them into little pieces," and told the Levines he knew that they had a large number of nieces and nephews, and that he would have them killed or kidnapped: "We know where they live and we'll pick them off one by one."

Carmen had allegedly gotten into the act, telephoning the Levines' family home at approximately 9:30 p.m. in

Nashville on Friday, June 23, 2000, two days after they had returned from Mexico with the grandchildren. After introducing herself to Mark Levine, she threatened him saying, "We know where you live in Los Angeles and I have lots of family there, so you better be careful." When Mark Levine responded, "Are you threatening me?" Carmen had hung up.

A few minutes later, Carmen called again, telling Mark, "By the way, I know exactly where you live, and Mexicans take their time."

After filing an "emergency petition" in the Davidson County Juvenile Court seeking custody of the grandchildren and termination of Perry's parental rights, the court granted the Levines temporary custody of their grandchildren. Perry, his father, and Carmen were also barred from "approaching or contacting the Levines, their family members or the children or the residence of any of them, or the children's school" and Perry was further ordered not to interfere with the Levines' "peaceful custody" of the children.

The judge granted Perry, his father, and Carmen the right to "reasonable telephone contact" and specified that any visitation had to be "strictly supervised" by both the Nashville Family & Children's Service and the Davidson County Metropolitan Police Department.

That action by Judge Green prompted Perry's new lawyers, John Herbison and Robert Catz, to fire their opening round on August 3, 2000. They filed a Petition for Return of Children under the International Child Abduction Remedies Act (ICARA). ICARA was enacted in order to implement the provisions of the Hague Convention. Both the United States and Mexico are signatories of this multi-nation treaty. It was adopted "to protect children internationally from the harmful effects of their wrongful removal or retention and to establish procedures to ensure their prompt return to the State of their habitual residence."

Under ICARA, for the children to be returned to Ajijic, Perry had to show that Mexico was their habitual residence. The Levines argued that Illinois was their residence, as they had lived there from 1996 to 1999.

In Perry's court papers were numerous affidavits and documents supporting his contention that the Levines were not supposed to take the children out of Mexico during the thirty-nine days of visitation, including a warrant for the arrest of the Levines and their son Mark, who was representing his parents in the lawsuit to terminate Perry's parental rights.

Desperate to get his children back, Perry asked the federal court for assistance. In his August 2000 complaint to the United States District Court for the Middle District of Tennessee, he asserted that the Levines had violated the Hague Convention. In the filing, submitted by Herbison and Catz, Perry requested that the district court expedite the return of his children to him pending a hearing, and immediately grant him access to his children, including telephone contact, so that he could have time with them.

Three weeks later, the Levines filed a sworn answer to Perry's demands, raising numerous defenses, including his failure to show up at earlier court proceedings in the United States, for which he had been held in criminal contempt. They stressed again in their court filing that Mexico was not the habitual residence of the children and that to return them to their father presented "a grave risk of psychological and physical harm as well as to place them in an intolerable situation"; further, the return of the children "would violate human rights and fundamental freedoms."

A week later, on August 30, 2000, Perry moved to get a summary judgment against the Levines on the grounds that they had wrongfully removed and wrongfully retained his children under ICARA. The Levines moved to dismiss the petition.

Getting the children back to Mexico was exhausting. Before it was all over, the court filings were over 1,300 pages and more than twelve inches thick as the paperwork flew back and forth between lawyers and the court.

The Levines in their court papers pointed to several surreptitious tape-recorded telephone conversations Perry had had with his children on July 4, 2000, after he'd learned that his in-laws were seeking permanent custody. In U.S. District Court Judge Aleta Trauger's opinion, that action caused the court to ultimately conduct private interviews with the children.

"I have been telling you all along that when they get you down there, they are going to try to file papers to keep you from me forever," Perry tells his son in one recording, sounding desperate and angry. Perry was also frustrated and hurt that Sammy did not refuse to be taken from his Mexican school by his grandparents. In another taped conversation Sammy told Carmen that he was happy being able to see his friends in Nashville.

The Levine court papers also claimed that Perry would shout at his son, but never at Tzipi and that "coupled with his paranoia about the boundless power and influence" of his in-laws, "it was driving him to the breaking point.

"He is demanding, abusive and controlling of Samson who, throughout, amazingly seems able to communicate an alliance with his father without really turning against his grandparents," the court documents say.

Finally, on September 1, 2000, the district court ruled that before deciding pending motions, separate in camera, or private, interviews would be held with Sammy and Tzipi with the assistance of a licensed clinical psychologist.

Court papers were then submitted by Wayne Palfrey, the director of Oak Hill School in Mexico, which both children attended. He stated that Sammy and Tzipi had a working and useful knowledge of Spanish and were successful in their course studies. At the time, Sammy had entered third grade and Tzipi was enrolled in kindergarten.

Palfrey said the children participated in school and extracurricular activities and that Perry and Carmen were also involved. "Sammy has continued with his cello studies and with horseback riding while Tzipi attends dance ballet."

By September 15, 2000, with the assistance of the clinical psychologist selected by the judge in Nashville, and with no lawyers or interested parties from either side present, each child was interviewed separately.

Sammy was first. He seemed happy and relaxed. In the sealed order scheduling the interview, the court had requested that the Levines not let the children know the purpose of the interview, and it was clear that they had honored that instruction.

Sammy expressed enthusiasm for his school in Mexico, saying "I love it; it was great." He added that he had learned Spanish and liked to speak it, liked his school, the climate, and being with his grandfather. He loved Carmen, who he said was "just wonderful. She's real nice with me and Tzipi." As for living in Mexico, "It's perfect weather all year round."

When asked if he was having nightmares, he stated that he was in the beginning, because he missed his dad and wanted to go back to Mexico. This was the only point when Sammy was close to tears, the psychologist observed. And when asked if Perry ever hit him, Sammy said only when he and his dad were fooling around.

It was the opinion of the psychologist that Sammy seemed totally unaware of Perry's alleged business problems in Mexico and the alleged use of guns by his grandfather, and that he was "substantially unaware of the turmoil surrounding the case."

Tzipi, who was 6, was less articulate but very relaxed during the interview. She was described by the psychologist as "playful and delightful in every way." Throughout the interview, she drew a picture of a little girl thinking about hearts. She said she liked speaking Spanish, loved her house in Mexico, and referred to one of Carmen's children as her "little brother." She enjoyed living with her grandparents, but missed her father. And what she would have liked most was for her father and "especially Carmen" to come.

She told the psychologist that Perry spanks her, but that her Mommy never did before she went away.

More than a month later, after the court allowed the voluminous amount of evidence into the record, the district court entered a fifty-two-page opinion granting Perry's petition and ordering the Levines to immediately return the children to him.

That of course didn't end it for either side, because then the United States Court of Appeals got into the act and stayed the order until October 10, 2000. Both sides appealed, another temporary stay was issued, and it wasn't until April 19, 2001, that its opinion affirmed the district court ruling, because "Samson and Tzipora have been separated from their father for almost one year now" and should be "reunited with their father with all due speed."

The court's order was very specific:

> *The children are to be flown to Mexico at the expense of the Levines to the Guadalajara, Mexico airport in the company of a family friend or lawyer to the Levines. No family member of the Levines is to accompany the children to Mexico. The Levines shall give written notice of the date, flight numbers and arrival time to Perry March through his counsel with a copy furnished to the court.*

Two days later, on April 21, 2001, the children were transported back to Mexico, and Perry met them at the arrival gate.

9

The Calm Before the Storm

Over the next four years, the Levines and Perry were in and out of court on a regular basis regarding grandparent visitation and other legal issues. By January 2002, the U.S. Supreme Court had declined to hear an appeal by the Levines. That ruling meant that they not only couldn't visit with their grandchildren, but couldn't even have telephone contact with them. In March 2003, the wrongful death verdict was overturned by a state appeals court, and on May 20, 2004, Janet March was declared legally dead for the second time.

But a month later, the court granted a default judgment against Perry on the Levines' claim that he was civilly liable for the intentional and wrongful death of Janet. And finally, after a three-day trial on September 7, 2004, that Perry also did not attend, the court awarded the Levines and their grandchildren six million dollars in actual and punitive damages against Perry.

Meanwhile, Perry was living it up in Ajijic. After his move to Mexico, he had quickly joined the hundreds of American expatriates who made their home in the tranquil haven, where stretching the American dollar was a way of life. He continued to thumb his nose at law enforcement. He had taken a cavalier attitude toward police and in particular, toward Carolyn and Larry Levine. The Levines were not only wealthy but they were also well-known in the tight-knit Jewish community of Nashville, and although Perry and his family were also Jewish, Perry's father, Arthur, always sarcastically and pointedly referred to the Levines in interviews as "the Jewish Mafia," with Carolyn Levine being "its Queen," and to Janet as "a JAP"—a Jewish American Princess.

Since Janet's disappearance the Levines had endured Perry's whining about the many court actions that they'd filed seeking visitation and custody of the grandchildren. The case ultimately made its way to probate court after Perry tried getting his greedy hands on the trust funds Janet had set up for her children.

Perry figured he was safe in Mexico. But unbeknownst to him, on December 7, 2004, a little over eight years after Janet had vanished, the squeaky wheel of justice finally caught up with Nashville's most notorious villain. That's when a grand jury found there was sufficient evidence to return a secret indictment against Perry charging him with second-degree murder, abuse of a corpse, and tampering with evidence.

It took another eight months of negotiations between the United States and Mexican governments, eventually involving the office of the Mexican president, before Perry could be deported by immigration authorities for alleged fraud. During that time, the grand jurors in Nashville, the witnesses who testified, and the prosecuting staff and police were sworn to secrecy.

On August 3, 2005, Perry's tranquil solitude erupted in the hot Mexican sun. Perry got up late that Wednesday, made some phone calls, and then, shortly before eight in the morning, nonchalantly made his way past his luscious outdoor kitchen to his lovely private pool and the spectacular tropical garden of his magnificent colorful hacienda with its Spanish ironwork gates, then past the villa with fifteen-foot ceilings onto the narrow cobblestone streets of the tranquil lakeside.

He meandered down the rustic streets, bumping into an occasional donkey, on his way to the picturesque bistro he and Carmen owned. Little did he know that he had been under twenty-four-hour surveillance for weeks by FBI agents stationed in Mexico, who were tracking his habits and movements.

As he neared the Media Luna Café, without warning, four cars with tinted windows sped to the curb, and eight men with guns jumped out and grabbed him.

Perry was helpless. He had been caught completely off-guard.

"They covered his mouth. Put him in a truck and took him away. They kidnapped him," Carmen sobbed hysterically, recalling Perry's arrest.

It took less than three minutes and Perry was gone, taken away in a van by Mexican immigration officials to the Guadalajara airport, where he was formally deported and handed over to FBI agents, who hustled him onto a plane to Los Angeles. Days later, Postiglione and Pridemore took over for the long journey back to Nashville.

It must have come as a shock when the roof came crashing down on him. Perry would no longer be living as a patron of his adopted paradise, but instead, as a "non-paying guest" of the suburban Van Nuys Community Police Station jail, thirty minutes from downtown Los Angeles, with murderers and rapists for neighbors.

10

Perry's "House of Cards" Collapses

It was one o'clock in the afternoon on Thursday, September 22, 2005, when Perry, looking pale after spending over forty days in a jail cell, made his long-awaited appearance in court before Davidson County Criminal Court Judge Steve R. Dozier, who would preside over his fate. Perry was eager for the bond hearing to get underway. He was confident it was his ticket to liberty.

Judge Dozier was considered a no-nonsense judge, one who had handled many high-profile cases. He'd decided to become a lawyer as a teenager after his grandfather gave him a book on family law. His father, Tom Dozier, a police officer affectionately called "the Major," had served on the Metro Police Department for fifty years. Dozier had experienced criminal cases from the perspective of a prosecutor, a defense attorney, a court clerk, and now a judge.

Seated at the defense table inside the well of the courtroom was John Herbison, the criminal and constitutional lawyer who had gotten Perry's children returned to Mexico after Larry and Carolyn Levine had "kidnapped" them five years earlier.

Herbison, the son of a preacher, is known to Nashvillians

as a streetfighter who battles tooth and nail for his clients. Well-regarded by his colleagues and clients, he represents some of the largest adult bookstores and night spots in Nashville. He is affectionately known to the vice squad as "Herbicide" and as a "whorehouse lawyer" by local police officers.

"Temperamentally, I enjoy tangling with the government. Philosophically, I don't think that the government should be choosing our reading material," says the six-foot, two-inch lawyer, who wears his brown hair shoulder length and his wrinkled suits as if he had slept in them. "I'm a liberal and I'm opposed to the death penalty."

After graduating from law school at the University of Tennessee in Knoxville, Herbison was attracted to criminal and tort law because "protecting individual liberty is very important to me. I am quite skeptical of government." His associates call him "a walking encyclopedia of legal cornucopia."

Next to Herbison sat William Massey, a prominent Memphis lawyer for more than twenty years. He had previously defended highly publicized clients such as a man charged with murdering a young girl left inside a hot van, and a well-known discount store owner who, the FBI alleged, had sold thousands of dollars' worth of stolen property to unknowing customers. At the time of Perry's hearing, Massey was also the president of the Tennessee Association of Criminal Defense Lawyers. His law partner, Lorna McClusky, while not as well-known as Massey, was equally brilliant. She made up the third chair at the defense table, seated beside Perry.

On the opposite side of the courtroom sat Thomas Thurman, the lead prosecutor and the deputy district attorney in Nashville, who had waited nine years to get Perry March into a courtroom. Thurman had been brought into the case "early" because at the time, he was a liaison with the police on their homicide squad's high-profile cases. "It was fairly obvious early on that Janet had been the victim of foul play," recalled Thurman, giving as examples the way her car had been found and the missing hard drive, which made it impossible to check when the twelve-day to-do list had been written.

A prosecutor for over thirty years, Thurman was a student of fishing and biology before he enrolled at the Nashville School of Law at night. After his freshman year, he applied for a court officer's job with Alan Cornelius, a criminal court judge. Thurman spent three years with Cornelius, learning and absorbing every case that came into the courtroom. It was there that he fell in love with prosecuting.

After finishing law school and spending two years in private practice, he moved over to the district attorney's office in 1977, where he was eventually appointed a deputy district attorney in 1989. Among his more high-profile cases was that of serial murderer Paul Reid, a 39-year-old Texas parolee and aspiring country singer, who was charged with killing three people at a McDonald's and two others at a nearby Captain D's seafood chain, as well as with two other murders at a Baskin-Robbins in Clarksville. Reid was later convicted of the murders and sentenced to death.

Seated next to Thurman at the prosecution table was Senior Assistant District Attorney Katy Miller, who'd gone to work in the district attorney's office after getting her license to practice law in 1981. She headed the family-protection team, specializing in domestic violence homicides.

The anticipation for the hearing to get underway was like an opening night on Broadway. Dozier's sixth-floor courtroom was packed with Nashvillians eager for a front row seat to catch a glimpse of Perry March. It was so crowded that scalpers could have sold tickets.

On hand were a number of lawyers who had nothing to do with the case, but merely wanted to witness the most talked-about defendant in Nashville.

Investigators who had worked diligently for nearly a decade to bring Perry to trial were also there, as were Janet's friends and her parents, Larry and Carolyn Levine. For the first time in over nine years they could stare at their former son-in-law as he shuffled into court in handcuffs, looking cocky and arrogant.

As the proceedings began, Perry looked back at his brother, Ron, his sister, Kathy, and her husband, Lee Dreit owich, seated in the gallery for moral support. But for the better part of the four-hour session, Perry kept busy scribbling in a legal-size notepad, projecting a carefree appearance. Occasionally he would yawn or sip water from a bottle, or whisper something to Herbison or McClusky. By all outward appearances he seemed smug and not at all concerned that the charges he faced could ultimately send him to prison for the rest of his life.

For the moment, getting the judge to set a reasonably low bond, somewhere in the neighborhood of $25,000, was what Perry's lawyers were aiming for.

Under Tennessee law, the only issue before Dozier was the amount of bond that would be appropriate to assure prosecutors that Perry March would appear at all future court dates. To make that determination, among the many factors Dozier was going to have to consider were Perry's length of residence in Nashville, his employment status, his history and financial situation, his family ties and relationships, his reputation, character, and mental condition, his record of court proceedings or failure to appear in court, the nature of the offense, the apparent probability of conviction, any prior criminal record, and finally, whether he was a potential flight risk.

To make as strong a case as possible for a bond to be granted, Massey began the questioning by calling former Metro Cold Case Unit investigator Mickey Miller as his first witness. Miller, a police captain and now the commander of the West Precinct, was, at the time Janet disappeared, the commander of the Personal Crimes Division and remained in that position until January 2003.

During the time of his involvement in the case, Miller testified, Perry was the only suspect that developed. March had repeatedly refused to allow the police to talk to his son or to cooperate and be interviewed himself, sending police a handwritten explanation of what he referred to as "the Janet incident."

Massey took Miller through numerous tips and possible sightings of Janet that police had received during the investigation, asking him to remember a tip about "a man from the neighborhood where the Marches lived," who, it was claimed, "had raped and murdered Janet March, and even kept a souvenir."

"I do not recall that," Miller replied.

Massey handed the police captain a document which Miller said indicated that the tip had come from Crime Stoppers on July 2, 2002. Miller read from the court paper. It described the person responsible for Janet's "demise" as "five-foot-ten inches to six-feet tall, thinning brown hair, separated, no children and never served in the military and was living in the neighborhood."

"Your Honor, that was an anonymous call with no reliability; it's hearsay," Tom Thurman interjected, cutting short any further response from Miller.

"Are you familiar with a gentleman by the name of Ronald Thacker contacting either police or the attorney general with news that Janet March had killed herself?" Massey asked.

Miller told the lawyer that he didn't recall that either. Massey pressed on with his questions. "You are aware, though, of sightings that people from the community have called in, saying that they've seen Janet March?"

"To the best of my memory, all of those were resolved to our satisfaction at the time," Miller said.

Although Janet had been declared dead, her body had never been found. It was the defense's theory that she was still alive and had merely wanted to get away from Nashville, Massey said. The defense hoped not only to convince Judge Dozier to order a reasonable bond, but to eventually persuade the jury that with all these sightings of Janet, "there's no proof at all that she is dead." She had been declared legally dead, but "it was by a default judgment in a civil case."

Massey was unrelenting. "Do you remember the incident of a sighting on James Robertson Parkway on August seventeenth, 1996?"

"It's a sighting of a gray Volvo, Your Honor, please, not Janet March," an exasperated Thurman interrupted. "Somebody called in and said they saw a gray Volvo on the parkway. Well, I go home that way and see one every day, but I don't know how you investigate that."

"If there's a gray Volvo outside and it looks like Janet in the car . . . we would've sent a detective out to look at it, 'cause we were on James Robertson Parkway," Miller said, referring to the fact that police headquarters was on the same road. Massey then asked if he was familiar with a Janet March sighting that Barbara Smith had made on August 24, 1996, at the Gerst Haus, a popular German restaurant.

"It was investigated at that particular time, and close to a year later, an employee who had worked with Ms. Smith gave us information that Janet was not there," Miller testified.

"What information was that?" Massey asked, ignoring the first axiom that a lawyer should never ask a question unless he knows the answer.

"The witness that we talked to said that she had worked with Barbara and that Barbara had admitted to her that she had lied to the police about that incident and that she only did it because she thought Perry was innocent and wanted to help him.

"We went back out and talked to Barbara after that. And Barbara changed her story somewhat, saying that, you know, she didn't really know if it was Janet or not, she wasn't sure. She softened it quite a bit the second time."

The zinger thrown at the defense came when Thurman got Miller to say on cross-examination that Barbara Smith was Perry March's father's girlfriend. "And she was faxing all kinds of information to Mexico to the Marches, about the case."

An interview done at Gerst Haus by detectives showed that not a single other person claimed to have seen Janet. "A year later we got information from a place where Barbara worked that she had made some admissions that she lied to the police. And we followed up on that, as well."

There were many other sightings of Janet over the years that, Thurman said, in the end filled at least ten volumes of reports. Joann Sachs mistakenly thought she'd spotted Janet in a field. Another woman on tour from Illinois claimed to have seen Janet on August 29, 1996, at Opryland USA. Two days later, a report had come in that Janet was seen in Destin, Florida. On September 6, 1996, Janet was again sighted in a Volvo near the American General Building in Nashville.

The sightings were never-ending. October 16, 1996, a man from Kentucky by the name of James Howard said he'd assisted Janet March on the interstate and that she had moved to Franklin, Kentucky, and was using a different name. With the help of Franklin police, they found the man, and it was determined that the person he'd helped was not Janet.

"Then there was a sighting at I-Twenty-four and Waldron Road that turned out to be a runaway from Rutherford County in Tennessee who had gotten off her medication," Miller said, ticking off still another Janet sighting.

She was seen at a Camden boat dock near Johnsonville, while another report had her at the railroad tracks by Lafayette Street. There was also a Paris, France, sighting and one in Athens, Greece, where the Olympics was going on.

"Actually, the Olympics sighting was reported by Perry March himself, by faxing a copy of a photograph of somebody at a cocktail bar in Athens. I wouldn't exactly call that a sighting," Thurman sarcastically told Massey.

Miller said that initially his investigators had gotten Interpol involved, trying to find any indication that Janet was out of the country, even though her passport was found with the Volvo.

He said that Perry "sort of led us to believe that maybe she left the country," and "had indicated that she was fond of Quebec in Canada. So we had Interpol check that out," Miller said.

Three years after Janet's disappearance, her parents had received an anonymous call from a man—police later determined he was in jail—"and he gave us the name of a woman named Sally Rhodes who lived in one of the Brixworth buildings," Miller said.

"I went out there and talked to her, along with one of the other detectives. And it was later determined that the person that she was referring to was two other girls who were living together, and that they were getting into domestic disputes.

"We had the girls come in and talk to the police at headquarters and it was determined that they were the ones, but neither young lady was Janet. One of the girls, ironically to me, did look similar to Janet. I believe that was the girl by the name of Jill King who was actually the lease holder," Miller testified.

"Detective Miller, it's fair to say that you don't have anyone to your knowledge in this case . . . that saw Perry March commit any kind of offense against Janet?"

"Not committing an offense . . . there were people along the line who mentioned his demeanor around Janet was aggressive."

"Did anybody say they saw Perry March kill Janet March?"

"No."

"What evidence do you have to tell the Court today that Janet March is dead?"

"It was a bunch of little evidence put together. It was almost like having a puzzle . . . and eventually when you get all the pieces, it kinda points you in the right direction. And that's what happened in this investigation."

Although Miller did not reveal to the defense lawyer the police theory of what had happened to Janet the night of August 15, 1996, he thought back to what police and prosecutors suspected happened to her.

It had long been speculated that Janet had confronted Perry with copies of the sexually explicit letters he'd written to Leigh Reames and a knock-down, drag-out fight had followed, after which she'd told him she would be seeing a divorce lawyer in the morning and that he was going to lose the house, his job at her father's law firm, and custody of the children.

Perry, it was conjectured, had picked up a wrench—possibly left in the kitchen when he'd assisted workers earlier in the day with a plumbing problem—and whacked Janet. Then, it was speculated, panic-stricken at the sight of Janet lying dead on the kitchen floor, he'd quickly gone over to his computer and typed out the twelve-day vacation to-do list, which would naturally be assumed to have been written by Janet. The print-out of the one-page list shows the time to have been 8:17 p.m. He'd then carried Janet to the trunk of his Jeep and covered her body in heavy-duty lawn bags, before coming back to the house and placing calls to his brother, Ron, and his sister, Kathy, telling them that he and Janet had had a fight and she'd left home.

Around 9:30 that night, Perry would have driven one mile to a large tract of land undergoing excavation that belonged to his client Sharon Bell, and buried the body on a hill. Once back at the house, he would have started the massive clean-up, using powerful disinfectant in all areas of the home, searching for any tell-tale signs of blood or any other evidence that could link him to the crime. When he was through, he tossed the cleaning paraphernalia—rags, bleach, and detergent—into the carpet, and rolled it up, to be discarded in the morning.

At midnight, he would have called Larry and Carolyn Levine to report that he and Janet had had a fight and that she'd taken off in the Volvo on a twelve-day vacation. After covering his tracks with his in-laws, Perry might have driven to the Brixworth Apartments parking lot, backed the car into a spot, removed his bike, which he had stashed in the rear seat, taken one last look at the Volvo before cycling back to his Blackberry Road home, and safely gone to sleep by the time Sammy awakened during the night crying that he was having a nightmare and jumped into bed with his father.

"That's bullshit!" was Perry's explosive remark when he

later learned of the police premise on how he'd killed his wife.

"Do you have personal knowledge that Janet March is dead?" Massey asked the detective, bringing him back to the reality of the courtroom questioning.

"No. I think I have a strong reason to believe that she's dead, yes. I think a little stronger than that, yes, sir."

Massey had one last question for Miller. He wanted to know if he'd ever interviewed Sammy about Janet leaving the house in that Volvo and waving to him as she left. Miller told the lawyer that Perry had adamantly refused to let police interview the boy, but "we would've certainly liked to've interviewed him."

On cross-examination by Tom Thurman, the police captain was asked if he knew of any credible sightings of Janet March that hadn't been investigated. "No, I do not," replied the detective.

Massey continued the hearing by next putting Ron March, Perry's brother, on the witness stand. Ron said that he believed his brother would stay in Nashville. Ron would help his brother financially by finding him an apartment and paying the rent and other expenses. He further explained that Perry had left Nashville in 1996 because of the media coverage of the case and the "extremely unhealthy environment" for the children.

Ron March acknowledged that he'd represented his brother in the Illinois custody case and the contempt order when Perry had failed to appear in court and left for Mexico. He also revealed that Perry had relatives in Illinois, Israel, and Mexico, and that he'd attended school in Singapore and had bank accounts in Belize.

Perry didn't score any points when Ron March admitted that his brother had forged his name to documents filed with the Probate Court in Davidson County and had also been held in contempt in that court. However, he emphasized that if Perry remained confined in jail, "it would severely prejudice him in preparing his defense" for the upcoming trial.

Ron did his best to convince the judge that Perry would show up for court proceedings if he were released on bail or bond, because of "my firsthand knowledge of him, and his desire to show his innocence."

Ron tried explaining away Perry's sudden decision to leave Nashville just weeks after Janet had disappeared by blaming his father-in-law, Larry Levine. "It was a very strained relationship . . . there was a lot of turmoil with his legal practice . . . and by moving to Illinois, he was hoping to start a new career . . . and earn a living there . . ."

The defense rested and the prosecution called as its first witness Laura Chastain, the deputy chief disciplinary counsel with the Board of Professional Responsibility, who testified about two complaints the disciplinary agency had received against Perry in his role as an attorney in Tennessee for his failure to respond to allegations.

Chastain testified that the hearing committee had found evidence to support disbarment, ticking off allegations and complaints. "That Mr. March had embezzled funds from the law firm in which he was working; that he had filed a frivolous pro se [representing oneself without the aid of a lawyer] lawsuit against his law firm; and he had been held in contempt of court on two occasions in the Probate Court for Davidson County; that he had failed to return his client's file—Esther Epstein's file; [and] failed to notify her that he was suspended, despite repeated requests, so that she could obtain another attorney to take over her case."

After Perry was disbarred, the witness said she received a letter from him dated August 13, 2000. Chastain was then asked to read the entire letter into the record:

Dear Ms. Chastain:
I was shocked to see the Order of Disbarment which you sent me. That was the first I had heard of it, a hearing or any of it. I guess that it . . . is some more home-cooking, and it shouldn't surprise me one bit.

I stopped long . . . long ago to expect even the appearance of impartiality out of any Tennessee political organ, and the Board is nothing but a political lickspittle, serving the powers that be, appointed by elected officials. What an independent judiciary and its own lap dog watch group. I'm impressed.

Self-regulation doesn't work. You know the view of the rest of America, and your organization will certainly be a prime example of that in my story. Shakespeare was right.

Unfortunately, you proceeded against me in error and without notice or proper service. I think it may've been tortuous and intentionally designed to divest me of a number of rights. That will be interesting to see, and I look forward to your public deposition on this.

Attached please find a copy of my faxed letter to you of June twenty-fifth, nineteen-ninety-nine, giving the Board my new mailing address and facsimile address in Mexico, an address that the Board and all of Nashville, Tennessee, were visibly aware was new.

Incredible that you would stoop to the oily tactic of sewer service in my bogus bar discipline case. By the way, I never heard of the Epstein matter before you.

That whacko filed a complaint, because I would not participate in her fraud on an insurance company. I couldn't take her grabbing her neck, screaming, 'Whiplash,' as she munched bagels and tried to bribe doctors to assign her a disability rating for a fenderbender.

Geez, you guys are a bunch a [sic] Keystone wanna-be cops. Please be so kind as to recuse yourself, along with Mr. Bracey, from handling my file. Venich, too; he has been in Larry's pocket since day one. Can't get a job as a real lawyer? How far does the Clement-Levine stein—slime go? We will see.

Please take this as a Petition to Set Aside the Order of Disbarment for lack of service, notice and proper process. But hurry, scurry around quickly, and try to figure a loophole to hold on to it.

What did I do wrong? Did I miss another deadline?

Can you throw this letter in the trash? Better not. I'm sending a copy of all of it somewhere you'd better not mess with. Big pile of poop you stepped in.

How can you argue technically that I had proper notice? You can't. It's a bald-face lie. I provided you with an address changed and you sewered me. That's it in a nutshell.

So, now get together and disbar me for merits or something else. Come on, you guys can do better than improper sewer service. Get creative. America will be watching. This is Tennessee, for God's sake.

Do I need to file something else? Tell me the rules to go by. You've got the oily keys. All I have is justice of course, second in Tennessee.

By the way, the address on this letter is my new address. You have my fax number. Thank you for your anticipated cooperation.

Truly,

Perry A. March.

Carbon copy: Eight-hundred-pound gorilla.

After receiving that letter, Chastain testified, she received some messages on her answering machine that bothered her.

"Well, I wouldn't call them messages; they were gorilla noises," she said. "Whoever was doing it was very childish," adding that while it was not unusual to get hostile or inappropriate communications from aggrieved persons, "it is probably the only letter that I've received like that."

Next to testify was Redina Friedman, an attorney in Chicago who had been appointed to be guardian *ad litem* for Perry's children in the grandparent visitation case.

The child representative testified that she'd had two or three conversations with Perry, both at her office and in his home, and that Perry told her that if she recommended that the Levines have any contact with the children, "he would not comply with those orders and that under no circumstances would he allow his children to have contact with the Levines."

At the second meeting with Perry a week later, Friedman testified, Perry told her he would no longer oppose the unrestricted visitation, "but wanted something in return. And what he said he wanted was a promise that the Levines would drop all civil litigation for financial issues, and in addition that Mr. Levine would assist him in getting back his law license.

"I told him I was not privy to those issues. I knew nothing about those issues. But then he told me that if I recommended any visitation or if the court ordered visitation for the children, that he knew how to disappear. He mentioned Singapore. He said he would disappear with the children to Singapore or Mexico and that the Levines would never see the children again and that he would not comply with any orders that allowed them contact with the children."

In other words, the children were Perry's bargaining chip.

"And did he make good on that promise?" Thurman asked her.

"Yes, he did."

Friedman went on to say that the next day she'd received a fax from Perry, again telling her he was "very unhappy" with her recommendations and that he had no intention to comply with it.

The day that Friedman reported her recommendation to the court, Ron March informed the judge that Perry had relocated to Mexico with the children.

By August 1999, Friedman said, Perry had been held in criminal contempt for failing to appear and for failing to produce the children in court.

Friedman later heard from Perry by telephone. "The gist of the conversation was that I should be very careful about what I say about him, and that I would be sorry . . .

"And I said to him, 'Are you threatening me?' And he said words to the effect of, 'Take it any way you want it, but you need to be very careful about what you say about me.' "

Friedman testified that she'd "felt threatened by the call and reported it to the FBI and to the Chicago police."

Thurman then brought out another significant piece of testimony regarding a statement made by Sammy in either December 1996 or January 1997 during an interview with another court-appointed guardian ad litem, Ralla Klepak.

Friedman said that as part of her investigation, she'd conferred with Klepak. Klepak told her what Sammy had once said: that the night his mother disappeared, he had heard his parents fighting. "He did not see them, he only heard them fighting. And then he fell asleep and when he woke up the following morning, his mother was gone. He saw a rug rolled up, somewhere in the vicinity of the kitchen, and later that day, the rug was gone. He made no mention of saying goodbye to his mother, waving goodbye to his mother and nothing of that nature at all."

That conversation with Sammy contradicted a media interview conducted with the boy some four years after Janet had disappeared.

It was an exclusive interview by Larry Brinton of WTVF conducted in Mexico. "The female producers and anchors did not think we should run the interview with Sammy, since he was only nine years old," Brinton said. "A child psychologist was called in as a consultant on the matter, who agreed, and the interview never ran at that time." (That interview was, however, later shown to jurors during Perry's murder trial.) When Brinton conducted the interview, Sammy and his young sister were living in Ajijic and the children were under the total control of their father. In the interview, Sammy told Brinton that he'd gone to bed at eight o'clock the night of August 15, and that his mother had come up and given him a good night kiss, and that she was carrying some luggage. "She took her bags, went downstairs, got in the car and drove away," the youngster told Brinton.

Sammy goes on to say in the interview that he'd watched his mother leave from his bedroom window and that she'd then gone down to the basement and out to the garage and driven off. "I waved to her and she waved to me when she left."

Sammy had been under the supervision— and influence—
of his father for several years, and it was Brinton's contention
that Perry had not only made up the story that Janet was alive
when she'd left home, but that he had convinced his young
son of it.

C. J. Gideon's testimony followed Friedman's. He advised the court that Perry had been held in contempt at
least five times, that there was also an outstanding attachment order—meaning property could be seized—and that
he had submitted forged documents to the court. Gideon, a
Nashville attorney, had been hired by the Levines and was
involved in the probate and wrongful death civil proceedings. Gideon also testified that Perry had an outstanding civil
judgment against him in the amount of six million dollars.

The testimony of Samuel Chavez, Perry's former busi-
ness associate in Mexico, was devastating. He testified that
Perry had wanted him to falsify affidavits regarding Gayle
Cancienne's allegations that he'd stolen money from her.
When Chavez had refused, Perry told him, "If you report
me, I will kill you the way I killed my wife."

According to Chavez's testimony, Perry had a gun with
him when he'd made the threat, and another attorney, Jose
Alberto Sandoval Pulido, had been present and overheard
the statement. Perry warned them, "I mean what I said."
Chavez said he'd taken Perry's threats "serious enough to
report it to the FBI."

Chavez had met Perry through Perry's father, Arthur,
shortly before Perry moved to Mexico. The elder March had
visited Chavez to discuss an urgent care facility for the many
retirees living in Ajijic, and he indicated that his son was a
specialist in the inner working of billings for medical institu-
tions.

Chavez testified that after meeting Perry, a partnership
had been formed between the two men, with Perry listing
himself as a financial planner who dealt mostly with offshore banking.

In some ways the partnership had been a match made in

heaven. Chavez was forced to admit during questioning that he too had been disbarred. He had received a thirty-month suspension of his law license in Indiana based on a federal conviction for bankruptcy fraud conviction.

Eventually the two men had had a falling out, Chavez testified, "after I found out he tried to kill me, I got rid of him. I was already firmly convinced by information that was given to me by various governmental sources and investigators that I had hired, with regard to the incident in which my children and I were almost killed, and I was satisfied that Mr. March was involved in that.

"And based on that, I locked him out of his office. I sealed his offices and I took possession of all the documents that were in there."

Chavez said he'd later agreed to meet Perry at his office in La Floresta. "I went with the distinct purpose of telling Mr. March that I had concluded, based on interviews with other individuals, that he was in fact, the individual who set in motion the assassination of myself and my children."

Chavez said he'd turned over some paperwork Perry had left in the office to the FBI and the district attorney's office with regard to his offshore banking activities, indicating that Perry had close to half a million dollars squirreled in various accounts.

Because Perry's constant threats were causing Chavez problems, Chavez testified, he'd wanted Perry "out of Mexico." Believing that Chavez was behind the move to have him deported, Perry warned his former partner that if it didn't stop, Perry "would feel compelled to act. I took it, of course, as a threat."

The state's final witness was Sergeant Pat Postiglione of the Metro Nashville Police Department, who testified that he'd been assigned to the Cold Case Unit and that he'd escorted Perry from California to Nashville after he was deported from Mexico. Postiglione further testified that Perry had been interested in knowing the facts of the case and whether anyone else was indicted. During his conversation with the detective, Perry had offered to make a deal and said that he would plead guilty and take between 5 and 7 years in prison "so he could close this chapter in his life" and "to get this behind me."

To his lawyers and in interviews, Perry denied over offering to make a deal, and said he would never pursue it with the district attorney because he was innocent, and if he made a deal he would have to admit he'd killed Janet.

In an interview with NewsChannel 5 after the bond hearing, Perry called the case against him a "house of cards," and said that he welcomed the chance to clear his name.

At the conclusion of the four-hour hearing, prosecutors asked for a bond of $2.5 million, based on the testimony of Sergeant Pat Postiglione and others. The defense, on the other hand, tried to show that the state's case against Perry was weak.

Dozier said he needed more time before ruling on Perry's request. The judge agreed to view the WTVF interview with Larry Brinton that had been introduced by the defense, and another videotape from WSMV–Channel 4 that showed a contradictory report before issuing his decision on bond.

Five days later, on Tuesday, September 27, in a detailed six-page decision, Dozier methodically gave his reasons for why he was setting a bond of three million dollars—to "reasonably assure" that Perry would be present at his jury trial:

The court has heard no proof as to the length of the defendant's prior residency in this jurisdiction but it is apparent that the defendant has not resided in this jurisdiction within the last nine years. There has been no proof of any employment options currently available to the defendant. The defendant is disbarred from the practice of law. There has been absolutely no proof of the defendant's current financial condition. The defendant's family ties are to other states and countries. As to the defendant's character and reputation, his attitude towards courts in which he has been involved speaks against the defendant in this regard.

Dozier also cited Perry's "multiple contempt court findings," testified to by C. J. Gideon, which indicated that he did not have a good track record with the courts. The judge also pointed to the testimony of Redina Friedman, the children's representative, who mentioned in her testimony Perry's willingness to "get lost in Singapore," as well as his threats to her.

There was also no testimony from "persons within the community to vouch for the defendant's reliability," the judge wrote.

> *The court heard proof that the defendant has displayed a blatant attitude of disregard toward the courts and its orders. This is evidenced by the numerous times he has been held in contempt and from the language of the letter he sent to the Board of Professional Responsibility. The court heard proof that the defendant has contacts in other jurisdictions such as Chicago, Mexico, Israel, Belize and possibly China.*

The only positive consideration that weighed in Perry's favor, the judge wrote was that until now, he did not have a criminal record.

Dozier wrote that if Perry could make bond, it had to be secured by at least three different bonding companies and that he would impose the following conditions: Perry had to surrender his passport; have no contact with any potential witnesses listed in the indictment; not leave Nashville; and wear an electronic ankle monitor.

11

"Do It When They're Both Together"

Perry despaired that he would be unable to post the three-million-dollar bond, the amount Judge Dozier indicated was needed to secure his release. He realized he was going to have to remain in jail until the trials against him had concluded.

As he sat in his 8×10 cell for twenty-three hours a day pondering his next move, what infuriated Perry was the contentious battle that was being waged elsewhere at the courthouse in two civil cases—one surrounding the multi-million-dollar wrongful death suit and personal property issues, and the other involving the child custody dispute.

An appeals court judge reversed an earlier circuit court decision regarding who owned what personal property belonging to Janet and her family. The judge described the acrimonious relationship between the parties as "trench warfare."

Claiming that Perry and his family had taken possessions from the Blackberry Road dream home that rightfully belonged to the Levine family, the Levines were seeking $200,000 in compensatory damages and an unspecified amount in punitive damages. Asking for punitive damages is a tactic used by lawyers to intimidate the other side—to let them know they mean business.

In filing the suit against Perry, and his brother, sister, and father, the Levines were actually hoping to recover their daughter's possessions. Among the items the Levines wanted returned were a painting by Janet called *Two Lawyers*, a drawing of a man at a dessert cart, *The Mind Over Platter Cookbook*, a priceless late-nineteenth-century desk (an "antique secretary") that Mark Levine had gotten from his grandmother and which Janet was storing for him, wedding china, a black-beaded evening bag with multi-colored flowers belonging to Carolyn, a cross-stitched baby quilt with a nursery rhymes hand-sewn by Janet's grandmother, a wooden footstool with a woven twine top, and an Encyclopædia Britannica.

At some point in the nasty proceedings, even the wedding pictures of the once-happy couple became a bone of contention, with Perry finally allowed to keep only those photos of himself and his immediate family. He also got to hold on to a bag of lace tablecloths and doilies, linens, two light fixtures, and two mezuzahs—religious symbols that were affixed to doorways of the house.

But what was eating Perry alive was a court decision a month earlier, on August 22. Nashville Juvenile Court Judge Betty Adams Green had granted the Levines temporary custody of the children. Perry was enraged over the decision, convinced that once again the Levines had influenced the judge to rule in their favor.

Perry struck back, ordering his lawyers to file an appeal, which was to be argued in another courtroom a few days after the bond hearing. In his original affidavit to the juvenile court, Perry's contempt for the Levines was loud and clear. He specifically wrote that he did "not [underlining in original] want my children to have any contact with Carolyn Levine, Lawrence Levine, and Mark Levine because said contact will cause my children irreparable emotional distress and harm."

It was also Perry's desire that Samson and Tzipora reside with his brother, Ron, and Ron's wife, Amy, in Wilmette, Illinois.

Alone in his cell and virtually isolated from the outside world, Perry's hatred of the Levines intensified. He was positive that they were behind the relentless effort to have him deported from Mexico and prosecuted for murdering their daughter. He wanted to settle the score. He wanted the Levines dead.

Perry became so obsessed with getting back at his former in-laws that he made the second self-destructive tactical error since his arrest—one that eventually would cost him dearly.

Not even his lawyers were able to understand his motivation. "Perry contacted me from jail in Los Angeles in August 2005" John Herbison said. "He had just arrived from Mexico and was to fly back to Nashville on August twelfth to face charges of murdering his wife. It started out as a pretty good case from the defense perspective. There was no physical evidence; the statements he made to police were not inculpatory. It appeared to be a weak circumstantial case.

"But things took an unfortunate turn on the plane ride back from Los Angeles, when he had conversations with the two detectives. The civil suits between him and the Levines got to him, and by the time he was locked up in jail, it was more than he could handle. And by then, he was his own worst enemy."

Herbison said that as Perry's attorney "he was off the charts" when it came to representing him in the criminal cases.

Already angry at being confined to a cell, Perry started to vent his hostilities about the Levines to Russell Nathaniel Farris, who occupied the cell next to him on the fourth floor of the Special Management Unit of the Metro Jail.

Farris was sinister-looking, with his bald head, tattoos running up both arms, and a bizarre question mark tattoo on the middle of his neck.

Photos of Janet March released by Nashville police during the early stages of the investigation. She was described as 5'4", 104 pounds, with brown hair and brown eyes. Her family offered a $50,000 reward.

Janet's car that Perry abandoned at Brixworth Apartments, three miles from the March home. Perry backed the car into the parking spot so that the license plate would not be seen by passersby to delay police.

An inventory of the contents of Janet's car, showing that Janet had not packed a hairbrush, toothbrush or bras, suggesting to police that a man, not a woman, had packed Janet's suitcases.

Perry (left) owned a mountain bike and was an avid bicyclist. Police theorize that Perry put the bike in the Volvo when he drove it from his house to Brixworth Apartments and then got on his bike and returned to his home after temporarily disposing of Janet's body.

Detective Brad Corcoran (left) and Commander Mickey Miller, who initially headed up the investigation.

While searching Perry's computer, police found that the hard drive was missing. Perry told police that either his father or his father-in-law removed it. Both men denied involvement.

Perry's Turn For Janet's 12 Day Vacation

1. Feed the Children nutritious food - 3 meals per day
2. Coordinate Deneane and Ella
3. Pay Deneane and Ella
4. Buy Raffi's Birthday present
5. Get Sam to and from Raffi's party on sunday
6. Do Children's laundry
7. Be with Children all day - don't pawn off on Mom and Dad
8. Keep list of Sammy's Birthday party RSVP
9. Go through Bill Drawer and pay bills
10. Call Shaun Orange $$$$ and dead trees
11. Bell South Mobility
12. Video Place
13. Make sure Children have bath everyday
14. Read to Tzipi
15. Do educational activities with Sam
16. Spend quantity and quality time with your Children not
    your guitar or computer or clients
17. Pay Dr. Campbell
18. Get OPEs back
19. Cancel credit card charges for computer crap
20. Change burned out light bulbs
21. Clean-up garbage area - children will get sick
22. Clean-up your closet
23. Call Steve Ward about driveway

        I agree to do all of the above before Janet's Vacation (in
response to Perry's cowardly, rash and confused vacation) is
over.

                        August 15, 1996

The 12-day to-do list that Perry claims Janet left him
prior to her disappearance on August 15, 1996, and
which investigators believe Perry wrote himself.

Exterior shot of the March house with Sammy's bedroom window circled. Perry had convinced his son to say in an interview when he was nine that he recalled seeing his mother wave at him from her car the night she was last seen, but Carolyn Levine testified that it would have been impossible for Sammy to have seen his mother.

Carmen Rojas, whom Perry married on March 31, 2001, two days before Janet was declared dead by a Tennessee court.

Courtesy Larry Brinton

Photo of Perry March taken on August 12, 2005, after he was taken into custody by Nashville police.

Arthur March, father of Perry. Photo taken on March 2, 2006, shortly before he gave a 150-page video deposition outlining to prosecutors how he aided his son in disposing of Janet's body.

Perry became friendly in jail with Russell Nathaniel Farris and convinced him to kill his in-laws, Larry and Carolyn Levine—Perry believed it would give him the best chance of beating the murder rap against him.

Fletcher Long, the defense attorney for Arthur March, reminded him that the tapes between Arthur and Farris were damning to his defense. It was going to be hard to convince a jury to ignore the recorded conversations between Arthur and Farris about killing the Levines.
Courtesy Joshua Wilkens / Robertson County Times (Springfield, TN)

Detective Bill Pridemore (left) and Sergeant Pat Postiglione (center) receiving congratulations from Chief Ronal Serpas for their relentless work over the past several years to bring closure to the 1996 Janet March missing person case.

Perry had first met Farris the night of August 12 when Pat Postiglione and Bill Pridemore brought him back to Nashville and he was locked up. "When he first got in, Perry was rather meek, almost timid," recalled Farris, who'd sensed that the rookie was new to confinement. "He asked me to make a phone call for him. I made two other calls for him and then as he got used to his surroundings after a few days, he talked to me about Mexico and how it was to live there.

"We talked about jail. He didn't know much about being in jail, and he wanted to know more about prison life, how things were in prison and if I thought he would be able to make it in prison."

That was how their friendship had begun. Communicating with each other wasn't easy, but with time on their hands, the two men devised clever ways to talk. Farris explained that almost everyone in the unit was housed alone in a cell and came out once a day for recreation. "It's called 'house alone, rec alone,' " he explained, meaning a prisoner was alone both in his cell and at recreation time. The only opportunity the two men had to talk initially was when Perry passed Farris's cell and spoke to him through a little crack in his door.

"Mostly he talked about his case," said Farris. "Then we figured out that our cells shared an air-conditioning vent in the middle of the wall that connected our two cells, and by actually standing on the commode, we could talk through the vents. We were also able to exchange notes. Our cells were so close together that basically all we had to do is tear strips of bedding sheets to make a little rope and tie something heavy on the end. It's what everybody in jail calls fishing. And we would just slide the rope with the message down the walkway to the next inmate and put it in his cell."

Farris had an extensive criminal history. A former Tire Barn employee, his arrest record dated back to 1995. He was 28 years old when he met Perry and already had six felony convictions, four theft convictions, one robbery conviction, and one for reckless endangerment, besides a misdemeanor theft conviction on his rap sheet.

His most recent arrest had been on April 23, 2005, and he was awaiting trial on five new felony charges, including three counts of attempted murder stemming from the shooting of two people, and two counts of robbery for allegedly holding up a supermarket and robbing a man at gunpoint. Farris was facing substantial time—15 to 25 years on the attempted murder counts and 8 to 12 years on the robbery charge in state prison, if convicted.

For some reason, Perry thought Farris had been charged with first-degree murder. "I didn't tell him that. He told me that," said Farris. "Perry must have checked me out by maybe asking an officer at the jail what crime I was charged with, because the jail computer erroneously listed me as having committed first-degree murder instead of attempted murder."

Over the next couple of weeks, Perry began to feel more comfortable, speaking frequently with Farris about his ongoing problems with the Levines. Then Perry's mind went into overdrive. He realized that the Levines were his greatest obstacle to freedom. There was only one solution: he had to kill them.

Farris would be the perfect hit man because of his knowledge on the use of guns. Day by day, Perry revealed more of his plan and confided to Farris that the Levines were the "biggest thing in his case" and that if it wasn't for them, he could "beat" the second-degree murder charge. He complained to Farris that the Levines had money, that they had pressured authorities to bring the case, and that they were going to testify against him. Perry kept saying that his chances of beating the rap improved from 40 to 90 percent if Carolyn and Lawrence Levine were dead.

After a number of these conversations, Perry promised his unlikely jail-pal financial assistance and a place to live in Mexico—where he would be "treated like a king." He promised him the profits from future criminal endeavors that they could conduct in Mexico. Perry boasted that he had already kidnapped for profit the children of wealthy parents while living in Mexico and said they could make big money snatching residents off the streets.

He talked to Farris incessantly for more than a month about killing the Levines. But to do the job, he knew that Farris had to make bond. Perry promised he would help him secure his bond of more than $250,000. How Perry was going to arrange to pay the bond was unclear.

Farris, meanwhile, worried that Perry might not use him as his hit man and assured Perry that he was "fixing to get out . . . that he had friends to help out."

The plans were progressing when an unexpected thorny situation came up. Jeremy Duffer, an accused child rapist, was suddenly placed in the same cell with Farris, complicating Perry's discussions with him and putting a damper on plans. A few days later, Duffer was moved to a single cell next to Perry, and talks between Perry and Farris resumed.

Perry made it clear that the Levines must die. He told Farris not to act until there was a "chilling-off period of thirty to forty-five days" from the date he was released on bond. Perry eventually provided Farris with his father's telephone number and e-mail address, instructing him to contact Arthur March in Mexico after he was released from jail. Perry came up with a code phrase—*buying* or *selling the BMW*—for Farris to use when contacting Arthur March about the murder of the Levines.

Soon after Perry enlisted him, Farris began to get cold feet about the nefarious scheme. On the one hand, he wanted out on bond, so he was willing to play along with Perry. But he realized that if the Levines were killed, he could be blamed.

On the next visiting day, he told his mother, Vickie Farris, about the plot hatched by Perry. Disturbed by the developments, she called Lawrence Levine and informed him of the murder-for-hire plot. Farris also let his lawyer, Justin Johnson, know about the secret conversations. He in turn alerted prosecutors and police of the murder plot and agreed to cooperate with authorities.

At first authorities were uncertain about whether the jailhouse snitch was telling the truth. But after providing Postiglione, Pridemore, and Thurman with enough details about the proposed scheme, Farris convinced them that he could be relied on with his information.

Prosecutors made no promises to Farris, who merely hoped that his assistance would lead to a reduced sentence. But after tipping off authorities, arrangements were made to allow Farris to tape-record his conversations with Perry. Farris would hold a tape-recorder to the air-conditioning vent as the two spoke.

The audiotape officially began rolling on October 6, 2005, nearly two months after Perry's apprehension. In the tapes, Farris is heard sweet-talking Perry. He reassures Perry that he knows how to take care of the Levines, and that he's the boy to do the job. Using his relaxing voice, Farris carefully chooses words to show enthusiasm. While Farris's tone conveyed caring, the two con artists tried outdoing each other. Recorded in seven hours of talk over two days, the two men cover a variety of topics from Duffer's abrupt banishment from Farris's cell to plans for murdering the Levines.

Perry, of course, started off by taking credit for Duffer's ouster by claiming he'd informed a case administrator at the jail, who was a good friend of his, that Duffer was "just unbearable," was "just a loony tune," was "gonna be in trouble pretty soon," that "Nate [Farris] is a good boy" and "you've got to get [Duffer] out of here."

The story Perry gave Farris was that the administrator's wife once worked for him as his secretary when he was an editor of the Law Review while attending Vanderbilt University Law School.

Farris had been on the third floor of the jail being briefed by detectives on how to operate the recorder when Duffer was taken away. When Farris got back to his cell, Perry gave him the good news. "They ambushed him," he tells his friend. "A black captain came up here, opened the door, and cleared Duffer's shit out."

As the conversation continued, Farris hinted to Perry that his bond was about to be lowered, making it do-able for his family to perhaps post the money to get him out.

"We've got to talk about our situation," Perry whispered to Farris. "Are you thinking about it? I'm one hundred and ten percent on board with everything we've talked about. I can't tell you how excited I am, okay?"

"It's just— Man, Perry, you know this is all I've been thinking about. . . . especially now that I'm fixing to get out. . . . it's real heavy on my mind and . . ."

"Well . . ." said Perry, "set some rules, set some parimeters."

Farris started to respond, but Perry cautioned him to "Talk low . . . you're talking too loud." What Perry then tried to convey to Farris was that his chances of being acquitted of Janet's murder depended on whether the Levines could testify against him.

With the Levines alive and ready to testify, Perry said, "I've got a forty percent chance of walking, forty."

"That's not good enough, forty percent ain't good?" asked Farris.

"Please listen to what I said at the beginning. Hear me all out. I'm just trying to explain to you what we have to deal with. Okay? . . .

"What we're going to do is, we're going to get real smart, right now. . . . We're gonna do it real smart, guy. . . . I'd rather take a shot at forty percent . . . you know . . . even if I get convicted, I'll get fifteen years. I don't want to die and neither do you."

But Farris was concerned "that the colonel, your dad, will . . . say, 'Well, I don't know you. Get the hell away from me.' "

Trust me, "They don't know you right now," Perry said, "but they will. My dad is the totally coolest guy in the world. Let me just say this to you. If you showed up at my dad's door right now . . . my dad would feed you like a king and take care of you the rest of your life."

But for now "the most important thing is, you have to follow the rules," he said in a soft voice. "If anything happens . . . they're gonna come after you. There's no question about it."

"I thought about that too, Perry . . . but . . . like, I'm wanting to know how to do it."

"We'll have to put together an alibi," said Perry, cautioning Farris that once he does the job, to cool his heels and "chill out for a while. . . . You have to there, be ready when the cops show up to question you."

Perry promised he would write his father that night and that Arthur would receive the letter in about two weeks. "Okay . . . what name do you want me to use?" he asked Farris.

Farris, eager to please, replied, "Let's make up one now."

"All right, first and last name that you can remember, that's gonna be easy for you to use," Perry said.

Farris came up with the name *Bobby Givings* and explained that the last name Givings was "just an old, old friend of mine from pre-school."

"Tomorrow, I'm gonna make a call to my dad. And if not tomorrow, it will be Monday or Tuesday. It's going to be on an unmonitored direct eight hundred . . . and I'm gonna tell him that a buddy of mine—I'll think of a story—Bobby Givings is gonna give you a call, so take good care of him.

"I'm gonna write a letter to him and tell him the same thing. I'll probably make up some story about how you wrote me and . . ."

"Let me stop you right there . . . Okay, when this happens, when I get rid of these motherfuckers and I call your dad, he's gonna know what happened. He's not gonna flip out, then, is he?"

"My dad has killed about three hundred people in his life. My dad was a Green Beret colonel. Let me tell you one thing . . . trust me when I tell you, I know for a fact, my dad is a soldier, okay? He's at the end of his days. You know, he's seventy-six. He wants nothing. He would give himself up for me in a blink of an eye. . . . That's where he is in his life."

"You know, Perry, what I'm worried about is . . . catching both of the Levines together."

Perry cautioned Farris that when he killed the Levines, to make sure that his children were not in the home.

But Farris's concern was whether he could kill both of them. "Say I got to him and not her, would that still help you?"

"Do it. You have to do it when they're both together for it to help me," Perry implored his hit man, giving Farris the Levines' West Meade home address and providing him with detailed directions.

But when Perry remembered that the Levines' home was being renovated and that they had moved to a nearby apartment complex, he suggested, as an alternative site, his father-in-law's law office, which was "a stone's throw away," and gave him the address.

After much conversation, Farris agreed with Perry that the perfect spot to bump off the Levines was when they were "both in that house . . . if they answer that door."

"Listen, you're the pro. I'm leavin' it up to you," Perry said. "Deal with them."

"Okay, but, like . . . I've got to have some kinda contact with your dad," Farris wearily said.

With that, Perry gave Farris his father's telephone number. On the tape, Farris can be heard scribbling the number on a piece of paper. "His name is Colonel," Perry reminded Farris. "I'll tell you what to do with my dad. . . . Let me give you a confirmation word for my dad."

He then devised a unique code name and phrase for Farris to use when he made contact with Arthur March. Perry explained it to his partner-in-crime this way: "My dad's dogs all his life [were all] named . . . Oni. Tell him, 'Oni number two waited till we got back from Davos to die.' "

Perry explained that his father would know what that meant. "Oni number one they gave to the Japanese Oak Hill Police Department. . . . We got another dog, Oni number two. After my mom died . . . my dad took us skiing to in . . . this place called Davos, Switzerland. When we got back . . . Oni [number two] was laying at the door, and he died that night from cancer, but he waited for us to get back. . . . That story will let him know who you are. That should be more than enough."

Perry gave Farris three other passwords to use as backups
that his dad's maid's name was Marta, "Uncle Mike from
East Chicago," or "Morrie Mages' ski sale every summer."

To set Farris's mind at ease that his father was a stand-up
guy, Perry swore that "if I called my dad and, if I had a clear
line and I'd say, 'Dad, come up here and shoot the Levines,'
my dad would be up here and shoot the Levines."

"He'd shoot 'em his self?" Farris asked in amazement.

"Yeah, when they kidnapped my kids, my dad got on the
phone with four mercenaries, four mercenaries, four fuckin'
mercenaries. They were gonna come in, kill the fuckin'
Levines and grab my kids and take 'em back to Mexico. . . .

"Here's the thing. The key is that they don't connect you
to me. . . . They're gonna keep me in here for sixty days, or
ninety days, just to investigate me. . . . They won't be looking for you in Mexico. . . . The key thing here is to make
sure that whenever they launch the investigation, that there's
no way that they can put us together, trace the guns. 'Cause
you're gonna be a good boy.

"My dad will stash you as long as it's necessary . . . He'll
love ya. . . . My dad would take care of you like a son."

"He's not gonna flip out about this?" Farris asked. "Turn
me in or something like that?"

"What you have to remember is to avoid news pressure
on the television," Perry said. The only way to avoid that
is to leave no evidence whatsoever, get rid of the evidence
the best you can. Don't be implicated."

Farris, who was not savvy about crossing the border,
questioned Perry as to how to respond if asked why he was
visiting Mexico.

"Just tell 'em you wanna get pussy," Perry said.

"Aw, you can tell 'em that?"

Perry laughed and the two men went over the details of
the planned hit.

"The best way to find them is to, like, hang around where
their house is," Perry said.

"How will I go about gettin' rid of their bodies? I mean,
should I just set 'em on fire after they're dead or somethin'?

You know what I'm sayin'? . . . It's gonna be pretty scary for me to leave 'em there. I've got to put 'em in my car or somethin', and that's really gonna spook me. But look . . . if they're both in that house, Perry, if they answer the door, it's over."

Perry kept reminding Farris that "When somethin' goes down, within an hour . . . somebody is going to put us together. You've got to be prepared for it. . . . Face the fear." He again told Farris to wear gloves to avoid leaving gunpowder residue, and to use a silencer.

Elated that plans for the hit were moving ahead, and that soon his name would appear in the news, Perry said all he could think of was "walkin' away from all of this . . . and get[ting] my kids back."

After some small talk about candy bars and prison life in general, Perry got back on topic. "So here's what you're gonna do," he told Farris. "Once you establish a rapport with my dad . . . Before you're ready [to go], you're gonna have my dad send a message through an e-mail, which is, *'Bobby Givings is gonna buy the BMW'* . . .

"What makes my stomach hurt is when Bobby Givings buys the BMW. It's gonna be all over the news. It's gonna be all over the national news . . ."

"You just promise me that once I do leave, that I'm gonna be okay in Mexico."

"You establish that yourself with my dad . . . when I get out of jail, you're set up forever in business.

"Just think of the BMW . . ." Perry told him again.

12

"Hello, Colonel . . . This Is Bobby Givings"

On October 7, the second day of their taped conversation, Perry rattled on about how he was going to tell his father that "Bobby Givings wrote me a nice letter and he's gonna be callin' him . . ."

Then out of the blue, Perry sounded worried that the authorities would "keep incoming letters" and that they could be used as evidence against him in court.

"What do you mean?" Farris asked.

"Do they take scans of them or pictures of them?"

"I don't think so," Farris said, explaining that an employee of the jail sifts through thousands of letters every day and that he seriously doubted she was instructed to copy all of his incoming mail.

"Remember . . . they're gonna focus like fuck on me, and my dad too. At the beginning they will. No question they're going to. You've gotta take it as a rule. . . . And you've gotta be real clean with that record."

Farris changed the subject and got Perry to talk about the federal custody lawsuit that Herbison was filing. If Perry is in jail, Farris asked, who gets his children?

"They'd first be returned to my father in Mexico, who in

turn would give them to my brother, Robert, or they'd wind up with Carmen," Perry replied. "Don't worry about that so much. What I'm really concerned about is another question I have in mind . . ."

Perry then got into a serious discussion with Farris about the charges facing him once he was released on bond, and the importance of his keeping a low profile. Farris indicated that he planned to stay clear of people involved in his case who might spot him on the street. "I'm gonna be a law-abiding citizen . . . because I've got a bigger picture," he said.

To draw attention elsewhere, Perry would "look like I'm fightin' for my kids. Let me tell you this: I'm gonna also be doing more about my case's bullshit. I'm gonna write a letter to people about how I'm gonna win my case . . . to create a paper trail."

For more than an hour, Perry gave Farris detailed lessons on how to use the Internet, from sending and retrieving e-mail to setting up a Hotmail account and communicating with his father on the computer.

"We're gonna be fuckin' outrageous," Perry said. "I'm telling you, it's so much fun. You go to an Internet café, go to a Borders bookstore, you can do anything, find *E-Mail for Dummies*. . . . There's really interesting places you can go to . . .

"Let me tell you. I just thought about this. It's gonna be so easy for me to be able to give you messages about the car . . . Everything's good on the car, we're ready . . . You know what I mean?"

Farris was about to get released when Perry suddenly suggested that they use alternate code words. "We have 'Bobby Givings' and a car, and we want another name and another scenario. . . ." Perry said. "So think of a name and I'll think of another scenario."

"Perry, I've got the name . . ."

"Hold on one minute, hold on, give me a second. I'll think this through . . ."

"Okay."

"Nate? Use a Spanish name."

"Okay, what about 'Jesus'? . . . That's easy for me to remember, 'Jesus,' you know."

"Perfect, 'Jesus' is perfect."

And for a last name, Farris came up with 'Roldan,' explaining to Perry that he once knew a Mexican girl by that last name.

"Our password [will be] 'kissing dog' and 'diamond,' " laughed Perry.

For the next several minutes the two men talked about Bobby Givings, the BMW, code words, Jesus Roldan. "And remember me talkin' about starting a pottery business," Perry said, because "in Mexico they have all those pottery" businesses.

"So . . . if my dad writes you and says, 'Hey, Jesus, Perry said the pottery business is ready to go' . . . or 'Perry says he needs about another week to figure out something,' or 'Can you check on some pricing for the pottery?' That lets you know . . ."

". . . that you're checkin' on stuff, okay, yeah," Farris said.

The tape runs on and on with Perry and Farris trying to make each other feel good by spending their last minutes together in mutual ego-stroking. Eventually, Farris was moved to the Williamson County Jail in Franklin, Tennessee, about 20 miles from the Metropolitan Nashville Davidson County Jail, to make it appear to Perry as if he had been released on bond.

Five days later, on October 12, Arthur March spoke with Farris by telephone. Arthur was in Ajijic, and Farris was in Nashville, where he claimed he had recently gotten out on bond after spending jail time with Perry. During the recorded telephone conversation, Arthur confirmed that Perry had alerted him that Farris would be contacting him. Farris asked that he contact Perry and tell him that "Bobby Givings contacted you about the BMW."

In their first brief conversation, Arthur threw security

codes to the wind. He claimed that the Levines were the cause of his son's prosecution.

"You want to hear the latest?" Arthur said, sounding chummy. "This one I'll tell you. You know the prosecutor that's after Perry," Arthur said, referring to Assistant Attorney General Tom Thurman. "They couldn't get anybody in the prosecutor's office that would take the case before this, because they know there's no case. So what they did, what the Levines did . . . this guy was guaranteed, win, lose, draw, whatever. He resigns when it's over and he's got a job on one of the big law firms in Nashville.

"Hey, listen, this whole thing is a setup. They know they ain't got nothin' on Perry."

Without being asked, Arthur voluntarily provided Farris with the name of Perry March's children's school in Nashville. A rumormonger and an old gossip, Arthur then proceeded to make undignified remarks about a Levine family member.

But Farris got Arthur back on track by discussing with him his need for "an instrument," a gun, and information about the Levines' daily routine. Before hanging up, Arthur advised Farris to obtain a "twelve," meaning he should buy a twelve-gauge shotgun.

In their next recorded conversation, two days later, Farris and Arthur again discussed the plan to kill the Levines. Arthur talked to him about "a nine" (9-mm gun) and explained that "nines" are "absolutely illegal" in Mexico, and that it would be easier if he obtained the gun in the United States. He also cautioned Farris not to "bring in the large economy size . . . and it can't be a twelve."

"My preference is like a twenty-two . . . because it's easier to hide, " Farris confided.

"I could probably locate one, the question is getting it to you. It's just that they have road blocks. If I drive between here and the border, it's a matter of going through at least four, sometimes as many as six blocks. Now that doesn't mean I can't get through with it. From my experience, it's easier at your end than at this end."

Farris decided to lighten up the conversation, asking, "It's fun down there?"

"The sky is blue, the beer is cold, the women are hot," Arthur responded. "What the hell else do you need? Just remember, when this operation is over, you've got a home."

Farris got the discussion back on track. He needed a silencer because "it's gonna be quick and quiet." Arthur also pointed out that it would be best if the gun went through several people's hands first. "Make sure that when you clean it, you got your gloves. My suggestion is . . . you wear thin surgeon's gloves. You do not take them off at all."

Farris said he might need "a little bit of funds" when he got to Mexico. Arthur let him know that he lived on an army pension and didn't get paid until the beginning of the month, so "try to do it the last day of the month or one of the first three days, 'cause the end of the month is a difficult time. It makes it easier . . ."

He then assured Farris that after the killings, and "once you get here [to Mexico], you got no problem. I'm your support and you're covered. Your ass is covered."

Farris wanted him to make sure that Perry knew he'd "found the car he wanted and would probably be purchasin' it soon."

"Okay. You gonna take one or two out?" Arthur asked, meaning was Farris going to kill one or both of the Levines?

Farris was confused by the remark. "Excuse me?" he said.

"Just one, or the two?"

"Two. It's got to be two."

Before ending the conversation, Arthur wished Farris "Good luck" and reminded him to be careful about Carolyn Levine.

"She's the smart one. She thinks there is nobody gonna touch her. And she has a built-in protection. It's called the Jewish Mafia. And she's the queen.

"You have to understand . . . they are very self-secure because they've got money. They use it. And they only got one thing. They want those kids. They could care less about Perry."

After speaking with Farris, Arthur March sent an e-mail to his daughter, Kathy, indicating that "Bobby G" had called him. According to Perry's earlier instructions to her, she was in turn supposed to print the e-mail and send it to Perry at the jail. But in a recorded conversation, intercepted by authorities, Perry later changed his mind and said he didn't want the mail sent to him.

On October 20, Arthur again spoke with Farris. Farris was informed that Arthur had spoken with Perry. Then the two finalized their plans.

"I've got me an instrument," Farris says. "I got me a silencer, too . . . the silencer cost me a little bit, but that's okay. I've done a little bit more surveillance and uh, I'm about ready to do this."

"So will it be next week or the week after? Is that when you're plannin'?" Arthur asked.

Farris said he intended to make the hit the following Tuesday or Wednesday.

"That'd bring you in here. And that's fine, and I see I get my money on the first, so we're in hallelujah land."

As Farris and Arthur maintained their dialogue, state authorities obtained permission to intercept Perry's telephone conversations at the jail. A day after Arthur learned from Farris that the hit was about to take place, Perry, using the agreed-upon code name and phrases, discussed with his father the plan to murder the Levines.

Perry was getting suspicious and, in speaking with his father, warned him not to send e-mails or phone calls about Bobby Givings.

And when Arthur mentioned to his son that Farris would be in Mexico "next week," Perry interrupted him, saying he didn't want to talk about it because "he was going to arrange for the sale of the car."

By October 25, Farris called Arthur with good news. "I'll probably be with you tomorrow. Everything looks good from up here, depending on the weather tomorrow. I'm gonna get this done. I'm not gonna ride a bus. I'm gonna take a plane from here, and I'm gonna go to Houston . . . and from Houston to Guadalajara."

Arthur told Farris he would pick him up at the airport, wished him luck and said, "Once you get here, you're home free."

"How will I recognize you?" Arthur asked.

"I've got a slick bald head. And uh, I've got a question mark tattoo on my throat. And I'll wear a yellow shirt. That way you can see me from far. I already know what you look like. Perry showed me a picture of you."

"I'm waitin' for you, buddy. Good luck."

Two days later, on October 27, Farris telephoned Arthur at 12:05 p.m. and in a brief conversation said he was calling from Houston, was about to board Continental Airlines flight 2046, and would be at the Guadalajara International Airport about 2:30 p.m.

"Have you finished the job up there?" Arthur asked.

"Yeah, that's done. Everything is done."

"How come it's not on my computer?"

"I don't have a clue about the computer," Farris responded.

"Okay, I'll check the news later," Arthur said before hanging up.

As Arthur March approached the arrivals gate to meet the would-be hit man, FBI special agents waited to greet him.

Special Agent Kenneth Sena had had Arthur under surveillance for a number of weeks, at the request of the police in Nashville, and had been monitoring his every movement for the time throughout which the phone calls between Farris and Arthur were taking place.

"Arthur March left his home around twelve-thirty p.m. and arrived at Guadalajara International Airport by one-o-five, and I made contact with him about three o'clock that afternoon," Sena said.

The agent approached 78-year-old Arthur and said he wanted to ask him questions about his presence at the airport.

"Arthur was physically shaken and turned pale," Sena

later said. "I found him to be evasive in his answers, but physically shaken. He had to sit down, and I gave him a second to catch his breath."

Arthur claimed he was at the airport to pick up a gentleman by the name of Bobby Givings, who he said was "a friend." The story he told Sena was that two weeks earlier, he'd received a call from another friend whose name he couldn't remember in Nashville, asking if he would be willing to allow Givings to stay at his house for a couple of weeks.

No amount of questioning by Sena could shake Arthur's memory as to the name of this so-called friend. He kept insisting that all he could remember about the elusive Tennessean was that he had agreed to let his friend Bobby stay at his home, even though he had never met him.

It was a standoff. Arthur offered to give Sena the keys to his car, which was in the parking lot, and suggested that the agent search it. He even dared Sena to search his home for guns. Both offers were declined by the agent.

Sena told Arthur that Mr. Givings was being detained by Mexican Immigration because he was having some issues.

Sena left Arthur at the airport.

A day later, on October 28, Davidson County District Attorney General Victor Johnson III announced that Arthur and Perry March were being indicted on charges that they had tried to hire Russell Nathaniel Farris, also known as Bobby Givings, to kill Lawrence and Carolyn Levine.

Perry, already in custody for theft and the murder of his wife, was immediately booked on new charges of solicitation to kill. But getting the feisty Arthur March to surrender posed problems. He denied any knowledge of the plot.

13

Father Knows Best

Days after Arthur was indicted and charged with helping Perry kill his wife's parents, he made it known that he had no intention of returning to Nashville to face the charges. He insisted he had been framed by the FBI and prosecutors, who'd entrapped him. Arthur vowed he would not "go peacefully . . . like Perry," and that there would be bloodshed if an attempt was made to arrest him.

Arthur had moved to Ajijic from the United States in 1991 because he realized that the $2,100 a month he received from the army and another $1,300 a month in Social Security benefits meant he could live like a millionaire in the Lakeside community.

Walking around the Ajijic retirement resort town he had called home for the last fourteen years, his menacing pet Doberman, Oni, and a benign-looking cane that housed a razor-sharp two-foot blade at his side, Arthur challenged the police to come get him.

Back in Nashville, authorities were reviewing their options on how to get Arthur extradited, since it was apparent that he wasn't coming voluntarily. Prosecutors had learned that Arthur's visa was to expire on November 7, and that he had re-applied for a renewal. He was concerned that Mexican immigration, alerted to his indictment in the United States, might turn him down.

If the visa renewal was denied, it could not only cost Arthur his freedom, but he would lose his Mexican home and any chance he might have of gaining custody of his grandchildren.

Arthur's Mexican attorney, Edgar Palacios, was handling the visa renewal paperwork, and explained to him that he had obtained an *amparo*—a special Mexican injunction from a judge forbidding extradition—and that before he could be removed from Mexico, he was entitled to an extradition hearing where Tennessee prosecutors could be forced to divulge some of the evidence against him.

In short, Tennessee prosecutors were going to have to provide the Mexican government with enough evidence to justify his apprehension as well as reveal some of the strategies they intended to use at trial.

The lawyer also told Arthur that the audiotapes between Farris and Arthur were inadmissible because under Mexican law it was illegal for the government to wire a criminal to set up a citizen or someone lawfully living in Mexico.

Despite those comforting assurances, on January 5, 2006, President Vicente Fox of Mexico revoked Arthur's visa and personally signed the expulsion order.

According to Arthur, early that Thursday morning, just as it happened when Perry March had been arrested in August, two red vans with dark tinted windows pulled up outside the Media Luna restaurant. Arthur was outside walking his Doberman when six *federales* unceremoniously jumped out, beat him up, and tossed him in the back of one of the vans.

"Arthur fought back. There was a fierce struggle when the immigration authorities grabbed him and beat him up," Fletcher Long, his attorney, said. "I believe he pulled a small knife hidden in his belt. He didn't know who it was that was beating him up. By the time Arthur reached Houston, Texas, after having been placed on an airplane in Guadalajara in the custody of FBI agents, he was in rough condition, and never fully recovered from the whipping they gave him.

"But on the other hand, Arthur kept warning them ahead of time that he was armed and said he would use it and wasn't going to go peacefully, and he didn't."

After spending more than a week in a Houston jail, where Arthur chose not to fight his extradition, Sergeant Pat Postiglione and Detective Bill Pridemore picked him up and escorted him back to Nashville on Friday, January 13, 2006, arriving at 10:30 p.m. for booking. Arthur elected not to be brought before Night Court Commissioner Carolyn Piphus, saying he was sick and was finding it difficult to stand for long periods of time.

Instead, he was moved to a high-security jail cell in the medical section of the special management unit—he was on the fifth floor, one floor below his son.

Because Arthur had to rely on a jail-issued cane to walk, he was kept segregated from other inmates for their own safety, since the cane could be used as a weapon.

At 78, noticeably weak and frail, the five-foot, eight-inch, 159-pound, slightly built March was suffering from myriad health disorders, from a heart condition to high blood pressure, and was taking nearly two dozen pills a day. At his arraignment on January 19, Arthur pleaded not guilty to three felony charges that he'd helped his son plot the murder of Perry's former in-laws.

He was extremely unhappy and confused during the court proceeding when he learned from Fletcher Long that he would have to remain in jail for at least one month until a scheduled bail hearing, set for February 2.

But then on January 23, a forty-five-minute unmonitored meeting took place between Arthur March and his son, after the two inmates asked sheriff's officials if they could see one another. The visit was conducted without the approval of the district attorney's office. Although a guard was nearby, the officer was unable to hear what father and son discussed. They met together at least five other times over the next few days. A short time after the last meeting, the bail hearing was suddenly postponed.

Fletcher Long described his elderly client as charming, likeable, charismatic, honest, and genuine. "He is also a dangerous defendant. Arthur had a legitimate entrapment defense. If you listen to the tapes between Farris and Arthur, there was a lot of arm-twisting in the first two recorded tapes after October fourteenth by Farris talking Arthur into this situation.

"And Arthur was set up, cajoled, arm-twisted and entrapped by the government that would do anything to get Perry."

It was Long's opinion that the government had to decide whether to go to trial against Arthur and possibly lose, or get a hung jury and a mistrial, because if they lost, it would cause greater problems in trying Perry.

Instead, negotiations began on February 2 between Perry's lawyers—Bill Massey and John Herbison—and prosecutors. Massey and Herbison made a proffer—an offer of proof—to find out what Perry would get in exchange for pleading guilty. The talks were held in a conference room at the Central Division police station of the Criminal Justice Center near Pat Postiglione's office.

Massey said the government told him that in exchange for Perry pleading guilty and describing how the murder had occurred, they would let Perry plead to second-degree murder at the state level with a 20-year sentence, and conspiracy to violate the murder-for-hire statute on the federal level with a 20-year sentence, with those sentences to run concurrently, for an effective sentence of 17½ years.

Long felt that Arthur also had an incentive to make a deal. "With good time credit, that would allow Arthur to plead guilty to solicitation to violate the murder-for-hire statute, and under that particular sentencing range he would have a guideline sentence in federal court of zero to sixty months at sentencing," Long said. "I went to Detective Pat Postiglione and asked him if he would agree that if Arthur took a plea deal, would he testify as a witness for him at sentencing that Arthur's conduct was essentially conduct after the fact?

"What that meant was that Arthur would not have been in on the killing, and wasn't in on the planning of the killing of Janet, and that he was only going to render assistance after the killing occurred."

Long explained to Arthur that under federal court guidelines, sentences were determined in months and at this stage of negotiations he was looking at a prison term of anywhere from 32 to 48 months behind bars. And this was only if both he and Perry pleaded guilty. "Arthur wouldn't agree to it even though he was told that Perry was ready to accept the offer," Long said.

"Arthur wouldn't budge. He was the hold-out. Massey told me that I had to talk some sense into my client, because he was really holding up the train."

When the lawyers resumed negotiations the next day, it was suggested that perhaps if Arthur heard directly from Massey that his son was actually going to take the plea, it would convince the elder March to agree to go along with the offer.

"We knew that Arthur could be pretty hard-headed. Throughout that second day, Perry and Arthur kept telling us to go out of the room and leave them alone to talk. Finally, with Herbison and Perry in the next room, I had Arthur to myself in the room with Massey telling him that Perry was going to take the deal."

Long, who by now was exasperated at Arthur's reluctance in accepting the plea offer, laid it out for his client. "I told him that the bus was leaving the station. 'Your son is going to admit to everything and he is going to take his twenty-year sentence. Now you can get on board or you can go down alone. But if you elect to go down, you are going down alone with your son testifying against you.'"

Massey assured Arthur that Perry was accepting the plea deal and he anticipated that under those arrangements, Arthur could be looking at a prison term of 36 months.

Arthur had been worn down. "All right, I'll take the thirty-six months if it will save Perry, because Perry really needs help," he wearily said.

Just then, Perry unexpectedly burst into the room with Herbison behind him. "Dad, you don't roll on me. I don't roll on you. We will wear these jumpsuits as a badge of honor, a badge of honor. If I'm going to get twenty years . . . Fuck 'em. I'm going down swinging," Perry snapped.

Perry didn't fully appreciate what his exposure to criminal liability was, even though his lawyers had explained it to him. "After listening to those tapes, I knew that Perry had cooked his own goose, but he enjoyed the celebrity of it. He got caught up in the drama, and being in the middle of the biggest murder case in the history of Nashville," Long said.

Larry Brinton of TV's WSMV said Perry was so confident that he would never be charged with Janet's murder that even after two days of intense, almost round-the-clock negotiations, he refused to accept any offer. "He surely didn't think he was going to win. When he fled to Ajijic in 1999 he had a chance to stay out of the public eye and give the public and police a chance to hopefully forget about him. But he was so self-centered and big-headed that he continually kept going on the air with my viewers, reminding them of who he was and arguing about his innocence," Brinton says.

Back in 1997, prosecutors had also offered Perry a plea deal. All he would have had to do was plead guilty and accept a voluntary manslaughter charge, in which he would have faced up to 6 years in prison. But Perry had turned it down. "Fuck them. I didn't do anything," he said at the time.

No one will ever know for sure what changed Perry's mind about not accepting the latest plea offer. But Perry had a wild look in his eyes and started barking orders to Massey and Long.

"Bill, you and Fletcher go out there and tell the government I get fifteen years, Dad gets a year, or we go to trial. "If they're going to give me twenty years, they're going to have to work to do it. And Fletcher, you tell my damn brother and sister that they are not allowed to talk to Dad."

Months ago, Long had represented all of the March family in their civil personal property case with the Levines involving money damages. But he no longer represented them once he was retained to defend Arthur in the murder-for-hire plot.

Long believed that Perry's outburst was the result of pressure that Ron and Kathy had put on their father to plead guilty and give Perry up. He suspected they had received letters from the federal government saying they were now targets of an investigation and should retain lawyers.

"I told Perry that I couldn't tell Arthur whom to have on his visitors' list. If Arthur doesn't want to see Ron and Kathy, he can tell his jailers himself, but I'm not going to make that decision for him," Long said.

When the lawyers left that day, they all felt as if they had "been played by our clients," recalled Long. "Actually, it was Perry." Long was convinced that Perry had used the plea deal situation to get his father to keep quiet. "We had earlier become concerned with what Perry was really telling his dad every time we were asked to leave the room, as opposed to what we believed he was telling him.

"I knew right then and there that the government was mad enough at Perry, and that the iron was hot, and if Arthur was going to make a deal, I had to strike immediately."

As Massey was getting in his car to return to Memphis, Long let him know that he would accept a deal for Arthur of between 1 and 2 years if he could talk his client into it.

The 38-year-old Long, who admits he likes the sound of his own voice and enjoys "the theater of the courtroom," had heard all of the audiotapes before negotiations had begun. "It's hard to tell a jury to ignore what's on those recorded conversations between Farris and Perry, and between Arthur and Farris about killing the Levines," Long said.

His nickname among his Nashville colleagues is "the Preacher," and according to Long, "That's because, when I argue a case before a jury, I sound like I'm orating at a tent revival. And as impassioned as I am, and as well-spoken and charismatic as I may be, I wasn't going to beat those tapes, which were damning to Arthur's defense. By the time the judge tapped the gavel and sent the jury out to deliberate, I knew those tapes were going to be Mount Everest."

By the time Long reached the jail on the third day of negotiations, Arthur was meeting with his son Ron and his daughter Kathy's husband, Lee Breitowich, who had flown in from Chicago. "They were trying to get Arthur to give up Perry, and were keenly interested in having him make a proffer—and plead guilty. Arthur told me go to the government and 'get me something within a year or two and I'll take it.'

" 'I need to know what you plan to give, Arthur,' " Long told him. " 'If I am going to persuade them to give you a year or two, they're going to want to know the whole story, and I need to tease them and lay it out for them.' "

Long went to U.S. Attorney Paul O'Brien that same day with the story Arthur had proceeded to tell him: On August 15, 1996, Perry had called him in Mexico and told him that he and Janet had had a fight, she'd left him, and he needed help with the kids. "Dad, could you come up here?" he'd asked.

It took Arthur three or four days to make the trip from Mexico, arriving at Perry's Forest Hills home around August 20.

Arthur sensed that his son was in trouble.

"What did you do, Perry?" he asked soon after getting to his home.

"Come on, Dad. You know what I did," came Perry's terse response. "Look, Dad, Janet and I had a fight. She came at me with a knife, but missed. I picked up a wrench that was being used by the construction people and hit her in the back of the head. She fell down the steps and she died. I got rid of the body."

"This was the convincer, 'cause when he told me that, it was the first time I knew from him that she was dead. He never mentioned that he killed her," Arthur explained to his lawyer. "He used the term 'accident' " to explain the circumstances of Janet's death. "Perry just told me that Janet had had an accident and that she was dead."

At that time, Perry had neglected mentioning to his father that during the argument, the children were upstairs asleep. He also never mentioned placing Janet's body in a black trash bag, putting her in his car, and driving to a nearby construction site, where he buried her on a hill, and returning before his kids got up.

All Perry had told his father that night was, "I need your help to make sure that there's no blood around. Go get Clorox, because I'm afraid there might still be some bloodstains around the house. Let me show you where there used to be blood in the driveway and where there used to be blood in the kitchen headed out to the driveway."

And with that, Arthur told his lawyer, despite his father's crippling arthritis, Perry had stood watching him as he got down on his hands and knees, and scrubbed and cleaned up the area, including the gravel in the driveway, even though he didn't actually see any blood.

Perry's next assignment for his father came a couple of weeks later when Perry asked him to get rid of two items from his computer hard drive. "Perry gave them to me," Arthur innocently recalled. He explained to his lawyer that he didn't know the name of one of the items from the computer. Perry handed it to him and he placed it into a disposable garbage box and put it in a Dumpster parked in a strip mall in front of a drugstore. "The other was the hard drive. I disposed of it by throwing it in a wooded area near the house," he said.

It was the hard drive that police had been searching for at his home in mid-September that initially made authorities suspect Perry of the murder. While Perry had quickly denied having anything to do with its disappearance, he'd readily suggested to police that his father may have removed it. Arthur had been unable to defend himself, because at that time, he had taken a quick trip with his two grandchildren to Wilmette, Illinois, to stay with Ron and Amy.

After the police left, Perry took off to Illinois in the Volvo to join his children and the rest of the March family for the Yom Kippur observance.

Arthur said that it was on the way back to the Blackberry Road residence after the holiday that Perry stopped the car off of Interstate 65 at a hardware store, where a shovel and another bottle of Clorox were purchased. It wasn't until they were safely inside Perry's home that night that he again sought his father's assistance.

Arthur sat in the kitchen stunned, listening to Perry talk about what had happened to Janet.

"What did you do with the body?" Arthur wanted to know.

It was then that Perry nervously came clean.

"I placed the body on a property not five minutes from the house that belongs to Sharon Bell, one of my clients," he blurted out.

"You fool. Why did you pick a place to stash a body so close to you, that can immediately be traced right back to you?" Arthur asked.

"We're going to have to move her, Dad, because they are going to start construction soon."

Perry told Arthur exactly where the body was located. He told him how many paces it was from the tip of the road to the construction site. They drove there and Perry let Arthur out of the car. Holding a flashlight, he walked up the hill the exact number of paces.

"He told me it was up this little road, and I was to go ten to fifteen yards and turn left and go in. He said I should look on the ground and I would see where the body was," Arthur said.

While Perry safely stayed in his car and drove in circles around the area, Arthur went to find the body. He had no problem. "It was in this black plastic bag. We call it a leaf bag up North. It looked like there was some digging around . . . what proved to be the grave. It had dirt on top. I pushed a little bit of the dirt off the top with my hands, and then closed up the bag and pulled it down the hill. It was a slight hill where she had been placed. I took it to the other side of the road that we came in on and waited for Perry to come with his car.

"Perry finally stopped in front of me and took the bag and pulled it back. He opened the trunk to the car and grabbed one end. I grabbed the other, and we lifted the body and put it in back of the Volvo."

Fletcher Long imagines that if the cops had pulled up and said "Freeze!" while Arthur was pulling the bag, Perry would have jumped out of the car and said, "Daddy, what did you do? What did you do to my wife? You killed Janet."

"Perry was real brave, sending his elderly father up to get the body instead of letting Arthur drive around in the car. Perry wanted to make darn sure that if the cops showed up, he wasn't going to take the rap. It was going to be good ole dad. He would have put it all off on his father and driven off," Long said.

Arthur didn't actually look inside the trash bag, but "saw some bones. I didn't really want to know what was going on. It wasn't heavy. It was under a hundred pounds." He was able to handle it. "I had pulled it down a slope. After closing the trunk, we got into the car and went down the highway. Perry was driving and we drove north towards Chicago."

When they got past the Kentucky line, they stopped and found a motel. In relating the details ten years later, Arthur's memory on some key points wasn't good. While he could recall the big picture when it came to finding and re-burying the body, he had difficulty remembering the name of the motel that he and Perry checked into that night around midnight.

"The motel," Arthur recalled, was "a small family-run operation. It had the name something blue in it. I remember paying cash for the room, which was registered under an assumed name. It sure as hell wasn't Smith," he told Sergeant Postiglione.

"Perry, you go in there and go to bed. I'll take care of this," he told his son, who handed him the car keys.

It was after midnight when Arthur got into the car, went back out on Interstate Highway 65, headed north again, and started to the other side of Bowling Green, past the Corvette Museum.

Long said that from what he'd learned of the family dynamics, Perry was always the "I can't do anything right" guy. Perry wasn't as tough as his dad, as savvy as his dad, as street-smart as his dad. Perry would go and screw things up, and Arthur would have to come around behind him and fix it."

Arthur went looking for a stream or creek to dump the gruesome cargo but when he found one, he could see that it wasn't very deep. He got back in the car and went farther north until he found another creek, but it too was shallow and there wasn't enough water to deposit a body.

Dawn was breaking when Arthur pulled over to the side of the road and saw this "heap of brush" that was at least twenty yards long and ten to fifteen feet wide. Arthur had at one time been a farmer and knew the reason for the accumulation. It was obvious that a farmer was clearing his land for future planting and had amassed a huge pile of tree limbs and leaves.

"The farmer was going to burn it and clear his land," Arthur said.

"As far as Arthur March was concerned, Janet was going to be cremated, which to him was an acceptable burial method in Judaism, and that's how he sold it to himself," Long told the government.

"I went and I cleared away three holes in the brush pile. In the first one, I pulled out some of her clothes that were in there on the top. That's when I saw the bones. I knew it was a body. In the next hole, I shook it out and put Janet in. I flipped out the body from the leaf bag and could hear the bones shake out. Then I put the empty plastic leaf bag into the third hole. I closed up all the holes and was starting to leave when I saw a school bus at the crossroads. I got into my car and went back to the motel where Perry was."

Arthur explained that he hadn't put the remains all in one hole because sometimes plastic does not fully burn. "And he didn't want to leave any potential evidence," his lawyer said.

The next morning, Arthur told his son that he had put Janet "in a creek with some water, and nobody was going to get to it . . . that it was under water. I didn't want to go through the whole thing with him, and he never knew until now where I put the body."

"Yes, Arthur lied to his son and never told him anything differently," Long said. "That is why, when Perry told inmates like Cornelius King and others at the jail that Janet had been buried in water—he thought it was the truth.

"Arthur never trusted Perry, and knew he had a big mouth."

After hearing what Arthur had told his lawyer, U.S. Attorney Paul O'Brien contacted Fletcher Long, saying the government was willing to give Arthur an 18-months sentence to be served in a federal medical facility and 3 years' probation if he would plead guilty and testify in the two criminal cases against Perry.

It was a done deal, Long said. "My client looked better than he had looked previously in appearances because I think he was relieved of a great deal of anxiety and stress, knowing what the ultimate outcome will be."

So why did Arthur give up his son to the government? Long said it was to protect Ron and Kathy, and because he really believed that Perry needed help. "By 'help,' I mean that Arthur felt that by his taking the plea deal, he thought it would force Perry to take the twenty-year sentence they were offering for killing Janet.

"While it's true that Perry told him to take the deal, Arthur did it because he loved his children. His giving up Perry was not treachery . . . it was protection. He pleaded guilty because he loved his son. He had some tough decisions to make and he made them."

As soon as a plea agreement had been reached, it cleared the way for Arthur to go before U.S. District Judge Todd Campbell, where O'Brien read the dramatic plea bargain aloud to the judge and Arthur pleaded guilty to conspiracy to murder and aiding and abetting his son.

"The use of a jailhouse snitch is a time-dishonored way of shoring up a shaky case. Arthur March has done what he needs to do in order to receive a shorter sentence," Herbison said. "He purchased liberty on the layaway plan. He's giving a little bit of information now. We'll give other information in the form of testimony later. [Perry] is very saddened by his father's decision. Perry is still Arthur's son, and Arthur is still Perry's father. They still love each other, but have differing accounts of what happened."

Until Arthur changed his story, Perry had had the advantage, in that the state's case against him was circumstantial and, according to his own lawyers and a number of local defense attorneys, rather weak.

A few days after the plea deal, Metro police detectives Postiglione and Pridemore checked Arthur out of jail and, with Assistant District Attorney Tom Thurman, traveled about 55 miles north of Nashville past Bowling Green, Kentucky, to have Arthur show them where he and Perry had gone in 1996 to dispose of Perry's wife's body.

But after ten years, finding the precise location proved difficult for Arthur. One problem was that the highway lanes had been widened and the topography in the area had changed, making it virtually impossible to find the exact spot where the brush pile had been.

The one place that came closest, investigators believe, is now Kenny Perry's Country Creek Golf Course in Franklin, Kentucky.

Ronnie Webb, the golf course contractor who'd cleared the land for the course said that at one time there was such a road as Arthur had described. He also said that in 1996, there were brush piles near an old road and a nearby creek, and that the creek wasn't deep enough to put a body in.

Concern that Arthur might not be able to testify due to his ongoing health problems prompted prosecutors to schedule two days of videotape depositions from him on April 10, 2006.

During the 150-page deposition, Arthur came across as a devoted father who was ready to do almost anything for his son. And when Bill Massey began his cross-examination, he asked if Arthur had ever felt that he and his family were being persecuted.

"By the Levines. Yes,' he replied.

"What about the police? Did you feel that the police were acting on behalf of the Levines?" Massey asked

"They were just doing what the Levines wanted them to do, 'cause, as you know, Carolyn Levine is the queen of the Jewish Mafia. And she could do whatever she wanted. She's the queen of the Jewish Mafia in Tennessee and Nashville."

When Massey pressed him to explain the 'Jewish Mafia' remark, Arthur's reply was cutting. "What's to understand? If you don't understand it, I can't explain it to you. You know what 'mafia' is, what the word means? And, you know what 'Jewish' means? And you don't understand those two words together?"

Arthur was of Jewish descent and observed most of the religious holidays, so it was a surprise when he lashed out about the Levines and his perception of Carolyn. In his deposition, Arthur also claimed credit for wanting to physically hurt the Levines.

"The easy way to get [the Levines] was to take out the queen and no balls at all, her husband. You said you didn't know what 'Jewish Mafia' was, well, Carolyn was the queen. She had computers of every Jew and everybody sympathetic to Jewish things in Tennessee, in Nashville. And I'm told in other countries. I mean, other parts of the United States.

"The reason she had so much power was, she was the lady that distributed the money. You have a hole in your judicial system, I'm sorry to say. The hole in your judicial system is that the judges at the lower level have to run for election. To get money to run for an election, they need money. They can't run for the office without getting money. And the Jewish Mafia was a big contributor, and the one who doled out the money was Carolyn. And that's where she got her power, and that's what Larry was building his on."

Arthur divulged that he didn't like the Levines. "They were liars. They were political animals who used her position with the Jewish Mafia and his position with the Democratic Party to get what they wanted when they needed it.

Otherwise, how did you control two judges who had no business even being in this case?"

As for Janet March, Arthur called her 'the Jewish American Princess.' "They sent her up to [the University of] Michigan to get married to a nice Jewish boy, just like [Carolyn] did when she went up to get and meet Larry Levine."

In Fletcher Long's estimation, the only plan of the Levines since the war between the two families had begun ten years earlier had been to "impoverish the Marches," to where they could no longer afford Perry's defense. "It's classic warfare. All of this suing of the Marches for money and making them incur legal expense fees is because they are funding Perry's defense.

"It's been a brilliant strategy on the part of the Levines. And Perry, being cocky and arrogant, comes across in these proceedings as unlikable. Perry's decision to go to trial was the ultimate act of selfishness and narcissism, because he was saying, 'I don't care about anybody but me.'"

Arthur's lawyer contended that by turning down all offers to take a plea deal, Perry had angered his elderly father, because it was Perry who'd gotten him into this legal jam in the first place. For fourteen years, Arthur had lived in retirement in Mexico without incident, without a criminal history, minding his own business. But Perry destroyed that by involving his father in digging up Janet's body, re-burying the corpse in Kentucky, and then foolishly undertaking a conspiracy to kill the Levines.

"What is so inexcusable is that Perry, in changing his mind and rejecting the prosecutor's offer, and refusing to plead guilty, was now forcing his father to testify against him," Long said. "It was something Arthur never wanted to do."

14

The Theft Trial

On August 17, 2005, the day Perry March appeared in a Nashville courtroom for his arraignment to plead not guilty to the murder of his wife, prosecutors handed him a surprising document.

It was a two-page indictment that had been presented to the grand jury in Davidson County (Nashville) six years earlier, on June 4, 1999. Reading the document, Perry learned he was accused of collecting fees of $10,000 to $60,000 from the firm of Levine, Mattson, Orr & Geracioti, the law firm owned by his former father-in-law, between May 1996 and August 1998.

Specifically, it was alleged that when Perry left the Levine firm, he'd taken three clients with him, and that the money owed to the law firm was actually paid to Perry.

Perry claimed to know nothing about the theft charge. "Who has billing records from nine years ago?" argued his lawyer, Ed Fowlkes, a long-time friend of John Herbison who had been brought in to represent Perry in the theft case while Massey and Herbison had their work cut out for them in the conspiracy and murder cases. "It's not his fault, nobody's fault."

If convicted of theft, Perry faced up to 6 years in prison—and that would be on top of any sentence he might receive should he be convicted in the murder trial.

Fowlkes was convinced that, were it not for the fact that the identity of the defendant in the theft case was named Perry March, the case would have found its way into a civil court, not a criminal court. And he had doubts about Perry receiving a fair trial in Nashville, given the amount of publicity the case had generated since Janet March disappeared almost ten years ago.

Perry's attorney filed a motion accusing the district attorney's office of trying to gain a tactical advantage by waiting until his client had moved to Mexico before seeking an indictment on the theft charges. He took the legal position that Perry was denied the opportunity to gather evidence in his defense as a result.

Not only did Perry want the indictment against him dismissed, but he accused prosecutors of denying him the right to a speedy trial.

A hearing on the motion was held three months later, on November 16, 2005, at which time Judge Dozier heard testimony from two witnesses.

Michaela Mathews, an assistant DA with Davidson County, testified that the theft case had been investigated by the fraud division in her office because it was a theft from an employer.

The decision to seek an indictment was made in May 1999 because of the time that it had taken to investigate the case and to wait until all depositions in the unrelated probate matter had been concluded to determine if there was enough evidence to indict.

She explained that the initial referral had been made to the district attorney's office in 1997. The civil case depositions had not been concluded until November 1998. But then she'd received additional information about the case in March 1999, and shortly after that, the case had been presented to the grand jury, which returned the indictment in June 1999. By then Perry no longer was living in Illinois, but had moved to Mexico.

No attempt had been made to seek an international extradition, since it is very expensive, and would have been unusual in a theft case, Mathews said. And the fugitive squad was not told to serve the indictment until they'd learned he was back in the United States.

The second witness to testify was Collier Miller, a detective with the fugitive division of the Metropolitan Nashville Police Department. He testified that after getting a copy of the indictment on June 21, 2000, he'd entered Perry's name in the NCIC—the National Crime Information Center computerized database available to Federal, state, and local law enforcement to provide information about criminals—to determine whether there were any outstanding warrants in Perry's name throughout the United States.

Since Perry had no prior criminal history, he came up clean. The arrest warrant and the indictment were placed in a safe at the fugitive squad and held there until after his arrest on August 4, 2005, when he was back in the United States. It was only at Perry's arraignment that the indictment could finally be served.

During the hearing, it came out that Perry had been aware of the accusation of theft in 1998, while the civil case was ongoing. The judge noted in his decision of December 6, 2005, however, that Perry's moving out of the country "caused the delay . . . and that the state can not be faulted by the defendant's voluntary withdrawal from the country and thus making more difficult the service of the indictment."

He continued, "There has been no proof of an intentional delay by the state to gain a tactical advantage or harass the defendant. As soon as he was back in the United States, he was served with a warrant . . . The court finds that the defendant's Sixth Amendment right to a speedy trial has not been violated . . . [and] therefore the defendant's motions to dismiss the indictment are denied."

Before slamming the door on Perry, Criminal Court Judge Dozier also refused to lower the $250,000 bond he was being held on in the theft case, in addition to the $3,000,000 the judge had ordered him held on for the murder charge.

The trial date on the theft charges was set for April 17, 2006, with the conspiracy murder-for-hire case to start June 5 and the second-degree murder charges in the disappearance of his wife to begin on August 7.

The three lawyers, Herbison, Massey, and Fowlkes, got to work bombarding Dozier's court with a plethora of motions on what would be allowed into evidence, and a variety of other issues. There was no shortage of motions exchanging hands between defense lawyers and prosecutors, with Tom Thurman also filing his share of motions in February and March 2006.

Massey and Herbison wanted all of the recorded conversations between Perry and Russell Nathaniel Farris, as well as any other person in custody, dismissed. They also wanted to strike all statements Perry had made to Pat Postiglione and Bill Pridemore, from the time they'd picked him up in Los Angeles to when they'd turned him over to the sheriff's office in Nashville. The defense also claimed that the police had failed to give Perry his Miranda warning. They pointed out that his lawyers had not been present to provide legal counsel during the trip from California to the Nashville jail.

The defense also sought to have dismissed the three-count murder indictment, arguing that too much time had elapsed from August 29, 1996, when Janet was reported missing, to the filing of the indictment on December 8, 2004, eight years and three months later. In their six-page motion documents, the defense argued that prosecutors had "manipulated the timing" and as a result, Perry "has been prejudiced in his ability to defend" himself.

Prosecutors struck back. They advised the defense that at trial they intended to let the jury know about fifteen of Perry's misdeeds, including embezzlement of law firm funds, filing frivolous lawsuits, failing to advise clients that he was under suspension, being held in contempt of court, lying to Mexican officials about where he lived, forging documents, lying to an attorney about sending letters to a paralegal, lying to members of his former father-in-law's law firm as to why he'd left Bass, Berry & Sims, forging court documents, representing himself to be a licensed Mexican lawyer, using false information about his parents on a Mexican marriage certificate, misappropriating money from the Belize bank account of client Robert Duncan, defrauding client Gayle Boozer Cancienne out of proceeds from the sale of real estate and attempting to sell the property, forging a rental receipt to his landlord in Mexico, misappropriating more than $100,000 in 2003 from the sale of real estate belonging to Ted Axton in Mexico, and defrauding Helen Speak out of four thousand dollars.

The purpose of introducing this evidence was to show jurors that Perry was inclined to be dishonest.

Another motion filed by District Attorney Tom Thurman asked to take the deposition of Arthur Wayne March, who was "elderly and in poor health." But before the judge would rule on the motion, Fletcher Long was required to submit a two-page affidavit detailing his client's medications and his ailments, which included a bleeding heart valve, high cholesterol, rotator cuff problems in the right shoulder, a ruptured disc, osteomyelitis in his right ankle, and the effects of a hip replacement.

The lawyers also filed a series of motions seeking a reduction of the $250,000 bail that had been set in the theft case and, more important, they wanted Perry's indictment tossed out because of the six-year delay between his June 4, 1999, indictment and his August 12, 2005, arrest. The defense claimed in its motion that the state was manipulating the timing of the prosecution and was prejudicial to Perry.

Fowlkes also sought in still another motion that a subpoena be issued requiring Larry Levine and Michael Geracioti, one of the partners in the law firm, to produce all records of all accounts billed by Perry from 1994 to the present.

In demanding these documents, Fowlkes and his cocounsel, Michael Flanagan, wrote that

Arguably, the office of the District Attorney General became the Alter Ego of the Levine Law Office and as

*such the Levine Office became an Agent of the State. It
is patently unfair for the office of the District Attorney
General to prosecute on information provided by
Levine, Mattson, Orr and Geracioti and claim that the
remaining information is not in their possession.*

In the process of filing these motions, Fowlkes learned
that Perry's former law firm was actually holding on to
money belonging to him.

By late February, Perry's lawyers, in preparation for the
June 5 trial, indicated to prosecutors that they planned to use
an entrapment defense at his conspiracy and solicitation
murder-for-hire trial. "For an entrapment defense to work in
Perry's favor, he would have to take the stand and testify that
he was an unwilling person and had no desire to hire a hit
man to kill the Levines, but that he gave in to pressure by
Farris, a government informant who induced him to commit
the crime. The key phrase in entrapment is that he was an
'unwilling person,'" Herbison said.

All of the pre-trial motions seemed to be moving ahead
when a dispute suddenly broke out between Thurman and
the defense over the scheduling of the theft case, resulting
in still another motion. The defense asked that the judge re-
arrange the schedule, saying they wanted the murder case to
go first. Herbison argued that he was concerned jurors hearing the most serious charge against Perry would be exposed
to publicity generated from the theft and murder-for-hire trials. "It follows logically that the case in which Mr. March is
potentially subjected to the most severe penalty should be
tried first," Herbison wrote.

The defense was also equally aware that the tape recordings of Perry talking to Farris were very damaging, and if
the murder-for-hire trial resulted in a conspiracy conviction,
prosecutors would use that conviction to impeach him at the
murder trial.

It was the district attorney's strategy to maintain the April
17 date for the theft trial. If Perry were convicted, prosecutors
could use that to impeach his credibility in the other two cases.

In the end, with witnesses already subpoenaed for the theft case, Dozier decided that the original trial dates would remain as is, with June 5 scheduled for the conspiracy trial and August 7 for the murder trial.

As hearings for the theft trial got underway that April, Fowlkes learned rather quickly that representing Perry could be a handful. Although he found Perry to be cordial and pleasant, Perry had a proclivity to interrupt him as he was trying to go over the case with him. He would distract Fowlkes, disrupting his train of thought by handing him notes as he was listening to a witness respond to a question.

Exasperated, Fowlkes finally turned to his client. "Perry, have you ever tried a jury case?" he whispered.

"No," Perry replied.

"Then stay the hell out of this. You are killing us."

"Perry was out in the wilderness when it came to trials," Fowlkes later said. "He has never lived off the land, and I would not want to be stuck in the woods with him with only a piece of fishing line, a safety pin, and a pocket knife.

"My motorcycle mechanic, Panhead Phil, has a sign at his shop. It says, 'Labor: $50 an hour. $125 an hour if you watch. $225 an hour if you help. $500 an hour if you've worked on it before.' Perry March did all of the above."

Whatever Perry's reasoning, it was maddening for Fowlkes. And it only delayed the defense side of the theft case to the jury.

Fowlkes eventually maintained that it was Perry's understanding when he'd left the law firm that for the clients he took with him, he could also take the accounts receivable.

As it turned out, the money in dispute involved three checks in the amount of $23,000 that had come from two clients of the firm.

Perry said he'd taken the two clients with him, but never sent the firm any money because, he claimed, he was owed $80,000 in billings.

The lawyer argued that the $3,500 escrow account supported their point that there was a dispute over billing. "If anything, it's a civil case and a dispute over money," Fowlkes said. "He didn't steal a thing. Absolutely not."

The defense won two small victories when Dozier ruled that the jury could learn about the existence of the escrow account and that the case could have been heard in civil court.

For weeks, because of the immense publicity surrounding the cases, Judge Dozier had warned the lawyers about making inflammatory statements to the press. "I don't want to issue a gag order," Dozier said more than once.

At one hearing, Herbison was reprimanded after he was quoted in the media for calling a potential witness "an arrogant egomaniac."

"Your Honor, I stand behind what I said," Herbison declared to the judge. "I have made some remarks about the dog-and-pony show whereby my client was brought in an unshaven condition in clothes that he hadn't been permitted to have laundered for several days for a wholly unnecessary proceeding before the night court commissioner over my specific objections to the deputy chief of police. Yes, I stand behind that," Herbison said.

"Actually the witness I was referring to was Chief of Police Ronal Serpas. What I said was, 'As one fat white egomaniac to another, Bear Bryant, the former University of Alabama coach used to say, "When you get to the end zone, act like you've been there before." ' "

On April 12, a week before the theft trial was to begin, Dozier issued a gag order, citing leaks such as WTVF–Channel 5 airing "details" of Arthur March's deposition.

With all of the housekeeping chores out of the way, it was almost time to pick a jury. But before selection could get underway, Dozier delayed his decision on whether Thurman could ask Perry about his prior "bad acts." He eventually ruled that jurors could learn about some but not all of the acts Perry was alleged to have committed to show a pattern of behavior. That ruling ultimately factored into Perry's decision on whether to testify.

It took lawyers five hours to select a panel of seven

women and five men, along with two attorneys to hear the theft case. Given all the publicity that had been generated in the case over nearly ten years, Dozier admonished the jury panel not to read newspapers or watch television news, and not to discuss the case among themselves until they were to deliberate. He also ordered that the panel be sequestered until they were ready to render a verdict.

During the voir dire process, prospects were asked what they'd heard about the case and whether they would be able to put aside any biases and base their verdict on the evidence heard in the courtroom. They were also quizzed about any preconceived prejudices they might harbor toward Perry.

"Is there any reason why you can't set aside your bias or personal feelings and decide the case on what you hear in the courtroom?" Dozier asked potential panelists. "Don't put yourself in a position that will get you in trouble with me," he said.

About twenty prospects were excused for various reasons. One man was dismissed who admitted that he couldn't be fair, and another claimed to have a "strong opinion" about the case, but many got off serving just for hardship reasons.

More than twenty witnesses were scheduled to testify by state prosecutors, including Larry Levine and his wife Carolyn. The defense indicated that they would be calling Janet's brother, Mark Levine, as well.

During her opening remarks, Deputy District Attorney Amy Eisenbeck said that in 1996, Perry had needed money to start his own practice. At the same time, Perry and Janet were having serious marital problems, and it was doubtful that his in-laws, the Levines, were going to offer him any financial assistance.

"He had to look somewhere else for the money, and that's where the theft came in," Eisenbeck said.

It was then, the prosecutor said, that Perry instructed two clients—Paul Eichel and Elliot Greenberg—to pay him directly, rather than Levine's law firm, where the funds should have rightfully been sent. She argued that he'd stolen the accounts receivable to fund his new law practice.

Eichel, a nightclub owner, had given Perry a $3,000 check because he was asked to by Perry himself. Greenberg, one of Perry's best friends had paid him two checks totaling $20,000, also at Perry's request.

The defense, in its opening argument, played down the funds that Perry had pocketed, saying that he'd truly believed the law firm owed him the money when he left in September 1996. "This case is about money—legal fees, earned legal fees. It's a dispute among lawyers," Mike Flanagan, Perry's defense co-counsel, said, minimizing the problem.

Michael Geracioti, a partner at Levine, Mattson, Orr & Geracioti, testified that Perry had begun working for the law firm in the fall of 1991. He was unaware of the circumstances that had led Perry to leave Bass, Berry & Sims fifteen years earlier.

Geracioti also said that although Perry had become eligible to become a partner in 1996, the same year Janet disappeared, he couldn't come to financial terms with the partners. When Perry had unexpectedly taken off that September, Geracioti said he'd left the firm in "a lurch" with a backlog of several cases that needed work.

Greenberg testified that the Levine law firm had later sued him for the money he'd paid Perry. It was then, he said, that he realized Perry had merely been looking out for his own interests. "I tried to contact Perry, but he ignored me," Greenberg said. "I don't like Perry, but I'm not biased. What's fair to say is, I'm no longer friends with Perry."

In more than two hours of testimony on the witness stand, Larry Levine explained to jurors not only his relationship with Perry at the firm, but his feelings about him as a son-in-law. He spoke about helping Perry pay his way through law school, and that he and his wife had given him and Janet money more than once, including money to build Janet's dream house. He had even assisted Perry's father when his house went into foreclosure.

"I helped both him and members of his family," Levine testified. "There is a provision in the United States Internal Revenue Code that says you can go ahead and give a gift of ten thousand dollars per year, por beneficiary, Carolyn would give Perry ten thousand dollars a year, and Janet ten thousand dollars a year, and Mark [Janet's brother] ten thousand dollars a year," he explained.

Janet's father described for jurors the marital problems his daughter had been having with Perry, and that the couple would argue and come to his wife, Carolyn, as a mediator.

Levine told of how, around the same time that Janet disappeared, Perry had come knocking at his door seeking money to start his own law firm. "Within a week before Janet was gone, Perry said he wanted to go ahead and start his own law practice, and he wanted to come and discuss money with Carolyn and I. And I said, 'When do you and Janet want to come?' And he said no, he didn't want to come with Janet. And I said, 'Well every major decision I've ever made in the forty'—well, then it was thirty—'years that I've been married, about money, has been made with Carolyn."

Perry insisted and met with the Levines anyway. Perry gave them a list of start-up expenses that totaled $30,000, but never asked them for the money. Instead, he said he would take the money out of his pension plan.

It was Levine's suspicion that Perry really wanted to borrow the money from them, but was reluctant to ask.

"But at that point, Janet and Perry were fighting pretty good, so I said to Perry, 'Where are you going to get the money?'"

"Based on everything you knew that was going on in the defendant's marriage at the time, were you likely to give him the money?" lead prosecutor Eisenbeck asked.

"No," he replied.

Carolyn Levine was even more emphatic on the subject. "At the time, I knew that he and my daughter were having marital problems, and I was concerned about that, and I said, 'Perry, I think you've got the cart before the horse. I think you need to focus on your marriage before your career.'"

Larry stressed to jurors that Janet had decided to divorce Perry. She had asked her parents for a list of divorce attorneys and told them she could no longer live with Perry.

Levine testified that an appointment had been made for Janet to meet with a lawyer, but that she'd disappeared first.

While Levine was on the witness stand, a portion of Perry's November 20, 1996, videotaped deposition was played for jurors to prove that he had lied when he swore that he never took money from clients intended for the firm. Perry had said that his father-in-law had said he was "fine" with Perry taking $250,000 in accounts receivable when he left the firm.

"Absolutely false," Levine responded.

One of Perry's former associates, Peter Rosen, was also called to the stand and testified that he remembered Perry "telling me his wife really didn't want him leaving the firm." Rosen recalled that when he'd declined Perry's plan to join him in his new law venture on August 16, 1996, the day after Janet disappeared, Perry had told him he "didn't feel well and was going home."

Perry did not take the stand during the theft trial. After a day-and-a-half of testimony, and with jurors hearing a dozen witnesses, prosecutors argued in closing remarks that they should focus on attorney fees and how lawyers bill clients.

Defense attorney Fowlkes argued that the case should have been in civil court. "It's a bunch of sharks feeding on their own young; that's all it is. You've got lawyers suing lawyers, lawyers suing clients, and everybody scrambling around for a dollar. It's a civil case."

Forty-five minutes after the jury began deliberating, they were back in the courtroom. The foreman announced the verdict that Perry was guilty of stealing $23,000 from his former law firm.

It would be only the first strike called on Perry.

Jurors later said that Perry's 1996 probate deposition was the most damaging evidence against him.

"We're very pleased with the verdict," prosecutor Eisenbeck later said. "We think the jury did the only thing they could do, given the facts and the law in this case."

"There wasn't a person that Mr. March didn't deal with that he didn't betray, from clients, to friends, to partners, to in-laws. Everyone he came in contact with, he betrayed," prosecutor Ben Winters added.

Fowlkes on the other hand couldn't understand why all twelve jurors found his client guilty. "The Levines weren't deprived of a dime. They aren't out a dime. They haven't lost anything. They are the same way they were ten years later as they were ten years before."

The lawyer added that prosecutors would now use the conviction in the two later trials "which is obviously what this is all about. Surely you don't spend this kind of time and money on a theft case unless there's some other reason for it."

After Perry was found guilty in his first trial, Perry and his lawyers turned their attention to the next one, the murder-for-hire scheme to kill his former in-laws. Because his co-defendant father, Arthur March, had cut himself a deal with prosecutors, the defense filed a motion to sever his case from that of his son.

Perry had months earlier thumbed his nose at any plea offers that were made by the government, despite the recommendations of his lawyers. While rumors circulated that a proposed deal was again on the table, nothing ever came of it, and jury selection in the murder-for-hire case began on June 1.

15

The Murder-for-Hire Trial

Over 600 potential jurors were summoned to the Davidson County courthouse to be considered to hear the case of the *State of Tennessee* vs. *Perry Avram March* in his murder-for-hire conspiracy trial.

Judge Dozier and the lawyers were looking for an impartial group. Most of the prospective panelists admitted knowing something about the case, but the lawyers needed to determine how much they knew and whether they could keep an open mind.

One juror was excused after telling the judge his feelings about Perry: "I think he's a slimy guy and I couldn't do a good job. I couldn't be a good juror," he admitted. Others were excused after indicating during the extensive voir dire that they had already formed an opinion as to Perry's guilt or innocence, or had problems being sequestered for the duration of the trial.

Surprisingly, a few prospects claimed to have never heard or read about Perry or his legal troubles, which raised eyebrows among the lawyers, considering that it had been the most high-profile case in Nashville in thirty years.

Finally, after two days of tediously screening the jury

pool and weeding out panelists who didn't meet the criteria to serve, the jury box was filled with nine women and three men, with two alternates, who were sworn in by the court clerk.

Before opening statements got underway, Judge Dozier ruled that the state would be able to tell the jury that Perry was facing an additional charge for murdering Janet, whose body had never been found.

As in the theft trial, the defense again filed a motion stating an intent to use an entrapment defense—that Perry had been an "unwilling person" who was induced or persuaded to commit a crime by someone under the direction of a law enforcement official. Again, this meant that for the defense to be successful, Perry would have to take the stand.

Ready to testify were nearly two dozen witnesses. The list included FBI Agent Kenneth Sena, jailhouse informant Russell Nathaniel Farris, his mother, Vickie Farris, Farris's lawyer Justin Johnson, Carolyn and Lawrence Levine, Metro Detectives Pat Postiglione and Bill Pridemore, attorney Fletcher Long, and Arthur March.

Prosecutor Thurman began his opening statement by painting a picture of the case from the night of August 15, 1996, when Janet had disappeared, up to the events that had led to this trial. Thurman described the day Janet March disappeared: "If you were looking at Janet March's life on that day, you would have thought it was perfect," the district attorney said.

He detailed the couple's close relationship with her parents, their dream house, and the two lovely children they were raising. He told jurors how, after Janet had vanished, Perry and the Levines became adversaries, and that numerous lawsuits were filed between them to force Perry to grant the Levines' visitation with their grandchildren.

He told jurors of Perry's arrest, and that he was now charged with Janet's murder, nine years after she'd vanished. While awaiting trial on the second-degree murder charge, he told jurors, Perry had become friendly with Farris, who was in an adjacent cell. "They talked for weeks about killing the

Levines, but then Farris had a change of heart, told his mother and his lawyer, and agreed to work with authorities."

Thurman characterized would-be hit man Farris as "a small-time crook" who "had a life of crime" and that Perry had become convinced that his new jailhouse friend was the person to kill his in-laws.

"And you'll be shocked when you hear how cold and calculated he is when this man talks about killing the grandparents of his children," Thurman said to the jury. "You'll be shocked when you hear the excitement and anticipation when he thinks about it happening."

The defense, on the other hand, portrayed Farris as a hardened criminal who was facing a lengthy prison term on attempted murder charges and was desperate for a "Get Out of Jail Free" card. "So when he sees Perry March coming into jail, it's all over the news, it's just like a little rat starting to scratch at his cage. So he starts talking to Perry March," Massey told jurors in his opening remarks.

"That's the government's chief witness," Massey told the jury, adding that the plot to kill the Levines was "an imaginary plan that could never be carried out, because Farris was in jail the entire time."

The defense account of what had happened to Janet was simple: "She was pulling out of the driveway and waved, and no one's seen her since."

As for the Levines, he portrayed them as having come after the children "not once, but twice," making it sound as though the Levines were evil or sinister people.

Massey insisted that it was Farris who'd encouraged Perry, day after day, to do something about the Levines. "Nathaniel Farris is creating crime," the lawyer said. "He's setting people up so that he doesn't have to sit in jail anymore."

The first witness prosecutors called to the stand was Carolyn Levine. She described her relationship with her son-in-law and said she had "loved him like a son," but that after their daughter had disappeared, and when Perry had moved first to Chicago and then to Mexico, the relationship deteriorated.

Next on the stand was Harris's mother, Vickie, who testified that after her son told her of Perry's plan to kill the Levines, she'd become concerned and called Lawrence Levine.

In his testimony, Levine said that after receiving that call, he'd notified police.

"This was not the first time that Perry and Arthur attempted to kill us, so we were scared," Levine told jurors.

An objection was raised by the defense to Levine's comments that it was the Marches' second attempt to kill them. After a bench conference, Dozier ordered the statement stricken from the record.

But a few minutes later, having just been admonished by the judge not to repeat his previous testimony, Levine ignored Dozier's ruling and said it again in front of the jury, further angering the judge.

Enraged that Levine was purposely not paying any attention to his judicial warning, Dozier raised his voice and lashed into the retired lawyer for disrespecting the court ruling.

"What are you doing?" he asked. "I've tried to tell you. The state's tried to tell you. I don't want to have to try this case again."

Levine was no novice to courtrooms, having practiced law since 1961. But it was obvious that he'd deliberately repeated the stricken phrase a second time as a ploy to be sure jurors would not forget the statement. The tactic is often used by witnesses because even though the judge orders the statement stricken from the record and tells jurors not to consider the remark during deliberations, it is still difficult for them to strike the comment from their minds.

The much-awaited key witness Russell Nathaniel Farris was sworn in to testify about the tape-recordings of conversations between him and Perry before they were played for the jury. He told the court that the plan was that once he'd murdered the Levines, and Perry was acquitted of murdering his wife, the two men would become business partners in Mexico, carrying out "express kidnappings.

"He told me that he'd done several," Farris said. "He said it's a fast, easy way to make easy money in Mexico."

Although Farris was not allowed to repeat his claim that Perry had previously carried out kidnappings in Mexico, Dozier did rule, over defense objections, that Farris could relate to the jury future plans to conduct kidnappings.

Defense lawyer Massey tried portraying Farris as a hardened criminal desperate for a way out of jail. "Perry March was your ticket, wasn't he?" Massey sarcastically asked.

The would-be hit man told the jury that he'd never intended to kill the Levines and that the murder was Perry's idea. He'd gone along with it only because Perry had promised to help him get bail money if he cooperated. Fear that someone else might actually kill the Levines and blame him for the murders had caused him to bow out of the plan and inform authorities, he said.

The defense strategy, meanwhile, was to convince jurors that Farris had made up the murder plot because he was eager to cut a deal with prosecutors. His lawyer Justin Johnson testified that his client was facing 15 and 180 years for multiple counts of attempted murder and aggravated robbery, but that no promises had been made to him. Both Johnson and Farris also testified that they were looking for a reduced sentence in exchange for his recording more than seven hours of conversations with Perry about the planned murder.

Metro Police Sergeant Pat Postiglione testified about the coded references in the transcripts between Perry and Arthur March. He pointed out that Perry had gotten a message that the job would be completed in two weeks and that Perry, in his taped conversations with Farris, had never tried to stop the murders.

"There was a big push on codes and code words," Postiglione explained to jurors. " 'Purchasing BMWs' meant 'killing the Levines.' "

Arthur March did not testify at the conspiracy trial, but the recorded words from his five telephone conversations with Farris were played for the jury. Arthur March was speaking to Farris from Ajijic, and Farris, who was pretending to be out on bail, was in reality in the custody of detectives and prosecutors.

By the second day of the trial, jurors had yet to hear from Perry March. That all changed on Tuesday, June 6, when prosecutors played nearly seven hours of damaging conversations between the ex-lawyer and Farris, in which Perry solicited his fellow inmate to murder the Levines.

"You have to wait for the opportunity when they're together," Perry says.

"Yeah," Farris replies.

"And then you leave no trace of evidence. The thing you have to remember is that you've got to clear the house of kids. Make sure there's no kids there."

"Uh-huh."

"When you're ready, it's going to be, you're going to have my dad send a message through an e-mail, which is, 'Bobby Givings is going to buy the BMW.'"

"I'm one hundred and ten percent on board with everything we've talked about. I can't tell you how excited I am, okay?" Perry tells Farris.

But when Farris asks what happens if he only kills Lawrence Levine, Perry replies: "You have to do it when they're both together for it to help me."

Throughout the two days of taped conversations recorded on October 6 and 7, 2005, Perry made it clear that his chances of beating the murder rap jumped to 90 percent if the Levines were killed.

Jurors heard from two other prosecution witnesses: First, FBI Agent Ken Sena said that he was assigned to follow Arthur March in Mexico, and that he'd spotted him at the Guadalajara airport expecting to pick up hit man Farris.

Fletcher Long, Arthur's attorney, testified about the meeting with his client in which Perry had burst into the room and said, "Dad, you don't roll on me. I don't roll on you. We will wear these jumpsuits as a badge of honor, a badge of honor," he repeated.

The defense called but one witness—FBI Agent Bret Curtis.

"Farris thought that if he obtained information about March's case and passed it on to the D.A., he, Farris, might be able to get leniency in his own case . . . he hoped he could get a deal," Curtis said, reading from the notes he had taken at the time Farris was debriefed.

On the third day of testimony, before both sides rested their case, Massey, who had promised jurors during the selection process that Perry would testify, advised the court that his client once again chose to remain off the stand and was dropping the police entrapment strategy. Outside the presence of the jury, Perry took the stand to inform the judge of his decision, for the record.

During closing arguments, Massey went after Farris, reminding jurors that the plan could never have been carried out, since Farris was locked up. "These people were in jail. This was a made-up story." He kept arguing that it was Farris's idea to kill the Levines, and that he had pushed Perry into hiring him as a hit man.

The lawyer went over the bitter custody battles between Perry and the Levines. When his in-laws were awarded temporary custody of the children, he said, Perry went ballistic. "There was a deep anger here. Don't think I'm minimizing it.

"The state bought Farris's testimony. They offered him his freedom. This was a ruse to charge Perry March and get Farris out of here," Massey said. Jurors were told that Perry had never given the go-ahead to kill his in-laws.

In the state's closing remarks, Assistant District Attorney Katy Miller said it was clear from the taped conversations that it was Perry who'd sold the would-be hit man on the idea of hiring him to bump off the Levines.

"Perry and Arthur wanted the Levines dead," Miller said. "Perry March thought that once the Levines were gone, his legal problems would be over. He thought the criminal case would be dropped.

"He talked with Farris about Mexico, how wonderful it was and how his father would treat him like a son," Miller said.

As the lead prosecutor, Thurman was the last up to address the jury. He let them know that Farris had no intention of going ahead with Perry's plan. "It could have happened if that bond money had come through and Mr. Farris had been the person [Perry] thought he was—the murderer he thought he was—who would kill in cold blood."

Calling Massey's closing argument "absurd," he reminded jurors that "You can't erase the voice of Perry March," and of hearing Perry say he was "excited" and "one hundred and ten percent on board."

"It's time for justice," Thurman said.

Jurors deliberated the case late Wednesday for about two hours before going back to a hotel for the night. They had another go at the evidence Thursday morning for about four hours before rendering their verdict.

And striking another blow against the already once-convicted Perry March, the jury found him guilty of one count of conspiracy to commit first-degree murder and two counts of solicitation to commit first-degree murder.

As the verdict was read, Perry demonstrated no visible reaction.

"Hearing Perry March's statements on those tapes, I think, was tremendously damaging evidence," Thurman told reporters after the verdict was read. "I think that when Perry said Farris had to kill both of them to help his case . . . and the conversation he has with his father when his father said, 'it's going to happen next week' was the comment that made the conspiracy for sure."

The prosecutor called his star witness "very courageous in this situation to come forward and assist us like he did. He may have a career in Hollywood once he gets out of prison," Thurman observed.

Massey, although obviously disappointed with the verdict, agreed that the tapes did his client in. "I think the tapes were probably the most damaging piece of evidence that the prosecutors had, by far. We had our explanation and the state had their explanation of the tapes."

One of the jurors later concurred in an interview with NewsChannel 5 that the tapes had sealed Perry's fate: "Well, I think that's probably what convinced most of us that he was pretty serious about what was happening."

The juror said that after reviewing the facts of the case, the panel had taken only one vote as to Perry's guilt or innocence. "The whole group felt pretty much like everybody else did that the evidence was pretty much overwhelming about what Mr. March's motives were."

After the verdict, the buzz around the courthouse was that Perry himself had to take full credit and responsibility for the murder-for-hire conspiracy trial and for his conviction. "Had he kept his mouth shut after his August 2005 arrest and said nothing to anyone other than to his lawyers, this trial would never have taken place," attorney Long said.

"The prosecution would never have won the case without the testimony of Detectives Pat Postiglione and Bill Pridemore; two other inmates, Cornelius King and Reno Martin; a sheriff's deputy convicted of civil rights violations who overheard the plot; [Perry's] father, Arthur March; Vickie Farris; Russell Farris; his lawyer, Justin Johnson; the two FBI agents; the coroner, Dr. William Bass, who testified that when Arthur March picked up Janet's body and reburied it, her remains could have deteriorated and there would have been nothing more than clothes and bones—and neither would they have had my testimony and seven hours of audiotape.

"Perry provided the prosecution with all of these witnesses. That was the meat of the prosecution case, and Perry blew it . . . Perry convicted himself. He did everything wrong. He did everything you tell a defendant not to do. He made their case for them," Long said.

While Perry felt let down by the verdict, Massey said his client "never lost faith in the citizens of Nashville to hear this case and to hear the case fairly. Even as we left today, he had nothing to say at all. He put his fight forward. That's what Perry March wanted to do."

The Levines, who'd waited almost ten years for justice, were equally subdued as they left the courthouse.

Perry was to have been sentenced for his theft and murder-for-hire convictions in July, but in a last-minute motion, his attorney asked Judge Dozier to put off sentencing until after his upcoming murder trial concluded. Both the judge and prosecutor agreed.

The reason given by his lawyers was that any pre-sentencing testimony that Perry would give could potentially be used against him in the murder trial set to begin on August 7.

A new sentencing date was set for Wednesday, September 6.

Defense attorney John Herbison, concerned that the extensive media coverage of both the theft and murder-for-hire trials could taint the potential jury slated to hear the murder case, sought a change of venue to Memphis, where two members of Perry's legal team had offices.

"Mr. March is entitled to a fair trial. I will grant the motion for a change of venue. I don't think it's worth being an issue," Dozier said.

Three weeks before Perry was set to go on trial, the judge further ruled that jurors would be selected from the city of Chattanooga, about 133 miles from Nashville.

"The defense would have preferred that the case was heard by Memphis jurors, where about twenty percent of all criminal trials end in not guilty verdicts," observed Larry Brinton, who has covered trials in Tennessee for half a century.

"In Chattanooga trials, the reverse is true, and ninety-six percent of trials end in guilty verdicts, while only four percent go free."

But with the good news about the jurors being chosen from another Tennessee city, there was some bad news for the defense camp. Dozier ruled against defense motions to exclude Perry's audiotape recordings with Farris, and any statements he'd made to detectives on the flight from Los Angeles to Nashville after his arrest a year earlier.

Herbison had claimed that the statute of limitations was two years on Perry's abuse of a corpse charge and four years on tampering with evidence, but the judge similarly refused to throw out those charges.

16

Murder by Lawyer

Mystery, money, greed, and revenge. The Perry March murder case promised it all for jurors waiting to be chosen to hear the case.

On Monday, August 7, in Chattanooga, a pool of over 700 potential candidates was summoned to the Hamilton County Courthouse to select twelve jurors and four alternates who would decide Perry's guilt or innocence in the murder of his wife, Janet, ten years earlier.

After nearly eight hours of scrutiny by Judge Dozier and the lawyers to determine their qualifications, six women and six men were selected.

Perry took an active role in the jury selection process, often whispering to his lawyers about his likes and dislikes of a candidate, or scribbling notes on a yellow legal pad. More than half of the jurors questioned wanted off the jury after learning they would be sequestered in Nashville and would be housed at an undisclosed hotel for the duration of the trial, expected to take at least a week.

Some prospective jurors who made the initial cut claimed never to have heard of Perry March. Prospects who indicated they could not convict him without the body of the victim got bounced from the jury pool, since Janet's body had never been found.

Both sides briefed jurors about star witness Russell Nathaniel Farris. Prosecutors informed jurors that among the witnesses would be two criminals. The defense wanted to know from jurors how much weight they would give convicts who expected a lighter sentence in exchange for testifying against Perry.

Jurors were told that the case was based mostly on circumstantial evidence and that despite the lack of a body, they could convict a defendant of murder even though there was no blood, weapon, or other physical evidence. Successful prosecutions of "bodiless" murder cases, while rare, go back at least to 1792 in England, when a man charged with throwing his captain from a ship was convicted. The law in the United States is clear: a homicide case can proceed without a body.

The first case in the United States to pave the way for bodiless prosecutions was the 1959 conviction of investment consultant Leonard Ewing Scott, who was accused of killing his wealthy socialite wife, Evelyn Throsby Scott, even though no physical trace of her was ever found.

Since then, there have been hundreds of successful prosecutions of similar bodiless murder cases around the nation. In 1989, in Connecticut, Richard Crafts was convicted of murdering his wife, whose body was never recovered, after jurors heard evidence that he had run her body parts through a woodchipper. And in a highly publicized case in New York City in May 2000, jurors meted out guilty verdicts to mother-and-son serial killers Sante and Kenny Kimes, for murdering socialite Irene Silverman, even though her body was never found. Sante used the motto "No body, no crime," according to her son.

Then there's the case of Dr. Robert Bierenbaum, a New York plastic surgeon. His wife, Gail, disappeared in 1985, but it wasn't until October 2000 that prosecutors put the surgeon on trial for her murder. Bierenbaum, also a licensed pilot, was convicted of killing her and dumping her body from a small airplane over the Atlantic Ocean.

In all of these cases, there wasn't any smoking gun evidence—it was largely circumstantial. And it was circumstantial evidence that prosecutors in the Perry March case were going to rely on to bring about a guilty verdict.

The defense, on the other hand, explained to jurors as they questioned them that Janet had simply taken off and left home in August 1996, and that there was no proof she was even dead, much less that Perry had killed her.

After being sworn in, Dozier gave the panel strict instructions. He told the group that they would be provided with state-of-the-art video monitors, and transcripts of audiotape recordings. At the hotel, their television viewing would be limited, as would reading newspapers. He promised that their needs would be taken care of, but that once opening statements began on Wednesday, they would have to devote their lives to the Perry March trial until a verdict was reached.

With more than a hundred subpoenas issued by the defense and prosecutors and with the legal maneuvering on motions resolved, the trial was to start at the recently opened Justice A. A. Birch Courthouse.

But just before it could begin, on Wednesday, August 9, defense attorney Bill Massey stood up to inform the court of an anonymous letter he'd received the day before. The letter-writer, believed to be Barry Lee Armistead, stated that he had been Janet's lover, and was with her after she'd left Perry. Claiming that Janet had died from an overdose of sleeping pills and alcohol, Armistead confessed to having gotten rid of her body. "We've talked to him on various occasions, and we cannot corroborate anything this man says," prosecutor Thurman responded. "Based on his history and everything, we found him not to be credible."

One of Armistead's anonymous letters, sent to prosecutors, contradicts another by saying that Perry had killed Janet, and then called Armistead who'd helped Perry bury her body in a Cookeville landfill, about 80 miles away from Nashville.

Armistead turned out to have had prior convictions for

grand larceny, forgery, theft, and aggravated assault, and he was currently a guest of the state at the Riverbend Maximum Security Institution.

Dozier had Armistead brought to the courthouse from prison, where he spoke briefly with lawyers. He denied writing the anonymous letter, and the judge refused to delay opening statements any further. But it would not be the last time that the judge, lawyers, or Perry would hear from Armistead on this issue.

Thurman spent nearly half an hour outlining the state's case. "This case is about murder. It's about deceit. It's about abuse of trust. This is a ten-year odyssey that has finally brought us to this courtroom today asking for justice for Janet March. If you were on the outside, looking in on Janet March on August fifteenth, 1996, she had it all."

The prosecutor described the couple's relationship, mentioning their two beautiful children, Samson and Tzipora, and Janet's loving parents. "But her life wasn't perfect. Her marriage was disintegrating and she had an appointment the next day to see a divorce lawyer. That is an appointment that she never kept.

"You will hear from her mother, Carolyn Levine, who will tell you how [Janet] and Perry March met while students at the University of Michigan and how, after they graduated, moved to Nashville. And that the Levines took Perry March under their wings and paid for him to go to law school. They gave Janet March a house and provided financial assistance, and helped them build their dream house, and they had a very loving relationship, not only with Janet, but with Perry, and treated him like a son.

"That was all shattered on August fifteenth, 1996, when [their] daughter disappeared. You will hear that right after that, the relationship went quickly downhill. After that, Perry March left the city with his children and they went into litigation over visitation about the grandchildren and litigation over Janet March's estate.

"You will hear that some time on the night of August

fifteenth, they had an argument. That he had been staying away from home. We know that Perry March at nine o'clock called his brother and then his sister, saying that Janet had left. It was after midnight that he called the Levines and told them that they had an argument and that their thirty-three-year-old daughter had stormed out of their home saying, 'See ya,' and has never been seen again."

Thurman walked the jury through the ten-year history of the case: the twelve-day vacation to-do list, how Perry March and the Levines had gone to police on August 29 to report her missing, finding Janet's Volvo on September 7, the missing hard drive on Perry's computer, and Perry's conviction after hatching a plot with inmate Russell Nathaniel Farris to kill his wife's parents.

"You will also hear from a witness who saw Perry March riding a bicycle near where Janet March's Volvo was discovered. There were a lot of things wrong when the Volvo was found. Crammed down on the driver's side, upside down, was Janet's purse. It just didn't look right, police said.

"You will hear how devoted a mother Janet March was, and that she would never leave without calling her mother."

Thurman raised questions that jurors should ask themselves as the evidence in the case unfolded. Why hadn't Janet notified the divorce lawyer that she was going on vacation and canceled her scheduled appointment for the day after her disappearance? And why had Perry March changed his will and insurance policy in September?

"You will hear a bizarre conversation between Perry March and Sergeant Pat Postiglione, talking about wanting to work out a plea deal. 'I never did anything criminal with Janet,' he tells the detective."

Thurman described for the jury how Perry and Farris had met at the jail and that "before long, Perry March asks him if he, Farris, would get out on bond, would he kill Lawrence and Carolyn Levine? . . . But Farris gets cold feet and tells his mother that he's in a mess. She calls Lawrence Levine and says, 'The police need to talk to my son.'

"You will hear hours and hours of tape between Farris

and Perry March planning to murder Carolyn and Lawrence Levine, the grandparents of his children, who already lost their mother.

"You will also hear from another inmate, Reno Martin, an ex–police officer who was caught in a drug sting, who overheard that Farris was going to kill the Levines, corroborating what Farris was saying.

"You will hear from Cornelius King, a fellow inmate that Perry March befriended. One night he told him that he beat his wife to death with a wrench after she told him she was filing for divorce after accusing him of cheating on her. 'Yeah, I killed her. I hit her over the head with a wrench. She said she was going to divorce me, and I wasn't going to let that happen. They'll never find her body, because it's ashes and it's in water,' King quoted Perry March as telling him," the district attorney said.

Thurman's opening comments detailed for jurors that they would hear from Arthur March's videotaped testimony how Perry had asked him to clean his driveway with bleach to make sure there were no visible bloodstains.

The district attorney alerted jurors that they would also hear from Bobby Heller, a friend of Perry March, who would be testifying about an e-mail Perry had sent him in the spring of 1997, asking that he critique a mystery novel he was writing about the murder of an attractive woman in her early thirties with long dark hair. "The victim in the novel is just like a description of his wife. Is that something a loving husband should be doing after your wife disappears?" Thurman asks.

An excerpt of the manuscript, called "@*murder.com*," was later entered into evidence. In the novel, Perry had written that the victim, named Violet, is found

lying on the smooth pile carpet . . . she lay on her back, left leg tucked beneath her, her head facing the ceiling, hands to her throat, eyes open and bulging. The subtle reek of decay was just starting to become apparent in the corridor outside the study. Textured on top of the

*cadaverous atom h, d mino embarrassing smell loomed.
Violet had soiled herself und ruined her carpet, The
combination of body excretions and the creeping color
of death intruded on this cozy place . . .*

Jurors reading the several pages of the manuscript shown
to them by the prosecutor had to wonder whether the
grotesque death scene was a description of Janet lying on the
floor after she had been killed. And was Perry recalling in
his writing that his wife had soiled herself and stained her
carpet? Was the carpet the Oriental rug that witnesses in the
March home had observed the day after Janet disappeared?

"You will also hear evidence that strands of Janet's hair
and rug fibers were found in Perry March's Jeep, and that
shortly after she disappeared, he went to a tire store and had
fairly new tires replaced, even though they had twenty thousand miles left in them."

Thurman suggested to jurors that Perry had wanted the
tires replaced because he was worried that his tire tracks could
be used as evidence against him, and could be matched to
places where he had driven.

"At the end of the trial there will be no question in your
mind that Janet March is dead. That she was murdered and
that the murderer is in this courtroom. His name is Perry
March," Thurman said, pointing to the defendant before sitting down.

Bill Massey began his folksy, Southern-style hour-long
opening statement playing down the prosecution remarks.
"They don't have the evidence because it doesn't exist.
There is no direct proof that Perry March killed anyone," he
said.

Massey hammered away at this theme, saying that the
case against his client was "purely circumstantial . . . that
Janet's body has never been found, and there's no proof
she's dead."

As to why his client left Nashville the day after the hard
drive had been discovered missing, Massey cited the extensive media coverage of the case, saying Perry had wanted to

get his children away from the publicity. "There was so much police, so much media—'Where's Janet? Where's Janet?'—that he left and took the children to Chicago."

The defense lawyer highlighted Janet and Perry's marriage problems. "You will hear from Dr. Campbell, a psychiatrist they had been seeing, that during one session in particular, Janet was very, very upset with Perry, that he was not paying attention to things at home, that he wasn't taking care of the kids, that he wasn't taking out the garbage.

"One of the things Dr. Campbell told them was that 'You guys need a cooling-off period—maybe get away from each other for a while.'"

The night of the argument, Janet "was upset to the point that she said she was taking a vacation, and she made out a list of twenty-three things for him to do . . ." Massey said, reading to jurors from a list of items she had typed.

"Janet packed her bags. She was very upset. She got in her Volvo and she left. As she was backing out of the driveway, her son, Sammy, is at the window of his bedroom. Sammy sees her and she sees Sammy, and they wave to each other."

Massey said that during the trial, the defense planned to play an interview that Perry's son had given to NewsChannel 5 about the night his mother drove away in her Volvo and disappeared.

Massey brought up that "Lawrence Levine was a very powerful and successful attorney in the Jewish community . . . and that Janet was rather strong-willed. She had the artist temperament, and if you look at the note she wrote, you will think that she's tired of doing housework: 'I'm tired of taking care of the kids, I want you to do those things.' Janet had a nanny and a housekeeper for the house, and she didn't have a full-time job."

The lawyer pointed out to jurors the "bitterness, anger, and hatred" the Levines had for Perry March and his father.

Massey spoke of the police investigation, and the purported sightings of Janet. He told jurors of the psychic who had made contact with Janet and who claimed Janet told the mind reader that she was rolled up in a rug.

"So police, with everything else to look at. went looking at rugs. They questioned Marisol Mouly, who was at Janet's home the day after she disappeared. Perry March did not know she was coming over with her son Grant for a prearranged play date that Janet had arranged on August fifteenth.

"She says she remembered a rug was on the floor, and that Sammy was jumping on it.

"This rug thing came from a psychic," Massey incredulously told jurors.

The lawyer rehashed the extensive and thorough police investigation, pointing out all of the city and state parks and nearby lakes that were searched looking for Janet's body, including a quarry in Alabama.

"Finally, after eight years and three months after Janet March disappeared, they go to a grand jury and get an indictment against Perry March. And on the plane over from Los Angeles to Nashville, Perry tells Pat Postiglione, 'I'm scared to death. I don't want to face thirty years in jail. I've never been involved in any crime proceeding until this Janet March thing. I didn't do this, but I would take something less . . .'

"Perry is taken to jail and meets a man named Russell Nathaniel Farris, and he's got a big question mark on his neck, and he's been in trouble since he's been knee-high—serious trouble," Massey said, listing Farris's arrests and convictions.

Massey said that, after seeing Perry on the television news, "Farris decides, 'This is my ticket to not having to spend the rest of my life in jail.' So he got to talking with Perry March, and Perry March made a bad decision. That he did . . . because Nathaniel Farris talked him into the scheme, an imaginary plan, if you will, to kill the Levines because they were material witnesses to the homicide trial.

"They talked this over, and it was recorded, and Perry told him he [Farris] was going to get out of jail on bond."

Massey made two points regarding the plot—he told jurors that "Perry March wanted the hit to be delayed—

'Delay, delay, delay,' he said. And secondly, he told Nathaniel Farris that 'Before you do anything, you get my okay . . . I have to give you the green light.'

"And you will hear how this inmate hopes to have his case disposed of favorably, based upon his testimony against Perry March.

"That's what this case is all about," Massey said in recapping his remarks. "They have no direct proof that Perry March killed Janet. Did Perry March kill Janet March when they don't even know she's dead? Did Perry March abuse a corpse when they don't even have the body? Did Perry March tamper with evidence when they don't have this evidence?

"This case was put together using fortune tellers and inmate testimony," Massey insisted. "Psychics, cadaver dogs, and inmates—that's what this case is all about. And at the conclusion of this case, you will see that the proof does not rise to meet the level, that the government can not prove that Janet March is even dead, that the government can not prove that Perry March abused a corpse or tampered with evidence.

"At the end of this case, you will return a verdict that the truth demands, not based on sympathy—that Perry March is innocent of these charges."

As in the last trial, the first witness called to the stand by Thurman was Carolyn Levine. In over two hours of testimony, she described how she had attempted to resolve the rocky relationship between her daughter and Perry.

Fighting back tears, Carolyn spoke about the arguments the couple had had, and how the marriage was deteriorating. She testified to the appointment Janet had made with a divorce lawyer for the day after she'd vanished, and how Perry had stayed in a hotel for several nights before Janet disappeared.

"I knew the treatment that she had undergone for a number of years by her husband, so I had my suspicions. It was abusive treatment. Perry would belittle her in front of me, in front of her friends, in front of others. He was not good to her, let's put it that way. She wanted to make the marriage work. She was very comfortable telling him that she did not appreciate his slights," Carolyn Levine testified.

Recalling the night that Perry had called her at midnight, she testified that she wasn't surprised. "They had been arguing so much that when he told me they had another argument, it was like, 'What else is new?'

"I said, 'Perry, don't worry about it, I'm sure she just wants to cool off. She probably is driving around the block. Call me when she gets back.'

"I believed what Perry told me. I believed she was really upset and wanted to cool off. I guess I believed him because I wanted to. My mind was not going to accept what I inevitably came to believe."

But as the days went on and Janet had not returned, her parents wanted to go to police to report their daughter's disappearance. Perry told them that the police couldn't be trusted and they should instead hire a private investigator.

Carolyn Levine also became distrustful of Perry soon after Janet's abandoned gray Volvo was found at the Brixworth apartment complex about 3 miles from Perry's home on September 7. "I didn't see a toothbrush, a hairbrush, or any bras," she noticed after police had inventoried the bags in the car. "It seemed like a bag that a man had packed," she testified.

Carolyn identified for jurors the lurid letters that Perry had written to paralegal Leigh Reames while working at Bass, Berry & Sims, which she'd discovered in January 1997. They were among Janet's art supplies, where they had been placed five months earlier. The house on Blackberry Road had just been sold and new owners were preparing to move in. An assistant to the Realtor who was helping Carolyn Levine pack Janet's personal belongings found the envelope and handed it to her.

Carolyn Levine opened it and began reading the letters. She promptly recognized their importance to the police investigation and wasted no time in giving them to detectives.

She also testified about the years of bitter disputes and

litigation that she and her husband had had with Perry over his outright refusal to allow them to see Sammy and Tzipi.

"Did your son-in-law ever make any derogatory remarks to you about Janet after she disappeared?" Thurman asked.

"He said to me, 'That effing Janet has ruined my life,'" she replied.

John Richie followed Carolyn Levine to the stand and testified that he and a co-worker had installed a cabinet countertop at the March home. Janet asked if he would also repair a loose pipe in the kitchen, and for that, he'd borrowed a pair of pliers from Perry.

Deneane Beard, the March housekeeper, testified that when she'd arrived to do her weekly cleaning the morning after Janet disappeared, she noticed that the kitchen and other areas of the home were already clean. Beard also found it strange that Janet, who had long hair, had usually left quite a bit of it in the bathroom sink, but that none was found the day she reported for work. When she didn't see Janet in the home, Perry explained to her that she had gone off to California for a few days.

Next to testify was Marissa Moody, who'd arrived at the March home to drop off her son, Grant, for a scheduled play date with Sammy that Janet had arranged a day earlier. Sammy had answered the door, but Perry claimed to know nothing about the appointment. She testified to noticing an Oriental rug rolled up in the middle of the floor, and that Sammy was bouncing up and down on it.

Divorce lawyer Lucinda Smith was on and off the witness stand briefly. She testified about Janet's eleven o'clock appointment to meet with her on August 16, 1996, but that Larry Levine had canceled the meeting the day it was scheduled to take place.

Laura Zinker, a "very close friend," testified about Janet's marital problems, saying that Perry was emotionally abusive of his wife. "He would be very critical of her," Zinker said.

Mitchell Barnett, the architect who'd helped Janet design and construct her "dream house," spoke of her devotion to her children and how attentive she was to their needs during the building. He also observed that Perry seemed to be totally uninterested in the home.

Laura Rummel, a Realtor, was friends with both Perry and Janet. The night Janet had left home, Rummel said, Perry called her to say she had taken off after they'd had an argument. She also recalled speaking with Janet the morning of the day she disappeared. Her friend sounded "hurried and distracted." She further testified to meeting Perry a day later to discuss furnishing his new law office.

Diane Saks, a childhood friend of Janet, told of a run-in with Perry shortly after his wife's disappearance. "I remember one conversation where he said, 'Diane, do you think I killed Janet, and put her in the car, and left the kids home alone sleeping, and came back, and acted like nothing happened?'"

"Did you respond to him?"

"It was very disturbing. It took me by surprise that he would say that to me. And it was after that conversation that my husband got on the phone and asked him never to call the house again. That was the last time I spoke with Perry."

Thurman got Saks to explain to jurors that Janet would never have left home in the middle of the night. "She was very protective of her kids, very involved in their lives. She was never without Tzipi at her side. She was very protective of Sammy. She just did everything for her children."

"What about her computer skills?" she was asked.

"She didn't have very good computer skills," Saks replied, smiling.

"And what about her driving habits?"

"That was a bit scary. Janet was not a good driver. She never could back into a spot. That would not be something she would do."

Saks testified that Perry had become a suspect in her mind because he was "unresponsive" to those who were trying to help him find Janet. "He just didn't have any concern. He never reached out to us and didn't want anything from us. We were all frantically trying to figure out where Janet was and who she would be with. If she was troubled, she would have gotten in touch with her inner circle. It just didn't add up when he wasn't responsive to us. He just didn't show a lot of concern to where she was."

Another friend, Gabriel Freidman, took the stand, testifying that after she'd given an interview to a local reporter about Janet's disappearance, "Perry was upset with me because of what I said in the newspaper.

"We had a brief conversation and I told him I had no idea why he'd be upset with me, because I had not said anything derogatory about him and had not insinuated that he had done anything wrong. Rather I had said something positive about his wife and the mother of his children . . . that something had happened to her to prevent her from being at Sammy's sixth birthday party that was beyond her control."

She testified that Perry was "upset in general" and appalled at the community in Nashville for thinking that he could do something so terrible to his wife. "I told Perry about a trial in South Africa where a man lost his temper and threw a statue at his wife, killing her. He asked me what was the outcome of that situation, and I told him the man was found guilty."

Dr. Thomas Campbell took the stand to testify that he'd seen Perry professionally about thirty times between November 1992 and March 1994. He described the last session he'd had with the couple in 1996, shortly before Janet's disappearance, as "volatile," and said he'd discussed the idea of a trial separation with them.

Sammy's kindergarten teacher at the University School of Nashville gave her testimony outside the presence of the jury, but it was videotaped. Kim Scott told of Sammy's first day of school on August 26, shortly after Janet disappeared. Scott said that Sammy was devastated at school and was constantly crying because he missed his mom, and he said he hadn't had a chance to say goodbye.

Piece by piece, like a jigsaw puzzle, prosecutors spent the first day putting together their circumstantial case against Perry, calling over a dozen witnesses.

The thirteenth witness of day one to testify was Dr.

Stacey Goodman, who'd gone to college with Janet and Perry, and in fact had introduced the two. The Vanderbilt University Medical Center doctor testified that Janet's driving habits were not consistent with the way the Volvo had been found, backed into a space at the apartment complex. Like Janet's other friends, she told jurors that Janet would never have left her children and gone off on vacation without them. She also described a threatening phone call from Perry, who was "screaming and swearing" at her.

Goodman had filed a police report about the threats, and quoted Perry as telling her, "When I come to Nashville, I'm coming to get you."

Thursday, August 10, day two of testimony, began with a twenty-minute hearing outside the presence of the jury to determine whether paralegal Leigh Reames, the recipient of Perry's sexually explicit letters, could testify about them.

The defense was seeking to exclude the letters at trial, questioning Reames extensively about the evidence she had that Perry had written the letters. The prosecution wanted the letters admitted as evidence to show that Janet had possessed them and intended to turn them over to a divorce lawyer the day after her disappearance.

The court ruled that the letters sent to Reames would be admissible.

Reames testified that after receiving the three anonymous lewd letters, she'd turned them over to her supervisor. An investigation had determined that Perry was the author of those letters. She eventually left the law firm. To prevent a lawsuit, Perry had settled with Reames out of court, agreeing to pay her $25,000, though he only paid her about half that amount.

Questioned by defense attorney John Herbison, she never once glanced at Perry sitting at the defense table with his head bowed. "I felt the letters was [sic] threatening, emotionally," she said. "I found the letters offensive, yes, very . . . It was an emotional abuse."

Cornelius King, a 25-year-old inmate charged with first-degree murder, also initially testified without the jury present. He had been in the same protective custody unit where Perry was housed, and they had become friends. King testified that Perry had confessed to him that after an argument with Janet, who'd accused him of cheating on her, he hit Janet over the head with a wrench and disposed of her body by burning her remains and tossing her body in a lake.

King also testified that Perry began to worry about what he had confided, and filed a grievance against King with authorities. As a result, King was moved to another area of the jail.

Under cross-examination, King denied lying about his conversation with Perry in order to cut a deal.

King composed a two-page handwritten explanation to authorities about his conversation with Perry that was entered into evidence. (Spelling, punctuation, and grammar have not been changed.)

> *During a discussion between me and Perry March he had descuss how he had killed his wife and he asked me not to tell my lawyer or anybody and the conversation had started he told me that they were arguing because she had a feeling that Perry was cheating on her and she threaten to leave him and get a devorse and take everything. And he said that he wasn't going to have that he stated to her before he let her take everything he own he'd kill her and he said that's when he hit her over the head with that wrench and killed her and then he stated that you'll will never fine the body because he burned it into ashes and empted them in a lake. And he also state that you'll all will suffer when this is all over because he is to smart for you'll. And he said when he finish with you'll he is going to sue you'll for everything the state have he said when he finish with you'll he will own this city.*
>
> *He also stated that he have a way of maken people disappear so don't discuss this with nobody then he ask me 2 days later did I come back to the hole to try*

to get iformation to use against him I did anser him so
he lied on me and got me moved. Because he was feel-
ing guilty about what he had said.

Mr. Perry March also spoke of a Mr. Rino Martin a
guy with a Fed case that suppose to testify against him
he also said that if he testify against him he will have
him kill because he is sick of people snitching on him.

Dozier indicated that if the statements of these two witnesses were admissible, they would be called back to re-
testify.

Finally, with the jury present, former babysitter–nanny
Ella Goldshmidt testified through a Russian interpreter about
caring for the March children for six years. "In my opinion,
she was an ideal mother. She was smart, caring, devoted.
She never failed to sacrifice time for the children."

Goldshmidt testified to Janet's emotional state the day before she'd disappeared, saying Janet was "particularly upset." She told of Janet working at the computer all day. The
nanny went on to testify that when she'd shown up for work
the day after Janet disappeared, she'd seen a large rolled-up
rug blocking the entrance to the kitchen.

Under cross-examination, she told jurors that she'd never
seen Janet and Perry argue. She said Perry had seemed "visibly upset" about his wife's disappearance and that he'd told
her he was having trouble sleeping because he kept waiting
to hear the sound of her car engine in the driveway.

The prosecution continued to present its case, calling several detectives who'd investigated Janet's disappearance. It
was during the cross-examination of Detective David Miller
that tempers flared. The defense tried to introduce the results
of a polygraph test administered in October 1996 to Charles
(Clyde) Sumner, a construction worker who had worked on
building Janet's dream home a year before she went missing.

While Miller found him to be "honest and cooperative,"
there had been reports that Sumner was sexually attracted to
Janet and had had sexual fantasies about her, including spying on her from outside the home. Massey was attempting to

show that Sumner might have had a motive to kill her. Thurman was furious at Massey because, as a seasoned lawyer, he knew that polygraph tests are never admissible in court.

While Sumner had answered "No" when asked whether he'd been present when Janet was killed, and whether he'd done himself, he had shown deception on some questions put to him, argued Massey, who wasn't about to give up without a fight.

In the midst of the blowup between the two lawyers, Judge Dozier showed his frustration by exclaiming, "Jiminy Christmas," just as the jury was being led out of the courtroom for the luncheon break.

As soon as the panel had left the room, Massey moved to declare a mistrial based on Dozier's off-hand remark, claiming the judge favored the prosecution. Dozier denied the motion and also ruled that the defense could not let jurors know about the polygraph, saying he would advise them to ignore any mention of the test that they may have heard.

Another witness to testify on August 10 was Peter Rodman, a former radio personality and flight attendant. He told of arriving at his Brixworth apartment complex on August 16, 1996, and seeing a man "with curly hair in his early thirties," whom he later realized was Perry, on a bicycle at one o'clock in the morning. Rodman testified that after seeing Perry's picture in the newspaper, he'd called Mike Smith, his friend, a homicide detective with Metro Police.

Rodman testified that Perry had frozen up upon seeing him. "It was like watching a squirrel that didn't know which tire to run under," he said.

Private investigator Kim Garbler, who had been hired by the Levines in the weeks before Janet was reported missing, testified that at one point in her investigation, Perry had called her, indicating he was "unhappy"—this after she'd told him she was interviewing residents of the apartment complex where the Volvo had been found. She also thought it "strange" that Perry had referred to his wife in the past tense.

Throughout the testimony of witnesses, Perry sat motionless and expressionless.

And in a bizarre twist to end the day of testimony, the Metro Sheriff's Office confirmed that Perry had abandoned his Jewish faith and converted to Christianity while in jail. Metro Sheriff's spokeswoman Karla Crocker said Perry had been sprinkled with water by a non-denominational jail chaplain for a baptism ceremony.

With twenty-six more witnesses to be called before wrapping up its case, on Friday, August 11, jurors heard from Travis West, a bicycle shop manager who testified that Perry's bicycle could have fit in the front passenger seat of a Volvo. Police department fingerprint analyst Danny Morris testified that several unidentified fingerprints sent to him from Janet's Volvo did not match Perry's prints.

For the first time, jurors heard Perry speak when they viewed his November 1996 videotaped deposition. He insisted he was not being evasive when asked if he had killed Janet. "I think you're vulgar and insensitive," he replied.

The deposition was introduced to the jury panel by attorney Jon Jones, who had been hired by Lawrence and Carolyn Levine to represent the family after Perry had filed a probate petition seeking to get his hands on Janet's estate and his children's trust funds.

While Perry swore under oath in the deposition that he'd never hit Janet, his hesitancy in answering the question was strange. "I'm thinking, because I'm just trying to separate . . . I don't . . . I don't know. I'm sure there were times when I grabbed her arm." He also suggested several scenarios of what could have happened to his wife. "The truth is, I did not have an argument. The truth is, Janet did. But you can't dance with only one person."

Throughout the videotape, Perry claimed he still loved his wife, and kept referring to her disappearance as the night "she ran away."

He claimed Janet had taken his credit card with her before she'd left home and that he couldn't recall how the argument had started.

Perry's demeanor on the tape was hostile and confrontational, though at times he appeared bored as he was being questioned, resting his head in his hands and yawning.

Jurors also heard an interview Perry had given to local NBC affiliate WSMV reporter Annette Nole Hall, in which he declared his innocence. He characterized the argument he'd had with Janet the last time he saw her as "actually a relatively benign evening," claiming he hadn't argued the night she disappeared. "It wasn't a fight. We had plans for next week, we had plans for next month."

Karen Korsberg, an FBI hair and fiber expert, testified that two fibers found in the trunk of Perry's Jeep were consistent with those from a rug or carpet, but since she had not been provided with any samples for comparison, she could not say whether they had come from a rug in his home. She also testified to finding Janet's hair in the trunk of the Jeep.

During the afternoon session, the defense was handed bad news when Dozier ruled on the admissibility of Cornelius King's testimony, and the testimony of Leigh Reames and the letters sent to her by Perry. He ruled that they could be shown to the jury. He said that the letters could relate to motive and that the jury had to have them to understand the case. The judge also ruled, however, that the condom found with the letters would not be shown to the jury panel.

"Are the contents of these letters overly prejudicial when you weigh them against their probative value?" Dozier asked. "I think not."

Leigh Reames was then brought back to the courtroom, where she took the stand with the jury present and repeated what she had previously testified to the court about the disturbing letters.

Mark Levine, Janet's brother, testified about the many years of litigation surrounding visitation and custody of Janet's children after she'd gone missing. He told of his parents visiting the kids in Mexico and bringing them back to Nashville, only to eventually have to return them to Perry in Ajijic where he was living.

He also testified that Perry had allowed him access to his home computer, where he found a six-page memo written by his sister in which she'd detailed the way her husband had been mistreating and abusing her.

Janet's first cousin and the family insurance agent, Michael Levine, testified that after Janet's disappearance, Perry no longer wanted Michael to handle his insurance needs. He testified that Perry had wanted to be listed as the sole beneficiary of his wife's policy, rather than have it given to Janet's estate.

Because jurors were away from their Chattanooga homes, Judge Dozier ordered that the court hold a rare proceeding over the weekend. The first witness called to the stand on Saturday, day four, was Cheri Lee, the hairdresser for both Perry and Janet, who testified to an incident that had occurred a month before Janet disappeared, when Perry came into her shop, Salon FX, while she was cutting his wife's hair. "Janet seemed nervous and sort of cowered a little" when she saw Perry.

By far the most damaging testimony that day came from Arthur, whose videotaped deposition was played for the jury. "The first time that Perry told me about it [the murder] was at the house, when he asked me to clean up. He was afraid there was some bloodstains. That's the first time."

Arthur went on to say how he'd helped Perry dispose of Janet's body, first removing it from a nearby construction site near his home and later when he'd gotten rid of the body by placing it in a brush pile, where it was incinerated. "It would be burned and cremated, and there would be no body," Arthur said.

After Arthur's taped deposition was played for jurors, Fletcher Long followed his client to the witness stand. As a prosecution witness, Long repeated his testimony of what Perry had said about the two of them wearing "jumpsuits as a badge of honor."

Dr. William Bass, a forensic pathologist who'd started the "Body Farm" at the University of Tennessee, where cadavers are subjected to various situations to study the effects of decomposition, testified that in that August heat, a body in the same condition described by Arthur March would have deteriorated after three weeks, and there would be nothing left but bones.

Massey tried unsuccessfully in cross-examination to suggest to Bass that animals could have ripped open the trash bag and destroyed Janet's body. But Bass stood firm, saying that while dogs or coyotes would take body parts away from a grave site, it was unlikely that rats and raccoons would join in such behavior.

Jurors also heard from Jose Alberto Sandoval Pulido, a Mexican attorney who testified through an interpreter about a 2001 meeting in Mexico with Perry and another lawyer, Samuel Chavez. He related an incident in which Perry had been angry and threatened Chavez, saying "that if he did not help him, he would do away with us the way he did with his wife."

Andrew Saks, whose wife, Diane, had testified earlier, took the stand to relate the disturbing remarks that Perry had made after Janet's disappearance. "He had commented that he wanted to 'eff' the Levines and 'eff' the Nashville police."

When it was suggested by Massey during cross-examination that perhaps Perry had been handling stress "in an imperceptible way," Saks replied, "It was a very stressful time for all of us. It was such an odd reaction that Perry had, that it devastated me, that it struck me to the core. I was devastated by Perry's lack of concern, in my view, of Janet missing."

Redina Friedman, the guardian appointed by the Chicago court to represent the needs of Sammy and Tzipi, testified that Perry had become openly hostile when she'd recommended that his in-laws get visitation rights with the children. She was also troubled that there had been no pictures of Janet when she'd made a visit in 1997 to Perry's house in Chicago.

Robert Armstrong, the retail manager at Universal Tire in Nashville, testified that he'd sold Perry a brand-new set of tires for his Jeep Cherokee in August 1996, even though he'd informed Perry that the current set was still in good condition. "The tires were in extremely good shape," Armstrong told jurors. "I asked Mr March if he was having any problem with them, and he said he wanted a set of Michelins. I asked if he wanted to keep his old tires, and he said no, he did not want them returned to him."

In an unusual Sunday session, jurors saw three of Perry's fellow inmates take the stand. First up was Cornelius King, who told of his conversations with Perry. As he had when he'd testified three days earlier without the jury present, King told the panel what Perry had told him about "the altercation" with Janet that "got physical," ending with him hitting her with a wrench.

"He said that the body wouldn't be found, because it would be burned to ashes and poured in a lake."

"Did he seem to think that he could beat the case because they couldn't find the body?" Katy Miller, the senior assistant district attorney asked.

"Right," King replied.

Next was Reno Martin, a former Cookeville police officer who'd pleaded guilty to federal drug charges and was in protective custody because he had been a police officer.

Martin's cell was right next to Perry's. He testified that Perry was outraged after a local judge had granted his in-laws temporary custody of his two children. " 'It should have been them that I took care of instead of . . . ' " he quoted Perry as having said.

The inmate testified that Perry's face had turned ashen, "like he couldn't believe what he just said to me."

The defense challenged Martin's testimony. Massey's co-counsel and partner, Lorna McClusky, asked Martin if he had been convicted of selling information previously, and wanted to know if that was what he was now doing in this case, in hopes of getting leniency.

"No," he replied, insisting he was telling the truth.

"So you're the only one who heard these things?" McClusky asked, her voice dripping with sarcasm.

Finally Russell Nathaniel Farris, the 29-year-old star witness, took the stand to testify once more against his next-door jail-mate about the incriminating conversations he had between him and Perry, and between Arthur March and Farris posing as Bobby Givings, that had been surreptitiously tape-recorded.

Before prosecutors began to play the seven hours of tapes, the witness underwent a lengthy and stinging cross-examination by William Massey, obviously trying to break down Farris's story.

"You were looking at up to ninety-nine years in prison, if you were convicted, weren't you?" Massey asked.

"Yes," Farris replied, gazing at his mother, Vickie, seated in the audience. She had already testified that she had warned Lawrence Levine of the plan to kill him and his wife.

"You hated prison and you told Perry that, and you didn't want to go back. Isn't that right?"

"I think so."

Farris was adamant that it was Perry who'd talked to him about his case. But the defense lawyer implied that Farris had taken advantage of Perry by playing on his emotions. Massey's cross-examination of Farris was brutal. "But you came up with the idea of taking the Levines out?" he challenged.

"No, sir," Farris replied. "He brought it up to me. I was trying to make Perry feel comfortable with me. I was going to tell Perry whatever he wanted to hear for him to make my bond. He was going to try and make my bond for me, and he told me about this lady who was going to give him $50,000. Perry never got me out on bond. He did not get me in touch with nobody . . ."

"But you told Perry March that you would kill the Levines?"

"Yes, sir."

"You tried to inflame him and pull him into this deal. You told him he couldn't beat his murder rap with the Levines here?"

"This was his deal. It wasn't my story. I was playing a role," Farris replied.

Farris testified that after deciding not to go ahead with Perry's plan to kill the Levines, he'd gone to his mother and

his attorney before speaking with detective Pat Postiglione.
"They wired me up and I was given some recorders that
were placed in my cell while I was in court," Farris said.

"Perry on his own said the stuff about the Levines," the
would-be hit man testified.

"You pushed Perry . . ."

"No, sir. I was trying to make Perry feel comfortable. I
was trying to let him know that I was on his side."

"You lied to him?"

"Yes, sir. He told me if I killed the Levines, his chances
of beating the murder rap went from forty to ninety percent."

"You told Perry March that he wasn't going to get a fair
trial?"

"Yes, sir."

"Didn't you tell Perry March that the Levines had a hit on
him and he had to get them first?"

"No I didn't."

Most of the day six, August 14, session was taken up with
jurors reviewing the secretly recorded tapes between Farris
and Perry. Before they listened to the tapes, they heard three
witnesses: Kevin Carroll, an investigator with the sheriff's
department who'd helped set up the recording devices in jail
that captured the voices of Perry and Farris talking about
killing his in-laws; Kenneth Sena, the FBI special agent in
Mexico who'd monitored Arthur March's movements and
confronted him at the airport while he was waiting for the
arrival of Farris, aka Bobby Givings; and Sergeant Pat
Postiglione, who talked about Perry's August 2005 arrest
and their airplane conversation.

Postiglione testified that he had arranged for Farris to
record his conversation about plans to kill Janet's parents.
He further explained for jurors the code words used by Perry
and Farris, and between Arthur March and Farris.

In cross-examining Postiglione, Massey asked him if any
other suspects had ever been considered.

"No."

The detective then went through the process of how they
eliminate or "clear" suspects, starting with Janet's inner cir-

cle. "We were never able to clear Perry March, and that is why he remained the main suspect in the case."

"In 2005, did you have any direct proof that Janet March was dead?" Massey asked.

"No," Postiglione answered.

Scott Parsley, the court-appointed legal guardian for Perry's son Sammy took the stand and, out of the presence of the jury, told the court that the 15-year-old youngster was not willing to testify. Instead, it was agreed between the defense and prosecution that taped interviews the boy had given years earlier would be shown to the jury, and that it was to be considered unsworn testimony.

In a taped interview Perry had given in 1997, he indicated that his son had been asleep when Janet left home. "I didn't do anything. My son doesn't remember anything. I'm doing my best to protect him. He's six years old. He was asleep and he's living a nightmare. Leave him alone," Perry told journalist Annette Nole Hall, who worked with the NBC affiliate WSMV-TV, Channel 4.

When NewsChannel 5 interviewed Sammy in Mexico, he was 9, and he remembered vividly his mom walking out of the house in velvet pants and a white shirt and saying goodbye.

"She told me that she'd be back soon. She came in, gave me my good night kiss. She took her bags, went downstairs, got in her car and drove away. I waved to her, she waved to me, then she left," Sammy said.

The unanswered question was whether Sammy had been coached by Perry to give that response.

Sharon Bell was the last prosecution witness to testify. A former client of Perry's, she confirmed that 100 acres of land that she owned in Forest Hills, near his Blackberry Road home, was about to undergo development. It was on Bell's property that Perry had temporarily buried his wife before his father permanently disposed of the body.

After Bell left the witness stand, the prosecution rested their case, having called fifty witnesses to the stand. Now it was the defense's turn to state their case.

17

The Verdict

August 15, 2006, marked the ten-year anniversary of Janet March's disappearance, and the seventh day of Perry's murder trial.

The defense began putting on their case after the lunch recess. In all, they called nine witnesses in less than two hours to testify on Perry's behalf. The first witness to the stand was Robert Jackson, a local attorney practicing divorce law, who testified that on August 27, 1996, Perry had made an appointment to see him, twelve days after Janet disappeared.

Next on the stand was Kyle Sowell, the court deputy probate clerk, who testified that on July 30, 1999, his office had received a pleading, supposedly from Arthur March, with a cover letter accusing Lawrence Levine of murdering his daughter and "covering it completely and trying to pin it on his son, Perry." Since the document was not under oath it went nowhere.

Putting in brief appearances on the stand were four officers from the sheriff's department. Sergeant Sheila Stinson testified about a report that inmate Cornelius King had threatened Perry with bodily harm and, after an investigation, was moved to another area of the jail. Corporal Alicia Baldwin testified that although she was aware of problems between Perry March and Cornelius King, she was not privy to the details of why King was moved from his cell.

The other two officers, Steve Howard and Paul Roberts, who worked at the jail on the fourth floor, where Perry was housed, testified that King had thought he saw ghosts in his cell.

The defense brought on David Roh, another employee at the tire store where Perry had purchased the Michelin tires in 1996. He testified that if Perry had bought four new tires that he didn't need, he would have remembered that. Under cross-examination, Roh said "it's possible, but not probable" that someone else had checked Perry's tires.

After Roh's testimony, and with the jury out of the courtroom, Perry took the stand. "I choose not to testify," he told the judge.

He also let Dozier know that he didn't want his son to testify in the case. "My son has been in far too many courtrooms at his young age. I have no desire to put him into any further light than he has already been put in the past. I do not want my son in this witness stand," Perry said.

However, his lawyers and the prosecution did agree to allow the 1999 interview Sammy had filmed when he was 9, which contradicts an interview he'd given three years before, at the age of 6. In that interview he told a child psychologist he'd been asleep when his mother left the house and that he did not remember anything about her departure.

But in the 1999 exclusive interview, Sammy recalled his mother in her car waving at him, and waving back at her from his bedroom window.

"She told me that she'd be back soon. She took her bags, went downstairs, and went away," jurors heard the boy tell Larry Brinton. "She waved to me when she left. I got out of bed and went to the window to wave to her as she drove off . . . she said she'd be back soon."

After the panel watched the thirty-second clip of the interview, the defense rested its case and the state put on the first of four rebuttal witnesses to discredit Sammy's recollection of whether he'd waved goodbye to his mother the night she disappeared. Carolyn Levine took the stand.

She pointed out in her testimony that she'd gone up to Sammy's bedroom to see if the driver of any car could be seen from his window, and testified it was impossible for her grandson to have seen his mother wave at him.

"I could only see the top, the hood of the car. I couldn't see in the car," she said.

Kim Scott, Sammy's kindergarten teacher, was back on the stand, and recalled how sad Sammy had been after Janet disappeared, because he had not said goodbye to his mother.

Ralla Klepak, a Chicago domestic relations attorney, testified that in 1996, when she'd been appointed by the court during the custody and visitation battle between Perry and his in-laws, Sammy remembered hearing his parents having a "very bad argument." He'd also told Klepak that the morning after the argument, he saw a rolled-up rug at the front door.

With the jury again taken out of the courtroom, the prosecution called as its last rebuttal witness child psychologist Dr. J. D. Woodman. He stated that he'd seen Sammy as a patient twenty-eight times between 2000 and 2001. He testified that the boy had "favored" his father, wanted to please him, and was manipulated by Perry. "Sammy would lie to cover for his father," Woodman told Judge Dozier, who later ruled that his rebuttal testimony would not be presented to the jury.

The prosecution felt that after calling a total of fifty-four witnesses, they had satisfactorily wrapped up their case before the jury.

Defense attorney John Herbison then stood up and renewed their motion seeking a directed verdict of acquittal to the three charges against Perry—murder in the second degree, evidence tampering, and abuse of a corpse—which was promptly rejected by the judge.

The legal wrangling was finally over and the judge said that the jury would begin hearing closing arguments on Wednesday, August 16, the eighth day of the trial.

The courtroom was packed to capacity as Katy Miller began speaking to the jury about the fact that the body of Janet March had never been found. "Can there be any doubt in your mind that she's dead, and that the state has proven that to you? She's dead, and that she was murdered by this man," Miller said, raising her voice and pointing to Perry seated at the defense table.

Miller was very methodical as she went over the testimony during the trial. "What are some of the things you want to look at about how we know that Perry March killed his wife, Janet? His behavior immediately right afterwards. He didn't want the Levines to call the police.

"The first witness you heard from was the mother of the victim in this case, Janet March. Carolyn Levine, her mother, talked about Janet and how they met at the University of Michigan. Her daughter liked him. They eventually came to Nashville where Carolyn and Lawrence Levine paid for his tuition, his books and all of his expenses to attend law school. The Levines could tell their daughter liked him.

"Janet and Perry got married in 1987, and again they were supported by Janet's parents. They gave them a house to live in. Perry March graduated from Vanderbilt law school and got a job at a prestigious law firm. They had a child, Sammy, born in 1990. They had another child, Tzipi, born in 1994. Life was good for Janet and Perry March."

Miller brought out how Janet was a loving and caring mother, and reminded the jury of the testimony of many of Janet's friends. "Would a mother like this miss her son's sixth birthday? Would she miss her son's first day of school?" she asked.

"In 1993 Janet decided she wanted to build a dream house for her children, designing a house they could live in for the rest of their lives, a place where even the Levines could live in case they had to take care of them. That's how big the house was. She spent a lot of time making sure it was perfect. The house was a copy of a French country home, and she primarily designed the house.

"You heard from Dr. Campbell that in 1996 Janet and

Perry had serious marital difficulties. Marilyn Levine had told you earlier that they had mainly problems over finances. She wasn't worried about it, but in 1996 things sharply deteriorated, and they were having heated arguments. They would have to go outside so the kids wouldn't overhear them.

"Things were so bad that Dr. Campbell advised that the couple separate for a while, and Perry March was even spending nights in a motel to get out of the house. But not Janet, that was her house.

"The week prior to Janet's disappearance, that week she was very unhappy, crying every day, crying about the situation with her husband. You heard from Ella Goldshmidt, the nanny, and how the day before she disappeared, she was very upset. She described Janet as 'gray stone-faced,' and that she was, in the room where the computer was, which was very unusual for Janet and that she spent the day at the computer. Something was terribly wrong.

"And of course you heard about the last day in Janet's life. You heard from John Richie, who was working on some counters there, and that Perry had given him tools. And then she disappeared.

"That night Perry March calls four people—Laura Rummel, one of Janet's good friends, to say Janet left. Why would he do that? Why, if you and your spouse had a heated argument and one left, why would you all of a sudden call people and say, 'She's gone, she's left'? He calls his brother and sister, and Larry and Carolyn, and the story he eventually gives the next day with this twelve-day note is that Janet accuses Perry of having a vacation where he spends the night in motels and now she's fed up and says to Perry, says, 'See ya,' and she leaves this note that Perry March needs to do while she's gone, and it's called 'Janet's twelve-day vacation.'

"You heard about how the Levines struggled with what to do about Janet being gone—maybe she has taken a break. But in the back of their mind there is that thought that they just can't embrace.

"Perry didn't want the Levines to call the police. Carolyn Levine said, 'My husband wanted to do it from day one.'

"And then Janet's Volvo is found on September seventh, and they know that something is wrong. It's locked and Tzipi's car seat is in it. All of her possessions are there—her passport, credit cards, makeup, shoes—but no trace of Janet.

"You heard from a lot of her friends, and they painted a picture of Janet for you, and they told you how close they all were. These girls all grew up together, gone to school together, and they were good friends. And as they had their children and raised their family, they saw each other frequently. They gave you some insight into Janet.

"Her children were her life. You heard Diane Saks say that she never went anywhere without Tzipi by her side. You heard Marissa Moody talk about Janet arranging a play date for Sammy and her son Grant. Would a mother like this miss her son's sixth birthday, that she had sent invitations out and planned extensively? Would she have missed her son's first day at school? Would she have missed her son's actual birthday on August twenty-seventh?

"No, she would not leave her family and take the only car seat with her. No, she would not leave her family not knowing who would take care of Sammy and Tzipi. You heard how she would leave notes when she went away. There were no notes left in this case.

"Would she leave the home that she had planned and designed for three years? Her ultimate dream? And then you also heard that the day after she disappeared on August fifteenth, she had made an appointment to go see Lucinda Smith, a divorce attorney, to talk about getting a divorce. Why would she all of a sudden take a twelve-day vacation when she is planning on getting a divorce?

"You heard she was not a good driver and would never have backed into that parking space. The car is locked, but the keys aren't in it. Is this a robbery? Of course it isn't. If it was a robbery, someone would have taken the car, her purse, her credit cards, money. But nothing was taken. No fingerprints were found.

"There was a memorial service held for Janet November seventeenth, 1996. Her husband doesn't appear.

"The police investigate this case and although it is initially investigated as a missing person case, through the ten years, they are not looking for a live person. They are looking for a body. And Mr. Massey cross-examined the police in this case about the different places they looked, and what they did, using helicopters, dogs, following up on every lead they got, whether it was ridiculous, but might have some merit to it.

"You know that Janet came from a prominent family here—but her case was treated like any other case. The police were going to keep looking for her body until they find it.

"We know Janet March is dead because of admissions that Perry March made. We know she's dead because of what Arthur March told you through his sworn deposition that he saw the bones and he made sure they would never be found, and when he put them in that brush pile in Bowling Green, Kentucky, he knew it would be burned up.

"The state has to prove that Perry March killed Janet, based on the evidence that you heard, and for you to reach a conviction on that. What are some of the things you want to look at about how we know that Perry March killed his wife dead? His behavior immediately afterwards. He didn't want the Levines to call police. You heard Carolyn Levine talk about it: 'My husband wanted to call the police from day one, but Perry talked us out of it.' It's Janet's twelve-day vacation note. And as soon as those twelve days is up, they immediately went to police.

"What else did Perry March do that was odd? He said his wife had taken a twelve-day vacation. He calls his dad in Mexico and asks him to come up. He asks Ella Goldshmidt. 'I'm going to need you more now,' he tells her. He goes to an attorney about a divorce. 'Yeah, Perry March came and talked to me about a divorce after Janet disappeared,' the lawyer says. 'But you never heard that he divorced Janet, did you?'

"What else does he do that doesn't make sense? He refers to Janet in the past tense.

"On August twenty-first, he purchased new tires for his Jeep Cherokee from Bobby Armstrong. He testified that the tires were only about fifty percent worn. 'You don't need new tires,' he is told. Why would he do that? Was he afraid that the tire treads might be tracked to places where he had been with that vehicle?

"He moves to Chicago barely a month after his wife is missing. He refuses to let the Levines see their grandchildren. The Levines, who had been helping him, and all of a sudden he cuts them off? He opposes the beneficiary change on Janet's life insurance policy. The Levines want it changed to Janet's estate and children, and he opposes that."

Miller also brought out Perry's demeanor when he gave the deposition in November 1996. "Does he look like someone who is upset? That his wife is missing? The things he says on that deposition—does that sound like someone whose wife is missing and might be dead?

"And when Redina Friedman, the guardian ad litem in Chicago recommends that the Levines be allowed grandparent visitation, Perry March becomes furious with her, and his attitude changes. He talks about disappearing to Singapore, and shortly thereafter he does disappear. In 1999, he moves to Mexico, and the next year gets married . . .

"You heard from Peter Rodman, the witness who told you there is no doubt in his mind that at one-twenty a.m. on August sixteenth, 1996, he was getting home and was parking his car in front of the manager's office at the Brixworth Apartments, and he saw a man on a bike and he got scared. He was acting oddly. He got a good look at him and he told you he was ninety percent sure that the man is Perry March. Mr. Rodman described his big eyes and curly hair.

"You heard from Travis West, the bicycle man who told you how easy it would be to put a mountain bike in the front seat of a Volvo. Perry March was an avid bicycle rider. And you saw pictures of the Volvo and how easy it would be to fit the bicycle in the car.

"You heard from Arthur March. In his deposition where, based on Perry March's description, he would find Janet's body on Sharon Bell's property. You heard her talk about how Perry March was the corporate attorney for her and her husband, and that he knew the property was sold and that somebody could start building a home there at any minute.

"Other proof that we know that Perry March killed his wife, Janet? Admissions and statements he made to other people. Diane Saks, Janet's good friend—Perry March told her, 'Do you think I killed Janet? And put her in the car and left the kids home sleeping?'

"Kim Garbler, the investigator that the Levine family hired. Perry showed her a picture of Janet and said, 'She was beautiful . . .' Also she received a phone call from Perry March when he found out that she had gone to the Brixworth Apartments and was interviewing all the people who lived there. He was outraged: 'Who told you to do that? I want you to fax me a list of everybody you talked to and what they told you.' Why was he so upset about that?

"You heard from Jose Alberto Sandoval Pulido, the Mexican lawyer, about the incident when he had gone to a meeting with Mr. Chavez and they were taking about a business agreement, and Perry March got extremely angry and said 'he would do away with us the way he did away with his wife . . .' And then he said some words in English and Mr. Pulido said he understood the English, it was 'I killed . . .'

"You heard from Cornelius King, another inmate jailed with Perry March, who had related to him that he and Janet had an argument over cheating, and Janet said, ' "I am going to take everything and leave." So he hit her over the head with a wrench and killed her.'

"Mr. King had no idea about the Leigh Reames letters. He had no idea about the evidence that Janet March was collecting to take to her divorce attorney. He had no idea that Arthur March told his son that he had put her in water. That's what Perry thought up until we heard about what Arthur said: that he couldn't find water deep enough until he found the brush pile. But Arthur told Perry he put her in water.

"You heard from Sergeant Postiglione what Perry said coming back on the plane, that he wanted to plead guilty and that he wanted between five and seven years, because 'I don't think my wife will wait around any longer than seven years.' And he said, 'prior to the Janet incident I didn't have any criminal record.' He asked Postiglione that if it was an accident 'would I still be charged with second-degree murder? I didn't wrap Janet in a rug and throw her in an incinerator like everybody says.' Are these the comments of an innocent man?"

Miller brought out Perry's attempt to conspire with Farris to kill his in-laws, saying that his actions were those of "a calculating killer."

"Perry March wanted to kill witnesses in his murder case. 'If they're alive, I've got a forty percent chance of beating the murder rap. But if they're gone, I've got a ninety percent chance of beating it.' "

She brought up the Sammy tapes. "You saw the pictures of the house and the bedroom window. There is no way you can look straight down and see somebody driving a car going underneath that window.

"You heard from his teacher. He was crying, 'My mommy left me. I didn't get to say goodbye.' He was so upset, he wets his pants.

"The law does not allow you to take someone's life because you are angry and having an argument. He also abused a corpse, clearly, the way he disposed of Janet's body, carrying it in the back of his Jeep trunk. There were hair and rug fibers back there. I don't know if it's like in the novel where he wrote about strangling the attractive dark-haired woman and she soiled herself. I don't know if that is what happened to Janet and she was laying on that carpet. I don't know, but you did hear the testimony about a carpet rolled up.

"The destruction of evidence . . . the hard drive that was ripped out of the computer. You heard Perry March talk about that on his deposition. It sure is an enigma to me. Why was the hard drive ripped out? Because Mr. March knew if someone looked at that hard drive, they could figure out that the twelve-day note wasn't written by Janet.

"That's for you to decide. It's for you to decide whether he's guilty and whether or not he's guilty of all the charges. I ask you to find him guilty of all the charges. The cold case squad did a good job. Mr. March has had a fair trial. Decide this case on the evidence and nothing else. I ask you to find him guilty."

After a ten-minute recess, it was up to Bill Massey to convince jurors of his client's innocence.

"It is wrong to allow the Levines unfettered discretion and the use of the Nashville Police Department to chase psychic dreams. It is wrong to charge Perry March with a crime when the police department is still looking for a body in 2005. It is wrong," Massey began.

For nearly two hours, speaking without any notes, Massey paced back and forth in front of the jury box, his hands behind his back, making eye contact with the panel. "The law may say you may prosecute without a body, but you have to have proof. Let's see what the prosecutor has brought you. The government has taken an astounding and long and precarious leap to finding Perry March guilty of a homicide when they can't even show that Janet March is dead. And that is scary, that is frightening.

"Let's look and see some of the things that aren't in dispute. There were difficulties in the marriage—but difficulties are not a homicide. If he wanted to eliminate Janet, why would he be seeing a counselor? You don't need a leap for that. Janet wasn't happy; Perry wasn't happy—to the point the doctor said, 'Maybe you should get away from each other.' Perry had already been doing that, staying at a hotel. And in order to save hotel bills, he got an apartment. Everyone agreed it was a good thing to do.

"But then came August fifteenth, 1996. Janet and Perry had an argument—discussion, whatever you wish to call it—and Janet said, 'I'm leaving,' and she packed her bags and took her toiletries and left. And as she left, her son was looking out the window, and they waved to each other. And Janet March drove out the driveway in the Volvo. None of that is disputed.

"And Perry March is worried about his wife. He had been with her fourteen years. This is the leap the state is trying to get you to make. If that kind of jump can be made, then Perry March doesn't have a chance. He's worried, so he calls his friends. He calls his brother. 'She's taken a twelve-day vacation.' 'She's gone.' Everybody said, 'Chill out.' He calls Carolyn Levine. The state wants you to say that is suspicious conduct. That is ridiculous.

"Carolyn Levine's not worried. 'Let's see what happens in the morning,' she tells him. He tells her about the twelve-day vacation list Janet left. The Levines are worried about their daughter, Perry is worried about his wife, and they all agree to wait. But they want to tell you now that 'Perry March told us not to go to police.' They didn't want to embarrass Janet by calling the police and reporting a missing person. 'She'll come back.'

"Then finally, twelve days go by. What happens at the end of twelve days? Perry goes to see a divorce lawyer. That's undisputed. What does the government say? 'This is a plan.'

"The twenty-ninth came, and Perry March and Larry Levine and Mark Levine all came to the police department. That is undisputable. It is also undisputed that they got a private investigator. On the seventh of September, three weeks after Janet disappeared, her car is found at the Brixworth Apartments. In the Volvo was found the bags that Perry March said that Janet had with her when she took off. When she left, she was angry and she forgot her toothbrush. Did you ever go off on a trip and forget your toothbrush? It's not unusual.

"The Levine family, they were crushed, understandably. This is their daughter. She is not here. Her friends don't know where she is. Perry March doesn't know where she is. But Carolyn Levine says at this point that Perry March has become a suspect to her. Why? Because Janet March didn't pack a bra, so it looked like a man packed the bag. That's a big jump.

"The Levines couldn't accept the uncertainty that Janet left and got into trouble elsewhere. They couldn't accept that. They had to have an answer, and the only thing they

⟨⟨illegible⟩⟩ come up with to Perry March. Within thirty days of Janet's disappearance, Perry has become a suspect—and he is becoming offended by it. Can anyone blame him one bit for that? 'You think I killed Janet? I don't think so. I've been cooperating with all this all along.'

"And the police come with a search warrant on September seventeenth, and Detective David Miller calls on heat-seeking helicopters to search for Janet, and has thirty to forty police academy trainees covering this property. Miller said it was the most extensive search, and three Blackberry Road was searched down to its toes. You know what was found? Perry March's fingerprints from his house. And that is a fact. You don't have to jump to get that.

"Then, when Mr. March moved to Chicago to remove himself from the circled wagons of the Levines, Perry takes his two children with him. They follow him there and they bring suit up there, and eventually Perry visits his dad in Mexico and moves to Mexico with his children.

"There has been one resounding theme throughout this case: no body, no body, no body."

Massey pointed out that police had looked for Janet for ten years. "They have followed psychic leads. And police have found no evidence of Janet's body."

Carolyn and Larry Levine sat stone-faced as Massey ripped into the government case. He produced several poster boards listing names of lakes, rivers, quarries, parks, and buildings where police had searched for Janet.

And then Massey attacked key prosecution witness Peter Rodman. "Remember him? He is the guy that said some sensational things. He tells one of his policeman friends, Mike Smith, that back in August 1996, he saw a man on August sixteenth at one-thirty in the morning with short hair wearing a jogging suit, and this is the government proof. Rodman is flaky. His testimony does not rise to the proof without a reasonable doubt that it could be Perry.

"So now the case is brought before the grand jury and an indictment is returned, and Perry March is arrested. This is what they had.

"And then they said, 'Janet didn't back cars into spots.' That's the government proof? They assumed it was Janet. Maybe it wasn't Janet. Because Janet doesn't back a car in, is that proof?

"And then Perry March is brought back to Nashville. He's on a plane speaking to a seasoned detective. Both want information from one another. He said he was 'scared shitless.' He was trying to find out what they have, and when Postiglione won't tell him what they have, Perry says, 'okay, I'll plead guilty. Tell me what you've got.'

"Then, after they get Perry back to Nashville, they put him next to a snitch who is aware of Perry March's situation. This is probably the most important piece of evidence that the government has: the tapes between Nathaniel Farris and Perry March.

"You listen to the tapes. And you'll see that Farris is pushing Perry. Perry told Nathaniel Farris, 'When you get out, you delay . . . until I give you the green light.' But Nathaniel Farris didn't delay. He went right in and talked to Arthur March about getting a silencer and everything.

"When their case is finished, you should see a puzzle where the pieces fit together. That has not been done at all. The government wants you to make an astounding and long and precarious leap to find Perry March guilty of a homicide where they can't even show that Janet March is dead.

"Those tapes have to do with a man who has had his family stripped from him, removed from him, his policies taken and frozen, every aspect of his life made a nightmare. They want to show this and say to you, 'Look, look . . . he's just a bad guy.'"

After another short recess, it was Thurman's turn to start his rebuttal to the defense argument. For fifty-five minutes, Thurman hit back at Massey's acerbic remarks attacking the prosecution's case. "If the Levines are so rich and powerful, why did it take his office eight years to bring the charges against Perry?" he asked.

Thurman blasted the defense for raising "this Clyde

~~Pumper teams on a whole support miner man Perry March~~
It's what we call a red herring. Who is he? A person who
worked at the March residence a year before, in 1995. We
brought him in and he gave us two different statements, but
we cleared him.

"You heard from Dr. Campbell about the last meeting
Perry March and Janet had. That it was extremely volatile.
And what was Janet March doing? She had an envelope with
her name on it, and inside were those letters.

"She had found those letters and told Perry March, 'You
better come home early.' She was going to a divorce attorney
the next day. That night she confronted him. They had a fight
and he killed her. Talk about Perry's behavior afterward. . . . !
He went to a divorce lawyer twelve days later—covering his
tracks, maybe?

"You see him in that video clip where he says, 'No, we
didn't really discuss divorce . . . it was a rather benign evening." He really didn't think his wife would be gone more
than a couple of days at most. Maybe one day. Well, why
does he have his dad driving three days from Mexico to get
here? What if Janet comes back the next day? Why does he
need help when the Levines live nearby, and always cared
for the children when Janet was not available? He needed his
good old dad, the one man he could depend on to do his
dirty work and clean up the mess.

"Mr. Massey talked about Perry March's level of cooperation. What was his level of cooperation? He gave one written statement to police and was extremely nervous doing it.
As soon as he starts suspecting that maybe the police aren't
buying his story, as soon as he knows they are going to get
his hard drive, it's over. The hard drive is gone and the next
day, he is gone. That's the end of his cooperation.

"Another thing you heard a lot about was the Levines
having a court order in Chicago for visitation. You heard
from Redina Friedman that Perry took off rather than have
the Levines see the children and take a chance that they
might talk to the police. And then he took off to Mexico.

"Don't be trapped into thinking there is no direct evidence.

You heard those tapes. You heard Perry March say, 'I'm so excited . . . I've been praying for weeks . . .' He wants to say those talks weren't serious? And he made that extra step by calling his father and said, 'Yes, talk to this man . . . Listen to this man [meaning Farris] . . . Cooperate with this man.' And when his father calls back and says, 'It's going down next week,' he didn't say a word about stopping it. He said he didn't give the green light? He is not guilty of murder? He says it's wrong for you to consider this as evidence? Well it's not. So why is it important evidence? Because the law allows you to infer guilt from the fact that a person attempted to kill a witness just to destroy evidence. Is that the action of an innocent person—to kill witnesses?

"It is not wrong for you to consider that. It's very strong evidence. That's what the judge will tell you."

Walking over to a projector and using poster boards, he showed jurors that they did have direct evidence. "Yeah, we've got circumstantial evidence, but we've got direct evidence. Peter Rodman saw something that's direct evidence. He saw Perry March. Arthur March testified he saw Janet March's bones in a bag. That's direct evidence. You heard people testify that Perry March made statements that he killed Janet March. That is direct evidence. So don't be trapped into believing that because this is a circumstantial case, that you can't convict."

Thurman then listed twenty-three reasons for jurors as to why Janet March was dead. Using a PowerPoint presentation, he noted that "no one disputes that she was a wonderful mother, a caring mother, a mother who never leaves her children. Her family. How close-knit they were. How often they talked, how they interacted. Would she walk away from them? Her home? She spent a year on this beautiful home. There was not a single financial transaction from her bank account. Her purse, her ID and credit cards, are found. Is she going to leave and not take her purse? No legitimate sighting of Janet March. Her appointment with her divorce lawyer the day before she disappeared that she never canceled or kept. The play date Perry March had no clue she made for her son outlive to the day she disappeared. If she was going to leave, she would have told him. The twelve day note that she typed on the computer. But on the tenth day was Sammy's birthday party, but Perry March probably didn't realize that. Janet had already sent out invitations, and he isn't aware of that, so he writes a twelve-day note."

Thurman reminded jurors about the missing items in Janet's suitcase when the Volvo was found, telling the panel that Janet would never have forgotten to pack a toothbrush, hairbrush or bras. The prosecutor then brought out other significant testimony—the missing hard drive, the missing rug, Perry suddenly changing the tires on his Jeep five days after Janet disappeared, and his move to Chicago thirty days after she was gone. "Arthur March told you under oath that Janet March is dead and he disposed of her body. And Peter Rodman saw Perry March on a bicycle at the Brixworth Apartments where Janet's Volvo was found.

"Mr. Massey wants to let you think that Peter Rodman is some publicity-seeking guy. What was the testimony? That he has never given a single interview in ten years. That he was reluctant to come forward. Yet, we know that Perry March was an avid bike rider. He spoke of the direction he came from, up the hill, right where the Volvo was. He spoke of the jogging suit. Perry March had jogging suits. Rodman gave a description, it was a man with curly hair, in his thirties, big eyes . . ."

Thurman urged jurors to look at the crime-scene photos taken at the Blackberry Road home "right after he killed Janet March. You will see dust, footprints on the door coming out of the doorway. Footprints coming out sideways. They are very consistent with a person carrying something." Thurman suggested to the jury that the foot print pattern was caused by Perry dragging Janet's body to the back of his Jeep.

"So what did he do with the body right after he killed Janet? Look at the back of his Jeep," Thurman said, showing jurors enlarged photos on the screen. "You've got the fiber of Janet's hair. You can see the fiber there. We know she was put in a leaf bag. He probably found the remnants of a rug and dragged her body out to the Jeep. Look at the back of the Jeep. You can see the fiber there. We found the fiber of a rug. You can almost see the outline of a body in the bag.

"Where is he to go? Right over to the property he is familiar with, Sharon Bell's property. He represents her. He feels comfortable there. If someone stops him, he can say, 'I'm the attorney for Sharon Bell. I'm over here checking something out.' He puts the body where Arthur March said he found it. Perry was getting nervous they are going to start construction and he knew he had to move the body."

Thurman went over passages from Perry's @*murder.com* novel, asking the jurors, "What kind of a person writes that shortly after his wife disappears? Is that something you write? Or is that something that happened to Janet March?"

The prosecutor also reminded them that Perry had driven Janet's car to the Brixworth Apartments and backed it in so nobody would see the license tag. Pointing to an exhibit photo, he asked them to notice how far back the passenger seat is. "It's so far back because that is where he put his mountain bike, right in that seat. And that purse? Now is any woman going to put her purse like that—upside down, stuck in that pocket? I don't think so. What he did was, he stuck that purse there and was later going to put it in the passenger seat, but his bike was there and he forgot about the purse.

"Not many people would think that you would be a skeleton that quickly, but Dr. Bass corroborates what Arthur March said about Janet's body [—it] had skeletonized as a result of the heat in the few weeks she had been buried.

"We will never know what Perry March did in the two weeks before police began to investigate the case. Did he pour Clorox over Janet? We don't know, because there was never a crime scene if you clean up the blood. He had asked Arthur March to dispose of the hard drive. He had already cleaned up the driveway, but he had Arthur go out there and clean it again with Clorox. Perry said it was such a loud argument that he and Janet had that they went outside to argue so it wouldn't upset the children. It's very likely that he killed her outside. Or there could have been blood that leaked out as he was moving her body.

"It's been ten years that this man hasn't been held accountable for his actions on August fifteenth, 1996. This case has been called the Perry March case, but it's also the Janet March case. It's about her life and the memory she did not get to make and the experiences she didn't get to experience.

"You can't decide this case on sympathy or emotions for her. But you can do justice. It was ten years yesterday, ten years that this man should be held accountable for his actions on August fifteen, 1996. Ten years for me to stand here and ask you for justice for Janet March and each of you in your heart, in your mind, you know what that is. You know what justice is, and I just ask you to have the courage to return that verdict."

It was a powerful summation. Lawrence, Carolyn, and Mark Levine sat stoically in the courtroom as Thurman summed up, fighting hard to keep their emotions in check. Perry on the other hand, appeared bored, doodling on paper and yawning as if to let the jury know that Thurman's remarks were meaningless.

After Thurman sat down, Judge Dozier recessed for lunch. When court resumed an hour later, he instructed the panel about the law. He defined *reasonable doubt*. That it does not signify a mere skeptical condition of the mind. That it was a doubt based on reason and common sense. That it means that the proof must be so conclusive and complete that all doubt is removed from the mind of an ordinary person.

He explained to jurors in detail the elements needed to convict Perry of second-degree murder. He also told the panel that they could find Perry guilty of the lesser crime of voluntary manslaughter, reckless homicide, or criminally negligent homicide.

"To convict of second-degree murder, the state must prove beyond a reasonable doubt two elements: one, that the defendant unlawfully killed a person, and, two, that the person acted knowingly," the judge said. He also explained to the panel the definitions of abuse of a corpse and tampering with evidence, and what was required for jurors to find Perry guilty on each of those crimes. He also reminded the panel that an indictment is neither evidence nor proof of guilt.

The judge informed the jury that if they found Perry not guilty of second-degree murder, they could then consider the lesser offenses. The jury was never told that Perry had been convicted in June of charges stemming from the plot to kill Janet's parents.

And he told them they must not consider the fact that Perry did not testify and that his not testifying should not enter into their deliberations.

At 2:15 p.m. the jury was charged and walked past Perry and his lawyers. The alternates were dismissed with the thanks of Judge Dozier. Once out of the courtroom, the jurors were led down the hallway to a small, rather nondescript, skimpily furnished room where they would discuss the case for the first time.

No sooner were the jurors out of the room than sheriff's officers handcuffed Perry and removed him from the courtroom, placing him in a nearby holding cell on the sixth floor.

For six hours on Wednesday, the jurors talked about the case, but could not reach a verdict.

On Thursday, August 17, day nine, the jury resumed its deliberations and sent out a note asking to review the testimony of two witnesses: Jose Sandoval Pulido, the Mexican lawyer who'd accused Perry of threatening to kill him, and Cornelius King, who'd testified that Perry told him he had killed Janet.

With that, the jurors went back to the jury room while the lawyers paced the hallways outside the courtroom. When lunchtime passed without another note from the jury, the tension for Perry, locked in a holding cell, began to build. The consensus among courthouse observers was that it was going to be a long deliberation. Herbison and Massey went back to Perry's cell to speak to their client.

"We didn't want to give Perry any false hope," Herbison

said. We talked a little a lot about the potential issues that could be raised on appeal should there be a conviction. Perry seemed pretty upbeat and expressed his appreciation to all of us as we waited for the verdict. We tried encouraging him that the case went well, but that he should be ready for anything.

"'Don't show any emotion when the verdict comes in. Stay cool. If we get a bad result, we'll just appeal it. Don't react one way or the other.'"

Awaiting the jury's decision was a horrible time for the Levines, who had gathered at one end of the hallway, talking among themselves and with friends, trying to be calm as they waited to hear whether there would be justice for their daughter. The Marches, on the other hand—Perry's brother and sister and her husband—decided not to attend the last day of the trial.

What the Levines didn't know as the hours dragged on was that the jury was hard at work, discussing every aspect of the case, voting, and making progress. But it must have crossed their minds as they sat on those hard benches in the hallway—what if there was a mistrial? Can we go through this again? And worse: What if Perry is acquitted?

Then in the afternoon, the jurors sent a third note, asking for clarification about the law surrounding "voluntary manslaughter," which is an intentional killing committed under circumstances that mitigate the homicide, although they do not justify it. The classic example is that of a husband who comes home and finds his wife in bed with another man and kills both of them.

Although Dozier did not give jurors an example to guide them, he explained the nature of that crime.

Finally, at 4:30 p.m. on Thursday, after deliberating for thirteen hours over two days, the jury foreperson signed the final note to the judge.

The foreperson pushed a buzzer twice, signaling to court officers outside the jury room that a unanimous verdict had been reached. The sound of the buzzer reverberated to the outside of Courtroom 6A on the sixth floor where, in a few

moments, the decision by the jury would end a ten-year saga
for the Levines, the detectives, and the prosecutors.

As word quickly spread throughout the floor and then
the building that the March jury had voted on all three
counts of the indictment, the crowd rushed in and scram-
bled for seats.

The front row of the spectator section was taken up, behind the prosecutors, with Detectives Pat Postiglione and
Bill Pridemore, and other police officers who had worked on
the case.

Postiglione and Pridemore admitted they were nervous,
even though they had been in countless courtroom situations.

"You never know with a jury," Postiglione said, recalling
that fateful day. "You just can't tell with a jury. They come
back into the courtroom, your heart is pounding, your hands
are sweating. You're watching the foreman, the jury. Are
they looking at us? Are they looking at the defendant? Are
they looking at the floor and avoiding eye contact all together? Ten years comes down to ten seconds."

Nearby in the room sat the Levines—Larry, Carolyn, and
Mark.

All eyes focused on the door behind the defense table,
waiting for Perry to make his appearance in the courtroom.
As he walked in the room, a hush fell over the wood-paneled
room, leading from the holding cell.

"This is it," Herbison told his client.

The tension in the room mounted as everyone sat motionless, staring at Perry and waiting anxiously for the jury to
come in and let the world know his fate.

"We have received a note from the jury. They have
reached a verdict," Judge Dozier said. He then addressed
Perry and those in the courtroom, reminding them that there
was not to be an outburst of any sort until after the jury had
rendered its verdict and left the courtroom. Dozier warned
that any spectator who created a disturbance would be removed.

One by one, the twelve-member panel walked to their

mainland coots, never once looking at Perry, their eyes focused on the floor.

It was not a good sign for Perry that the jury didn't look at him. Traditionally, when jurors avoid looking at a defendant, it's an indication that the verdict is guilty.

With the jury seated, Judge Dozier asked that Perry stand while the foreman read the verdict.

"We the jury," the foreman intoned, "find the defendant, Perry Avram March, as to count one, guilty of second-degree murder."

Without interruption, the foreman went on to find Perry guilty of the second and third count of the indictment: abuse of a corpse and evidence tampering.

Perry stood stoically at the defense table, in stunned silence, never blinking an eye. It felt, in some ways, like an anticlimax. Carolyn stared at the jury, and then looked at Perry. While she and Larry had never made eye contact with Perry during the trial, preferring to sit in their seats with poise and confidence, Carolyn did glare at him as the verdict was read. And there was a glimmer of satisfaction on her face as he was found guilty.

Once Perry was led swiftly out a side door to be taken to his jail cell, the scene inside the courtroom turned to bedlam as friends and relatives hugged and kissed and breathed a sigh of relief that justice had, at long last, been served.

For the first time since it had all begun ten years earlier, the Levines spoke publicly as cameras and microphones were stuck in their faces.

Larry Levine read a prepared statement after Carolyn hugged Thurman and Miller. "On behalf of my wife, Carolyn, and my son, Mark, I would like to express our profound gratitude to Tom Thurman . . . who continuously gave us hope justice would be pursued for Janet over ten years." They also thanked a long list of law enforcement officers "for their excellent work over many long hours, months, and years, too, to find Janet and the cause of her death."

Tom Thurman was pleased with the outcome. He explained to the media why he had finally decided to indict

Perry when they did. It was the fear that witnesses might begin to lose memory of the incident, or even die.

What Thurman found most compelling was seeing Perry's father testify against his own son, though he was disappointed that Perry did not take the stand to testify in his own defense.

Katy Miller was "just so happy for the Levines."

"It's been a long tough case for everyone involved," Massey said after the verdict. He said that the taped conversations between Russell Farris and Perry were by far the most damaging pieces of evidence.

"If you had Cornelius King alone, that's one thing. If you had Reno Martin alone, that's one thing, But the prosecutors didn't rely on either of those men. The combined testimony of Farris and Arthur March was too difficult to overcome."

John Herbison's assessment was right on target. "Perry was brought here with a weak case. The state built much of its case after Perry was back in Nashville."

Even though there was a conviction, the Levines struggled to find closure. Janet's body has never been recovered. "For the Levines, there's still that void," Detective Bill Pridemore said. "Hopefully some day we can fill that void."

As for Perry, after becoming a Christian a few weeks earlier, he wasted no time in converting back to Judaism. Detective Postiglione chalked up Perry's latest antic to trying to manipulate the system. "If you are able to convince the Tennessee Department of Correction you are a practicing Jew, it can send you to certain prisons. But I don't think any prison is good," he said.

"I think Perry is a sociopath. I believe he has no conscience. I don't believe he has any remorse whatsoever. He attempted to manipulate me on the airplane. And that's what he's doing now."

Peter Rodman, a key witness, also spoke out after the verdict. "He kind of twisted things around, but he liked to do that with all the witnesses," Rodman said, calling Perry "a punk."

"He's worse than a punk, really. He's a punk with a sense

of entitlement. As though you have an argument with your wife, you're entitled to abuse her.

Two weeks after his conviction, Perry wasn't about to let bygones be bygones with the Levines. The disbarred lawyer filed a handwritten lawsuit against his former father-in-law's law firm, saying he was owed money from working there.

In the eight-page lawsuit, with the return address listed as the Metro Jail, he demanded that the firm of Levine, Mattson, Orr & Geracioti provide him with a complete accounting of all funds and bank accounts that bear his name.

With the guilty verdict, there was good news and bad news for the Levines. The good news was that, as a convicted felon, all Perry's rights as a parent were stripped away—no amount of lawsuits would change that, and the children would remain with their grandparents. The bad news was that it wouldn't prevent Perry from continuing to file lawsuit after lawsuit against them while in prison.

18

The Sentencing

Perry sat at the defense table in his yellow prison jump-suit, scribbling notes, cracking jokes with his lawyers, scheming, and looking smug. Not even the clerk's solemn pronouncement to those assembled, around one o'clock that afternoon, to "All rise," signaling that Judge Steve Dozier was about to preside over the sentencing, could move him to respectfully stand.

Courtroom 6A was packed with police officers, detectives, and members of the district attorney's office who, for ten long years, had worked on bringing justice for Janet and putting her killer away for the crime.

Seated in the audience were many of Janet's friends, her parents, and her brother, Mark.

But before the sentence could be imposed, it was time for Carolyn, Lawrence, and Mark Levine to make known their feelings about Perry in their victim impact statements, which would tell about the years of devastating grief they had suffered as a family. In a departure from the norm, it was ultimately decided not to have them read their statements, which were instead submitted as part of Perry's official sentencing record, and would follow him over the years while in prison.

Lawrence and Carolyn Levine wrote:

In taking the life of their mother, Perry March deeply scarred his own children for the rest of their lives . . . it was shocking to think that Perry could be so depraved. But there was no time to mourn Janet then. We were concerned for her children, our grandchildren, who had lost their wonderful mommy.

There are no adequate words to describe the immeasurable pain and suffering we have endured over the past ten years—the bitter tears, sleepless nights, the sharp curtailing of our social and community life, and the kind of grief and anger that tears at one's soul.

Before he murdered her, Perry was emotionally and psychologically abusive to Janet for more than five years. She finally confided in us, and for hours, weeks and months, we listened to her tear-filled stories. By the summer of 1996, she could tolerate it no longer and finally asked Carolyn to go with her to see a divorce lawyer. Instead Perry March took her young life, the mother of his two children, and cruelly encouraged Sammy and Tzipi to believe that their mother had run away, abandoned them, and was still alive somewhere and that their grandparents were evil.

Perry threatened that if we did not 'call off the f— king police' his words, of course, we would never see our grandchildren again. Later on, he offered us visitation, but only for a steep price. He wanted one half of our property, he wanted Janet's property, and he wanted all the children's assets that Janet had set aside for them. We refused and had to resort to legal action.

Janet's brother, in his statement, wrote:

Who can doubt Perry March is a sociopath? He has no conscience and no concern for anyone but himself. His arrogance and cruelty to my parents and to his own children is legendary.

Saying that Perry "created a reign of terror for many, many families and small children," Mark went on in his statement to reveal that

> *Janet's murder fundamentally changed all of our lives. For me, there will always be a sense of guilt. Janet told me in no uncertain terms in June 1996 that Perry had told her twice, "I will kill you." And while Perry's threats upset me so much, I angrily told my parents about them, I unfortunately dismissed the comments as the bitterness couples express when they are on the verge of divorce.*

Massey went through Mark's statement with a pencil, objecting to several remarks, which he called "inappropriate," such as his rhetorical question in calling Perry "a sociopath."

First to speak as the proceeding got underway was Tom Thurman, the lead prosecutor who, because of his tenacious handling of the case for nearly ten years, was nicknamed "the Thurmanator."

Thurman did not mince words with the judge. He told him that Perry March was a dangerous offender who had led a life of crime since killing his wife ten years earlier, and should be sentenced to the maximum under the law for his crimes.

Bill Massey, Perry's lawyer, asked Dozier to consider Perry's background. He was well-educated, had always held a steady job, had never been in trouble before, and had been lured into the plot to do away with Carolyn and Lawrence Levine by Russell Nathaniel Farris. The lawyer proposed that Perry should not even get 20 years, because that would mean he would be 65 or 70 years old before he could get out of prison. Massey's suggestion was that Perry should be given a lesser sentence.

Dozier listened intently to his arguments and when Massey had stopped his effusive rhetoric, went for the jugular, crushing any semblance of hope that Perry would make it out of prison before he was 80.

We have someone who has committed a murder, committed a theft, moves out of the country and when is brought back, begins planning other murders. You don't set out to kill witnesses if you're not guilty of murder.

"It appears to the court that he has no positive thoughts or kind thoughts about anyone involved in this case other than himself. He has some strange audacity to pray to God about assisting in the conspiracy to kill the Levines. In terms of this whole case in general, it's often said that of those who have much, much is required," Dozier said before imposing sentence.

He continued about Perry's time in the Nashville jail and his plot to have Farris kill his in-laws. "That sort of nonchalant attitude toward killing two people, in the court's opinion, is what a dangerous offender is meant under the statute and case law. But it's not just two people. It's the grandparents of your own children. This is occurring after he had already killed his wife."

And what disturbed Dozier was Perry's lack of genuine remorse.

Perry may have thumbed his nose at Dozier before the sentencing started, but it didn't deter the judge from socking it to the defendant standing before him.

All eyes in the courtroom shifted to Perry. Judge Dozier asked: "Perry March, is there anything you wish to say before sentencing?"

His lawyers had prompted Perry not to respond when asked that question, since an appeal was planned, and they didn't want him saying anything on the record that could later be used against him.

"No, Your Honor," he said quietly.

With that, Dozier handed Perry the full 25 years for the second-degree murder of Janet; another 7 years for tampering with evidence and abuse of the corpse; 24 more years for conspiring to kill the Levines; and 5 years on the theft charges that would run concurrent with the other sentences. In total, 56 years, and Perry would be eligible for parole in three decades—around the year 2040.

While there were no loud cheers in the courtroom, the sentence did not come as a surprise to Perry or his lawyers, who'd expected Dozier to give him about 60 years.

When it was over, Perry was led quickly out of the courtroom and back to the Metro Jail, his home for the last year. His next stop would be the Charles Bass Correctional Complex near the Riverbend prison in Nashville, where for thirty days he would undergo both medical and mental evaluations before being assigned to a state prison facility.

Outside the courtroom, there were smiles all over. It was now a time to heal. Thurman was delighted at the sentence. "Finally justice has been done. I think it's a very fair sentence and richly deserved, and is based on the facts and the law."

"We've waited for a long time for this day. Janet was a loving daughter, a devoted mother, a caring sister, and a good friend," Carolyn Levine said, reading from a prepared statement on behalf of her family.

" 'Happy' is not the appropriate word to describe our feelings. I don't feel happy. We're pleased with the verdict, but I'm also very sad. Sad that our former son-in-law and the father of our grandchildren . . ." she started to break up. "I regret that I didn't recognize his darker side sooner.

"Although it is their mother who should be raising them and giving them her loving guidance, we hope we can help them grow into adults in the way that Janet should have."

Bill Massey took the sentence meted out to Perry in stride. "He expected a heavy sentence and so it did not come as a surprise. He is looking forward to his appeal. This system will vindicate him."

As for the lengthy prison term, the lawyer anticipated no problems for his client. "I think he will cope. Perry's a fighter, and he'll adapt."

And Tennessee Correction Commissioner George Little let it be known that when Perry is moved to the state prison system, he won't be getting any special privileges. "Mr. March will be treated as any other inmate coming into the system."

"I'm gratified to see him get what we always suspected he deserved," Pat Postiglione, lead detective with Bill Pridemore, said. "His smirking and laughing thirty seconds before his sentence was imposed is incredible. He's never shown the first second of remorse to us. He really doesn't get it. But now he's getting ready to meet the real world in terms of prison life. He has no idea what he is in for."

Bill Pridemore noted that Perry was "eligible for parole in thirty years."

"But that doesn't mean he'll get out in thirty years," Postiglione added, "because we'll be around to voice our opinion as to whether he needs to be back into society or not."

Postiglione believes that inmates he comes in contact with should be cautious of getting too close to Perry in prison. "He thinks he can manipulate the inmates. This has been his modus operandi from day one. He thinks he can manipulate whoever he comes into contact with, be it his family or other inmates. In the conspiracy case, he tried to manipulate the inmates, and I'm here to say that's not going to happen."

With Perry on his way to state prison, the focus turned to his father, who was set to be sentenced nine days later.

Days before the September 15 date, the Levines' victim impact statement was leaked to the media, in which they refer to Arthur March as a "despicable human being" who not only had shown no remorse, but who had expressed regret that he himself did not succeed in killing them. While Arthur's attorney, Fletcher Long, wouldn't publicly comment on the leaked letter, it did appear to court observers that the Levines were attempting to derail the plea deal presented to U.S. District Judge Todd Campbell back in February.

In the agreement between defense attorneys and federal prosecutors, Arthur was to get an 18-month prison term, followed by three years' probation in exchange for his testimony in Perry's conspiracy murder-for-hire trial and at his murder trial.

But when sentencing day rolled around, Campbell made an about-face: he threw the book at Arthur. His sentence was tripled, even though Arthur had effectively made the case against his son. He gave the 78-year-old former pharmacist a 5-year sentence for his role in conspiring with Perry.

Fletcher Long was outraged. "When we first presented the deal on February seventh, 2006, Judge Campbell was shown the eighteen-page plea agreement and didn't say a word. He had no problem with the deal. But he waits until sentence day, after Arthur has cooperated, after he has testified in state court, after he has given up his son and given information that led to his conviction and now tells us Arthur can withdraw his guilty plea and go to trial.

"That is unacceptable. The federal government reneged on its deal. Arthur lived up to his end of the deal. On February seventh, Arthur hadn't cooperated and hadn't testified in open court. For the judge to call us in on September fifteenth and then use Arthur's cooperation against him is wrong. In the proffer process, Arthur was supposed to be completely honest and not leave out anything. For the judge to now say that the conduct by Arthur is too serious and that he cannot ignore the violent nature of his crime so he can't give him eighteen months defies belief.

"The judge didn't learn anything new on September fifteenth. The only new fact was that Arthur had cooperated and that it had led to Perry's conviction.

"Arthur saw it all go down, and he predicted it. 'The Levines are too wealthy and too powerful. They'll never let me get eighteen months,' he told me before sentencing."

When the deal with Arthur went south, he said to his lawyer, "I've been fucked. I've been fucked. I told you that Carolyn Levine ran the Jewish Mafia. They've gotten to the judge. I knew they'd never let me get 18 months."

"At the sentencing hearing, Larry Levine got up and was about to cry as he read his statement," Long recalled.

Your Honor, I know the government made a deal in order to get Perry March. But they say "The apple does not fall far from the tree." We believe that Perry March's sociopathology stems from his father, Arthur March. He is a despicable human being. The crime for which Arthur March has been convicted was apparently the third time he had tried to kill us. In 2000, when we were in Mexico, he personally threatened us and our son Mark by shouting at us, "You'll never get out of Mexico alive." Then after the Mexican police left the scene, Arthur March, armed with a forty-five-caliber gun, chased our car at high speed.

Levine told the judge that he, his wife, and his grandchildren, who were all in the car, were lucky to have lost Arthur in the streets of Guadalajara

because he later publicly admitted that had he caught us, he might well have killed us. The FBI warned us to leave Mexico immediately, but not by way of Guadalajara because Arthur and Perry March had probably sent people there who were "armed and dangerous to get us."

Levine reminded the judge that he'd learned of the second plot during the conspiracy murder trial when Perry had bragged to Farris that his father hired mercenaries to murder him.

Arthur March is a frighteningly dangerous man. He has no remorse for trying to murder us. His only regret is that he did not succeed. We believe this sentence is far too light, given the plots against us, the crimes to which Arthur March has already confessed to.

As long as Arthur March is alive and out of prison, we will understandably fear for our lives and the lives of our family.

Did Larry Levine have something to do with Judge Campbell changing his mind? Fletcher Long is convinced that he did. "How do you say that Larry Levine didn't have something to do with it? The Levines were consulted throughout the plea deal process. They have to be. I've been told that by Tom Thurman. The Levines didn't like the deal, but they agreed that it had to be made in order to get the bigger fish. And for them to stand up at sentencing and whine and cry and say they are scared for their safety and that if Arthur gets out they are scared he may kill them and that they want him to get as long a sentence as possible, is nothing more than old-fashioned going back on your bargain . . .

"What Arthur did for Perry was deplorable. But the government made a deal and broke their word. Arthur handled himself with tremendously more honor than the government."

Paul O'Brien, the assistant U.S. attorney, was understandably upset by Judge Campbell's decision, but he noted, "the judge saw otherwise and we respect his decision. It happens. I can tell you as a prosecutor, it's happened to me before. It's happened in the past and that's just the nature of plea agreements."

There are many in Nashville who believe that Judge Campbell proved that a prosecutor's deal is not necessarily a final deal and that he has the legal authority to toss such agreements out the window. There are others who feel that, given Larry Levine's clout with the Democratic Party, politics played a major role in scuttling Arthur March's plea agreement.

Arthur looked terrible at his sentencing. To his lawyer it seemed he was at death's door. "He was gaunt, he was brought into the courtroom in a wheelchair, he was unsteady on his feet. In the short year he was in custody he had aged twenty years and looked more like he was ninety-three rather than seventy-eight."

On Friday, October 6, Arthur was transferred from the Grayson County Detention Center at Leitchfield, Kentucky, to the Texas Federal Medical Facility which was formerly known as the Fort Worth Medical Center.

His projected prison release date was May 15, 2010. But

his serious medical problems persisted at the Fort Worth prison, a low-security facility for inmates with medical needs. And there, on Thursday, December 21, Arthur died of "respiratory failure" after serving 3 months of his 5-year sentence.

"If you take away a man's reason to get up in the morning and live, his condition can deteriorate rapidly. I think that's what happened. He had a lot of life experiences that made him very interesting to talk to. He certainly didn't like the Levines. What you saw with Arthur was what you got," attorney Long said.

"He didn't make it a habit to sit around and cry over spilled milk, blame his son. Arthur loved his children, unconditionally. He thought of Perry as kind of a ne'er-do-well, naïve, unsophisticated, unsavory individual that he always had to come behind him to clean up."

Three days after he died, Arthur was buried at a graveside service in Beth El Cemetery in Portage, Indiana, with Perry's brother and sister in attendance. Since it is against Tennessee Department of Correction policy to allow inmates to attend funeral services, Perry remained in his cell.

19

Epilogue

In October 2006, Perry was moved to the Northwest Correctional Complex, one of the toughest prisons in Tennessee, near Tiptonville, about 120 miles west of Nashville. Perry exchanged his familiar yellow jumpsuit, signifying that he was in protective custody, for a blue shirt and dark blue pants to indicate he was a state prisoner.

He shaved his head, grew a beard and set to work in his 8-foot-by-10-foot cell filing lawsuit after lawsuit. In one of his many handwritten scribbled documents to Judge Dozier, he complained he didn't have access to a computer, the law library, and a copy machine. He also demanded that Dozier assign a lawyer to his Mexican wife, Carmen, and that the attorney meet with the judge. Lawrence Levine responded by reminding Perry that prison wasn't Club Med.

Sammy and Tzipi had remained in Mexico until shortly after their father was deported in August 2005. The deportation order that expelled Perry from Mexico for ten years also included his two children.

The deportation order further directed the Mexican authorities to turn Perry's children over to the United States Consul in Guadalajara. But Perry's father, Arthur, beat them to the punch and shipped them out of the country on an airplane to Chicago, where they were met by Perry's brother Ron and his wife, Amy.

To prevent the Levines from gaining custody of the children, Perry, while waiting in Los Angeles to be transported to Nashville, signed a handwritten "custodial rights and guardianship document" on August 8, 2005, naming his brother and his sister, Kathy March Breitowich, as joint guardians of the children.

Seven days later, the Levines were back in juvenile court seeking custody of their grandchildren. They were given temporary custody with an order from the court directing law enforcement in Tennessee and elsewhere to assist them "in immediately retrieving the minor children" from Ron March and his sister.

Despite some last-minute objections by Perry, the kids have remained with the Levines in Nashville since the evening of August 16, 2005. Perry has not given up fighting his former in-laws and is suing them again, using the ICARA, which got his kids back to him in 2001, to have them live with his second wife, Carmen. But unfortunately for Perry, the ICARA does not apply to his son, since he is over 16 years of age.

In still another suit against the Levines, he called them "child-abductors" and accused them of "malicious and sinister actions." In it, Perry also pointed the finger at the Metro police, Nashville Mayor Bill Purcell and even Senator Bill Frist, claiming they were all behind a conspiracy to have the Levines get custody of his kids.

Another handwritten filing made in October in federal court had Perry seeking to have his children sent back to Mexico to live with his wife, Carmen. That suit was eventually denied in February 2007, and Sammy and Tzipi continue living with their grandparents. And on June 14, 2007, Metro Juvenile Court Judge Betty Adams gave permanent custody of Samson and Tzipora March to their grandparents.

John Herbison went before Judge Dozier in late October to have Perry's murder and conspiracy convictions overturned due to overly prejudicial evidence used against him in both trials. Dozier took the matter "under advisement."

The judge, however, threw out Perry's motion to have his theft conviction overturned. And he later denied Perry's request for new trials in the conspiracy and murder charges.

By November, Perry claimed he was a pauper, too poor to pay the $230 fee when filing a lawsuit. A hearing was held where Detective Pridemore submitted to the judge recorded conversations in which Perry told Carmen March that she would be happy about his family finances.

In an excerpt of the conversation between Perry and Carmen that was played in court, he is heard saying to her, "There's some real positives . . . how do I put this . . . about our family's finances . . . you understand?"

"Okay," Carmen replies.

"You'll be very happy when I talk to you about this."

"Why will I be really happy?" she asks.

"Because it will take a lot of pressure off of you. You are going to have a lot more."

In other conversations, Perry talks about transferring property to Carmen and alludes to a $16,000 bank account and a condo that was sold for $80,000. Mentioned in the recordings is that Ed Fowlkes was paid $10,000, and that John Herbison and Bill Massey are sitting with $100,000 in their accounts.

Dozier acted swiftly and ruled that despite prosecution arguments, and the applications for offshore bank accounts and recorded conversations, Perry was indeed indigent and could receive legal aid.

Then in December, Perry filed a handwritten lawsuit against key witness Russell Nathaniel Farris, his mother, Vickie Farris, and his attorney, Justin Johnson, accusing them of lying about him to local and national media. He also charged that all three of them intentionally inflicted emotional damage on him. He is seeking an unspecified amount of compensatory and punitive damages.

Farris, the star witness at Perry's trials, was let out of jail shortly after Perry was convicted, pending the outcome of his separate robbery case. But a few weeks later his bond was revoked when an altercation with his girlfriend got him re-arrested. He was released again in February 2007, but then was wanted for probation violation after testing positive for cocaine. When authorities went looking for him, he holed up in a local hotel and after a six-hour standoff with police, surrendered on March 2, 2007.

At his sentencing, Farris wept. He admitted violating probation by using drugs and causing the armed standoff with police. Davidson County Criminal Judge Cheryl Blackburn then ordered him to serve a 10-year prison sentence which had been suspended in exchange for his cooperation in the March cases.

Inmate Cornelius King, who also testified for the prosecution in Perry's murder trial, was convicted in March 2007 of reckless homicide in the slaying of a Nashville mother of two who was killed by a bullet intended for someone else.

In November 2006, motions were filed in criminal court on Perry's behalf about newly obtained letters from Barry Armistead, an inmate in the Riverbend Maximum Security Institution who claimed to have had a relationship with Janet back in 1996. He said Janet had been depressed and taken a fatal overdose of sleeping pills, after which, he'd panicked and disposed of her body.

His name had come up the first day of the murder trial. Lawyers for both sides spoke with him, and Thurman said in court that anything Armistead said could not be corroborated. Based on convict Armistead's confession, Perry filed a lawsuit seeking a new trial, despite the fact that Armistead had made three very different confessions about Janet's murder.

In December 2006, Herbison, who, with Massey and his law partner Lorna McClusky, is working pro bono, filed a notice of appeal. "I don't know all the issues yet," Herbison says. "But we will urge most strongly in the murder case that the tapes of the conversations with Nate Farris and the admission into evidence of the conversation on the plane between Perry and the police should not have been presented to the jury."

Whether Perry will get a new trial after the briefs are submitted will be up to a three-judge panel of the court of appeals. Whatever the outcome, there is one thing John Herbison knows for sure: "If there is a new trial, I will not represent Perry March. I could, but I choose not to. I think I've had quite enough of the Perry March experience."

With nothing else to do at the penitentiary, Perry has shown no signs of letting up, showing off his legal writing skills and keeping the prison clerk busy at the same time with his lawsuits.

In one of his recent suits, filed on Tuesday, February 20, 2007, he accused Armistead of being the real killer.

The 47-year-old Armistead is serving time on aggravated assault charges. Perry again accused him of having an affair with Janet, giving her drugs that caused her to allegedly overdose, and, after she died, dumping her body.

Perry is asking that Armistead pay him and any other interested party compensatory and punitive damages and all other economic and emotional damages associated with the wrongful death of his wife.

And in the never-ending fight for custody of his two children, Perry was back in Nashville's juvenile court on Thursday, March 8, 2007, and in federal court asking that the custody dispute be transferred to a Mexican court and that the children live with their stepmother. Both judges denied Perry's request.

Still unresolved in court are questions about Janet March's estate. Perry's brother Ron is appealing a decision where he was ordered to pay nearly a quarter of a million dollars to the Levines.

Soon after Perry's last legal filings, he was transferred to the West Tennessee State Penitentiary at Henning. Initially, Perry's sister Kathy Breitowich said she was talking on the phone with him at the Northwest Correctional Complex, a minimum and medium facility in Tiptonville, when she heard some prisoners in the background, yelling, "Kill that Jon."

Herbison thought that perhaps prison officials moved Perry to a maximum facility because there was a gang of Aryan Nation inmates at Tiptonville who were not happy with Perry being there. While at Tiptonville, Perry had lived under the lowest security level possible at the facility.

But once at the Henning facility, about an hour from Memphis, Perry was initially placed in administrative segregation, and put in twenty-four-hour lockdown. A spokeswoman for the Tennessee Department of Correction said that Perry was moved there and placed in isolation because he had hatched a plot to get himself transferred to a less secure prison so he could escape.

"We received information that he was hoping to be moved to a minimum security annex facility. If that happened he was planning on escaping from that facility," TDOC spokeswoman Dorinda Carter said.

"What I can say is that the Department of Correction will work to ensure that everyone who comes to us stays with us in the amount of time the court orders them to," Carter said.

Perry's filings to have Carmen adopt her two stepchildren were turned down on May 22, 2007, when the Sixth Circuit Court of Appeals advised him that he had failed to pay the proper filing fee. Still unresolved is whether Perry's marriage to Carmen is legal.

Perry has gone so far as to file a federal libel, slander, and assault lawsuit against Fred Dalton Thompson of *Law & Order* television fame who considered a run for President. It seems that the former Tennessee Senator put out a news release years ago sponsoring a law about people leaving the country, and in the announcement wrote that Janet March had been murdered. At the time, Perry was the prime suspect in her murder and was no longer living in the United States. His lawyer, John Herbison, eventually persuaded him to voluntarily drop the lawsuit.

With nothing but time on his hands, and now only being

allowed to make one outside telephone call a month, Perry continues his claims. Janet's brother, Mark, in a television interview said: "He is going to try for the next thirty to fifty years to stay in our lives, to torture us through lawsuits. And I think all of us want to not think about him and never say his name again. I look forward to that."